The Routledge Guidebook to Gramsci's *Prison Notebooks*

Gramsci's *Prison Notebooks* are one of the most important and original sources of modern political philosophy, but they present great difficulties to the reader. Not originally intended for publication, their fragmentary character and their often cryptic language can mystify readers, leading to misinterpretation of the text. *The Routledge Guidebook to Gramsci's* Prison Notebooks provides readers with the historical background, textual analysis and other relevant information needed for a greater understanding and appreciation of this classic text. This guidebook:

- Explains the arguments presented by Gramsci in a clear and straightforward way, analysing the key concepts of the notebooks
- Situates Gramsci's ideas in the context of his own time, and in the history of political thought, demonstrating the innovation and originality of the *Prison Notebooks*
- Provides critique and analysis of Gramsci's conceptualization of politics and history (and culture in general), with reference to contemporary (i.e. present-day) examples where relevant
- Examines the relevance of Gramsci in the modern world and discusses why his ideas have such resonance in academic discourse.

Featuring historical and political examples to illustrate Gramsci's arguments, along with suggestions for further reading, this is an invaluable guide for anyone who wants to engage more fully with the *Prison Notebooks*.

John Schwarzmantel is Visiting Research Fellow in the School of Politics and International Studies, University of Leeds.

THE ROUTLEDGE GUIDES TO THE GREAT BOOKS

Series Editor: Anthony Gottlieb

The Routledge Guides to the Great Books provide ideal introductions to the work of the most brilliant thinkers of all time, from Aristotle to Marx and Newton to Wollstonecraft. At the core of each Guidebook is a detailed examination of the central ideas and arguments expounded in the great book. This is bookended by an opening discussion of the context within which the work was written and a closing look at the lasting significance of the text. The Routledge Guides to the Great Books therefore provide students everywhere with complete introductions to the most important, influential and innovative books of all time.

Available:

Hobbes' Leviathan Glen Newey

Galileo's Dialogue Maurice A. Finocchiaro

Aristotle's Nicomachean Ethics Gerard J. Hughes

Hegel's Phenomenology of Spirit Robert Stern

Locke's Essay Concerning Human Understanding E. J. Lowe

Wollstonecraft's A Vindication of the Rights of Woman Sandrine Bergès

Wittgenstein's Philosophical Investigations Marie McGinn

Heidegger's Being and Time Stephen Mulhall

Plato's Republic Nickolas Pappas

Descartes' Meditations Gary Hatfield

Forthcoming:

Thoreau's Civil Disobedience Bob Pepperman Taylor

De Beauvoir's The Second Sex Nancy Bauer

Mill's On Liberty Jonathan Riley

Routledge Guides to the Great Books

The Routledge Guidebook to Gramsci's *Prison Notebooks*

John Schwarzmantel

Routledge
Taylor & Francis Group

LONDON AND NEW YORK

First published 2015
by Routledge
2 Park Square, Milton Park, Abingdon, Oxon OX14 4RN

and by Routledge
711 Third Avenue, New York, NY 10017

Routledge is an imprint of the Taylor & Francis Group, an informa business

British Library Cataloguing in Publication Data
A catalogue record for this book is available from the British Library

Library of Congress Cataloging in Publication Data
Schwarzmantel, J. J. (John J.), 1947-
The Routledge guidebook to Gramsci's Prison notebooks / John
Schwarzmantel.
pages cm. -- (The Routledge guides to the great books)
Includes bibliographical references and index.
1. Gramsci, Antonio, 1891-1937. Quaderni del carcere. 2. Political science--
Philosophy. I. Title. II. Title: Guidebook to Gramsci's Prison notebooks.
HX288.G7S357 2015
335.43092--dc23
2014027726

ISBN: 978-0-415-71416-7 (hbk)
ISBN: 978-0-415-71417-4 (pbk)
ISBN: 978-1-315-73385-2 (ebk)

Typeset in Garamond
by Taylor & Francis Books

MIX
Paper from
responsible sources
FSC
www.fsc.org   FSC® C013056

Printed and bound in Great Britain by
TJ International Ltd, Padstow, Cornwall

CONTENTS

SERIES EDITOR'S PREFACE

'The past is a foreign country,' wrote a British novelist, L. P. Hartley: 'they do things differently there.' The greatest books in the canon of the humanities and sciences can be foreign territory, too. This series is a set of excursions written by expert guides who know how to make such places become more familiar.

All the books covered in this series, however long ago they were written, have much to say to us now, or help to explain the ways in which we have come to think about the world. Each volume is designed not only to describe a set of ideas, and how they developed, but also to evaluate them. This requires what one might call a bifocal approach. To engage fully with an author, one has to pretend that he or she is speaking to us; but to understand a text's meaning, it is often necessary to remember its original audience, too. It is all too easy to mistake the intentions of an old argument by treating it as a contemporary one.

The Routledge Guides to the Great Books are aimed at students in the broadest sense, not only those engaged in formal study. The intended audience of the series is all those who want to understand the books that have had the largest effects.

Anthony Gottlieb

*Series editor **Anthony Gottlieb** is the author of*
The Dream of Reason: A History of Philosophy
from the Greeks to the Renaissance.

PREFACE

Like many others, I first came across the name and ideas of Antonio Gramsci when I was a student in the 1960s, and read with interest and excitement the path-breaking study by John Cammett on *Antonio Gramsci and the Origins of Italian Communism*, which introduced me to some of the fundamental ideas of Gramsci's *Prison Notebooks* and to Gramsci's political activity and the historical context of his life and work. But it was only many years later, in the post-communist epoch of the 2000s, that I was able to engage more closely with Gramsci's thought in the course of preparing and teaching a final-year undergraduate module at the University of Leeds on 'Antonio Gramsci and the Theory of Modern Politics'. I enjoyed teaching that course and remain grateful to those students who took it, for lively discussion and stimulating exchanges which helped me (and, I hope, them) to understand Gramsci, as well as helping to convince me of the continuing relevance of his theories to our contemporary world.

Gramsci's *Prison Notebooks* are undoubtedly a classic text of twentieth-century political and social thought, and they deserve inclusion in a series devoted to introducing and explaining the great books of all time, but writing a guide to such a multi-faceted and at times complex text is no easy matter. I am very grateful to those scholars and experts who have helped me in this task. My first thanks are due to the staff of the Istituto Gramsci in Rome, who received me with courtesy and openness on my visits there, and whose help was invaluable. I owe a great debt of gratitude to the librarian of the Istituto Gramsci, Dario Massimi, for his friendly assistance and courteous welcome, and for making me aware of relevant literature in Italian that otherwise I would not have known about. Conversations with the director of the Istituto Gramsci, Professor Giuseppe Vacca, and with its vice-director, Professor Francesco Giasi, were inspiring and illuminating, and I am most grateful to both of them for sparing the time to share their expert knowledge with me, and to Professor Vacca for making available to me copies of extracts from some of his writings on Gramsci. Professor Vacca was also kind enough to read and comment on an earlier version of several chapters, and this was extremely helpful and encouraging. I am also happy to acknowledge the enjoyable lunchtime discussions with fellow researcher David Broder while I was working in Rome, which flowed all the more easily because of the wine consumed over lunch but helped me broaden my awareness of the history and problems of Italian communism and the Left in general.

I am also grateful to my old friend Professor Ernst Wangermann of the University of Salzburg, who encouraged me to take up the challenge to write this book, and who was kind enough to read some chapters in draft and who made very helpful stylistic and substantive suggestions which certainly helped improve the text. I have also enjoyed and benefited from discussion with friends with whom I talked about Gramsci and his ideas, and who encouraged me with their support for the project, in particular my former colleague Justin Grossman and my friends Professor Judith Pallot of Oxford University and Professor Janet Wolff of the University of Manchester. They all really helped, and so too did a number of other friends.

Finally I must acknowledge the help and support received from the successive editors and colleagues at Routledge with whom I have dealt. I received the initial invitation to write this guidebook to Gramsci's *Prison Notebooks* from the commissioning editor Andy Humphries, and I appreciated his encouragement and positive responses to my queries, and I am equally grateful to his successors Siobhán Poole and Rebecca Shillabeer and to editorial assistant Iram Satti, who have all been helpful and efficient at all times. I would also like to express my gratitude to James Thomas for his excellent work in copy-editing the typescript. His eagle-eyed scrutiny saved me from many careless blunders.

When I started preparing to teach my undergraduate module on Gramsci at the University of Leeds, a colleague in the Italian Department whom I had approached for advice told me he thought that Gramsci had 'gone off the boil' in recent years, meaning that interest in his ideas, which had been so lively in the 1960s, both in Italy and internationally, had waned. I would prefer to agree with Professor Vacca, who in his recent and highly valuable study of Gramsci's life and thought in the period of the *Prison Notebooks* talks about a 'new season' of Gramsci studies. The waning of Cold War passions and distortions, as well as the discovery of new documentation, sources and archives (used in the work of Italian scholars in preparing a new 'national edition' of Gramsci's works), have made it possible to approach the *Prison Notebooks* in a fuller and more objective way. I have benefited very much from this recent excellent work by Italian scholars, and their work is referred to at many points in this study. I hope that the present work introduces readers to Gramsci's highly original and exciting reflections on politics, history, philosophy and culture, which can help us make sense of our present epoch, different though it is in crucial aspects from the era in which Gramsci wrote his notes in the cell of a fascist prison.

REFERENCES TO GRAMSCI'S OWN WORKS

FSPN   *Further Selections from the Prison Notebooks.*
Translated and edited by Derek Boothman.
London: Lawrence & Wishart, 1995.

LP   *Letters from Prison*, 2 volumes. Edited by Frank
Rosengarten, translated by Raymond Rosenthal.
New York: Columbia University Press, 1994.
References to this two-volume work are followed
by volume and page number.

PPW   *Pre-prison Writings.* Edited by Richard Bellamy,
translated by Virginia Cox. Cambridge: Cambridge
University Press, 1994.

Q   *Quaderni del carcere*, 4 volumes. Critical edition of
the Gramsci Institute. Edited by Valentino
Gerratana. Turin: Einaudi, 1975. References to
this edition are followed by the number of the
notebook and the number of the paragraph (§),
and by the page number in the Gerratana edition.

QE   *Prison Notebooks*, 3 volumes (ongoing). Edited with
introduction by Joseph A. Buttigieg, translated by
Joseph A. Buttigieg and Antonio Callari. New
York: Columbia University Press, 1992, 1996,

1

GRAMSCI BEFORE
THE *PRISON NOTEBOOKS*

Antonio Gramsci (1891–1937) was one of the original members
of the Italian Communist Party (Partito Comunista d'Italia,
PCd'I), taking part in its founding congress in Livorno in January
1921. Before that, he had left his native Sardinia to study philology
and linguistics at the University of Turin, and had become
engaged in the politics of the Italian labour movement and joined
the Italian Socialist Party (Partito Socialista Italiano, PSI). Starting
in the years of the First World War he worked as a journalist and
theatre critic for the socialist press in Turin, and was an active
participant in the struggles of the working class of the city. He
played a leading role in the wave of strikes and occupations of
the Fiat car factories which took place in the so-called 'red two
years' or *biennio rosso* of 1919–20. He saw the factory occupations as
the possible beginning of a socialist revolution in Italy, inspired by
the revolution which the Russian Bolsheviks had made in October
1917. Along with other young socialist intellectuals Gramsci
founded the journal *L'Ordine Nuovo* (The new order) and his articles
for that journal developed the idea of factory councils as the

institutions through which the workers could run the factories and which could be the basis of a new type of socialist state. Critical of the failure of both the PSI and of the trade unions to defend and extend the factory council movement, Gramsci joined the PCd'I at its foundation, became one of its leaders, and was sent to Moscow in May 1922 by the party as its delegate to the executive committee of the Communist International (Comintern). It was while in Moscow, recovering his health in a sanatorium, that he met Julia Schucht, who was to become his wife and mother of their two children. In November 1923 Gramsci left Moscow for Vienna, and returned to Italy in May 1924, having been elected as a deputy (member of parliament) for the region of the Veneto in the elections of April 1924. Gramsci became secretary general of the PCd'I in August 1924. Since the March on Rome of October 1922 the fascists had taken power in Italy, and after having survived the crisis provoked by the fascist assassination of the socialist deputy Matteotti in April 1924, the fascists went on to consolidate their power through the violence of their armed gangs of *squadristi* and the intimidation of their opponents.

Antonio Gramsci's *Prison Notebooks*, or *Quaderni del carcere* to give them their title in the original Italian, are a series of notes and reflections written over a period of more than six years from 1929 to 1935, years spent in jail following the prison sentence handed down to Gramsci by a tribunal (a Special Tribunal for the Defence of the State) convened by the fascist government headed by Benito Mussolini. After what was essentially a show trial in June 1928, having been arrested in November 1926 despite his parliamentary immunity as a deputy elected to the Italian parliament, Gramsci was condemned to prison on trumped-up charges of subversion for twenty years, four months and five days, and similar sentences were handed down to the other leaders of the PCd'I with whom Gramsci was put on trial. He started writing his notebooks in February 1929, as soon as he had been able to get permission to write in prison, and filled twenty-nine notebooks (school exercise books) with his reflections on history, politics, philosophy and culture, as well as a further four notebooks filled with translations from German, English and Russian texts, which Gramsci used as language exercises.

Gramsci's *Prison Notebooks* are an undoubted classic of twentieth-century political thought, and they have had a huge influence over all fields of social and political thought and cultural theory. Gramsci is one of the Italian thinkers who have been most translated and studied throughout the world, and the *Prison Notebooks* have made concepts like hegemony familiar in a range of intellectual disciplines. This influence was a long time coming. Gramsci died in 1937, and the *Notebooks*, retrieved from Gramsci's last place of confinement by his sister-in-law Tatiana Schucht and sent by her to the Soviet Union, remained in an archive in Moscow until they were returned to Italy at the end of the Second World War. Large sections of the *Notebooks* were first published in Italian in the years 1948 to 1951, while Gramsci's letters from prison first appeared in published form in 1947. But it was only in 1975 that the first complete Italian edition of the *Notebooks* appeared, with full scholarly apparatus and identification of the many sources referred to in the course of more than 2,300 printed pages of Gramsci's notes. For reasons more fully explained in the next chapter, the *Notebooks* are not an easy text to read: constrained by the circumstances of his imprisonment, Gramsci was often forced to be allusive and cryptic in his references, and the *Notebooks* are composed of hundreds of separate sections of paragraphs, some long, some short, which cover a massive range of subjects. Compared with other classic texts of political and social theory, it appears as an assemblage of fragmentary reflections, and certainly not as a polished text revised for publication, with a beginning, middle and end of a coherent argument. A substantial English-language edition of parts of the *Prison Notebooks* was published in 1971 entitled *Selections from the Prison Notebooks of Antonio Gramsci*, edited and translated by Quintin Hoare and Geoffrey Nowell-Smith, and it is this edition which provides the structure for the present guide. While approaching the *Notebooks* through this set of selections does impart a particular perspective to the analysis of Gramsci's *Notebooks* (in a way privileging the political, historical and philosophical aspects at the expense of the themes of culture and popular beliefs which are also important), the justification remains that the Hoare/Nowell-Smith edition is still the way in which most English-speaking readers initially approach Gramsci's *Prison Notebooks*. The present guide is therefore oriented to that set of selections, designed to help readers encountering the text through that edition, while making reference also to the full text of the *Notebooks* in both the 1975 Italian edition and to the as yet incomplete English translation, which at the moment (2014) covers only the first eight of the twenty-nine notebooks, as well as to other English-language translations.

The remainder of this introductory chapter seeks to explain briefly Gramsci's political career and writings before his imprisonment. The next chapter gives an overview of the main themes of the *Notebooks*, and then discusses the structure and nature of Gramsci's prison writings, explaining the way in which they were written and the periodization of their composition. After that, the successive chapters of this guide follow the thematic ordering of the *Selections from the Prison Notebooks* (hereafter SPN), with chapters on intellectuals and education; history and modernity; politics and the state; and finally philosophy and Marxism. The only departure from the ordering of SPN is in the discussion of Gramsci's views on Americanism and Fordism, which are dealt with here in the chapter on history and modernity, whereas the SPN puts these in the section dealing with politics. The aim of the following chapters is mainly expository. It is hoped to give a clear explanation of Gramsci's ideas, with the addition of some critical analysis of how those ideas stand up in the conditions of contemporary twenty-first-century politics. A concluding chapter offers a brief and selective review of some of the ways in which Gramsci's *Prison Notebooks* have influenced wider political and social analysis, and takes up the way in which Gramsci presents the themes of the national and the global, the crisis of the nation-state, and his ideas of cosmopolitanism, themes which have become ever more topical since his day. If the present guide helps to clarify Gramsci's ideas and assists readers in their study of the *Selections*, and hopefully directs them to the complete version of the *Notebooks*, then it will have served its purpose. In the light of the discovery of new sources of documentation and helped by the work of scholars engaged in the preparation of the new (Italian) national edition of Gramsci's works, and the cooling of Cold War passions and distortions, it should be possible to arrive at a more balanced and dispassionate treatment of this classic of twentieth-century political and social thought.

THE EARLY GRAMSCI

Understanding the content of the *Prison Notebooks* requires some grasp of Gramsci's own life and political career, so it is necessary to give a short account of Gramsci's development before he was imprisoned in 1926 by the fascist regime, which was to keep him in prison effectively for the rest of his life, until 1937. Gramsci was born in Sardinia in 1891, and came to Turin as a student, to study (primarily) philology, though as his fellow student, and later leader of the PCd'I, Palmiro Togliatti observed, wherever there were lectures on interesting subjects, Gramsci was to be found there: 'I would bump in to him', Togliatti wrote, 'wherever there was a Professor who enlightened us on a series of essential problems' (Togliatti 2001, 140). Gramsci did not complete his studies at the University of Turin, committing himself to a career as a socialist journalist and organizer in the city of Turin, writing first for the socialist paper *Avanti!* (Forward!) and then joining with a group of other young comrades to set up the socialist paper *L'Ordine Nuovo*, which proclaimed its mission to be an organ of working-class culture and education, with those involved in it known as the *ordinovisti*, the 'new order people' (Rapone 2011). The core ideas of the *ordinovisti* are important for understanding the ideas of the *Prison Notebooks*, since there is continuity between the early Gramsci and the late Gramsci, in the same way, it can be argued, as there is continuity between the young Marx of the 1844 Paris Manuscripts and the later Marx of *Capital* (*Das Kapital*). In his early writings in the period of *L'Ordine Nuovo* Gramsci was concerned to articulate the idea that the working class could express and develop its own culture, and that Marxism did not represent a form of economic determinism but expressed such a new culture. Just as the French Revolution had been preceded by a long period of intellectual critique and undermining of traditional ideas, so too the socialist revolution was bound up with a process of intellectual renewal and transformation. This is well illustrated in Gramsci's article on 'Socialism and Culture', written for the socialist paper *Il Grido del Popolo* (The cry of the people) on 29 January 1916. In that article Gramsci wrote that 'every revolution has been preceded by a long process of intense critical activity, of new cultural insight and the spread of ideas through groups of men initially resistant to them, wrapped up in the process of solving their own, immediate economic and political problems, and lacking any bonds of solidarity with others in the same position' (PPW 10). He illustrated this with reference to the French Revolution and the ideas of Enlightenment figures like D'Alembert and Diderot. For Gramsci, 'the Enlightenment was a magnificent revolution in itself ... it created a kind of pan-European unified consciousness, a bourgeois International of the spirit' (PPW 10). But in the present situation of 1916, Gramsci wrote, a similar process was occurring, not a 'bourgeois International' but a new socialist consciousness: 'The same phenomenon is occurring again today, with socialism. It is through a critique of capitalist civili- sation that a unified proletarian consciousness has formed or is in the process of formation' (PPW 11). This article illustrates themes which were to be much more fully explored in the *Prison Notebooks*, namely the importance of ideas and forms of consciousness, and the need to form a new intellectual perspective as a precondition for radical political change. There is also the idea of getting beyond a limited perspective concerned just with 'immediate economic and political problems', and the need to articulate a broader philosophy which rises above what Gramsci in the *Prison Notebooks* would refer to as the 'economic-corporate level'.

One other theme was also raised in Gramsci's early journalistic writings which receives a far deeper and more extended analysis in the *Prison Notebooks*, namely the idea of Marxism not as a form of economism in which politics was determined by economics, but of Marxism as precisely the expression of human will and creative action, encapsulated in the term which Gramsci developed in the *Notebooks*, 'the philosophy of praxis'. The most famous expression of this idea in the pre-prison writings came in his article on the Bolshevik Revolution, which he saluted as 'The Revolution against *Capital*'. In that article Gramsci startlingly refers to Marx's *Capital* as being 'more the book of the bourgeoisie than of the proletariat', at least in the way in which it had been interpreted in Russia

(PPW 39). Instead of just passively waiting for the unfolding of history along a path determined by the iron laws of economics, with socialist revolution deferred until after the development of capitalism, or as Gramsci put it, in opposition to the idea that 'a bourgeoisie had to develop, the capitalist era had to get under way and civilisation on the Western model be introduced, before the proletariat could even start thinking about its own revolt, its own class demands, its own revolution', the Bolsheviks had shown a different path through their own actions (PPW 39). In Gramsci's words, 'They are *living out* Marxist thought – the real, undying Marxist thought, which continues the heritage of German and Italian idealism, but which, in Marx, was contaminated by positivist and naturalist incrustations' (PPW 40). Here again there is a core idea which received more extensive treatment in the *Notebooks*, the idea of the importance of practice and the rejection of the 'positivist and naturalist incrustations' which had, for Gramsci, distorted the nature of Marxism. It is true that in these early writings of Gramsci his use of Marx and Marx's writings was rather a polemical one, making an appeal to Marxism as a way of criticizing the passivity of Italian socialists and their failure to exploit the potentialities of the situation in the way the Bolsheviks had done in Russia in 1917. A careful study by Francesca Izzo of Gramsci's various readings of Marx shows that it was only with the *Prison Notebooks* that Gramsci engaged fully with some of the core ideas of Marxism, above all with the philosophy of Marxism (Izzo 2008). In his early journalistic and political writings, Gramsci was using Marx as an intellectual weapon in polemics against a range of political adversaries, in perhaps a rather superficial way, using Marxist ideas against liberal, conservative and nationalist politicians, for example against the Italian Prime Minister Giolitti and his protectionist economic policies which aimed at sealing an alliance between northern industrialists and southern landowners. Similarly Gramsci used Marxist ideas in opposition to nationalists like Corradini who sought to transform the idea of class struggle into the nationalist framework of the struggle of nation-states against each other, with Italy as a 'proletarian nation'. As Izzo makes clear, it was only in the *Notebooks* that Gramsci made a 'true and real "return to Marx"', grappling with issues of base and superstructure, and reformulating 'historical materialism' (not a term Marx himself ever employed) as the philosophy of praxis. In the *Notebooks* he explored the philosophical implications of Marx's work in ways which he did not do and could not do in those early writings, written as those journalistic articles were under the pressure of events, from day to day. It was with reference to Marx's 1859 Preface to *A Contribution to the Critique of Political Economy* and *The Poverty of Philosophy* that these ideas were developed. Those writings were the key texts on which Gramsci drew in the *Notebooks* and which 'constitute the source, the laboratory on which Gramsci drew in his discussion of critics of the philosophy of praxis, above all Croce' (Izzo 2008, 575). While it is true that this more profound engagement with Marx and Marxism comes only with the *Prison Notebooks*, the idea of freeing Marxism (and political analysis generally) from the deterministic and economistic 'incrustations' of pre-1914 Marxism, and seeing Lenin as the example of such a voluntaristic and creative Marxism is one which is certainly an important element in the *Notebooks* but also finds some expression in Gramsci's early articles, such as 'The Revolution against *Capital*' quoted above. In the early writings, Gramsci invokes the Marx of *The Communist Manifesto* and of *The Holy Family*, using these writings as examples of an activist creative perspective. In an article of 4 May 1918, also written for *Il Grido del Popolo*, Gramsci wrote that 'Marx did not write some neat little doctrine; he is not some Messiah who left us a string of parables laden with categorical imperatives and absolute, unchallengeable norms, lying outside the categories of time and space. His only categorical imperative, his only norm: "Workers of the world, unite!"' (PPW 54).

In his early journalistic writings, first for the periodical *Il Grido del Popolo*, then for the socialist newspaper *Avanti!* (whose editor at an earlier stage had been Mussolini), and finally for the journal *L'Ordine Nuovo* (whose first issue appeared in March 1919), Gramsci gave an analysis of the events of the day, and in those journalistic writings certain themes appear which he was to develop further in his *Prison Notebooks*. In his early writings Gramsci developed a critique of Italian society and of the failure of the Italian bourgeoisie to be a truly modernizing force. In Gramsci's analysis, the true face of capitalist modernity was realized through liberalism and a liberal society as represented by the Anglo-Saxon countries of England and the USA. In those societies a tradition of individualism spread ideas of autonomy and self-reliance. A truly liberal society, marked by civil liberties, was most conducive to the development of capitalism, and hence provided the best conditions for the growth and eventual victory of socialism. Gramsci's Anglophilia even led him to praise Baden-Powell's Boy Scout movement for fostering qualities of self-reliance and individualism (Rapone 2011, 145–50). Evidently Gramsci neglected or overlooked the imperialist ideology which the Boy Scout movement also developed. The corollary of his positive view of liberal capitalism as realized in Britain and the USA was his critique of Italy and the Italian character. Gramsci contrasted the Italian love of games of chance and the hope for fortune's wheel to bring a windfall with the English belief that individuals had to work for and deserve any reward (clearly this was before the period of the National Lottery in Britain). In Gramsci's analysis, Italy had not become a properly liberal society. The politics of Giolitti (the Italian prime minister) were marked by compromise, by economic protectionism rather than free trade, and by an endeavour to form an alliance of northern industrialists and southern landlords, with some attempt to co-opt the reformist leaders of Italian socialism into the alliance, and Gramsci saw this as the opposite of a progressive liberalism which would foster capitalist development. In an article written for *Avanti!* on 16 May 1918, Gramsci wrote of liberalism as 'a precondition for socialism, both ideally and historically' (Rapone 2011, 352). So for him Italy was a backward society in which the bourgeoisie was far from economically productive and dynamic. The character of the Italian people was marked by sentimentalism rather than force of character, and what was needed was greater discipline and stress on work rather than hoping for windfall gains from games of chance.

It is also interesting to note in these early journalistic writings of Gramsci his hostility to Jacobinism and to democracy, compared with his early praise for liberalism. In the *Prison Notebooks* Jacobinism (as we will see in Chapter 4 below) was praised as the politics which in the French Revolution had led the urban poor to support the demands of the peasantry, and which had pushed the revolution forward. In the early writings, by contrast, Gramsci's use of the term 'Jacobinism' is much more negative, seeing Jacobinism as the politics of an intolerant minority, imbued with abstract ideas which it was foisting on the population as a whole, so that 'Jacobin democracy is the negation of liberty and of autonomy' (Rapone 2011, 359). He saw the Jacobins as the typical leaders of a bourgeois revolution, not in tune with the masses, and imposing their own ideas in an authoritarian fashion. This was linked with a critique (by Gramsci) of 'democracy', as seen as an abstract idea: he stated that 'democracy is our worst enemy', because it tried to pacify or tone down ideas of class struggle (Rapone 2011, 352). Gramsci in these early writings was scornful of the defenders of democracy, whom he saw as articulating abstract ideas in a sentimental way, invoking the 'sacred principles of 1789' and ideals of justice, fraternity and liberty without seeing how those ideas were historically formed and situated, so that they were not universal truths. The defenders of democracy had come to justify the First World War, legitimizing it as a democratic war, and preaching a gospel of democracy which elevated these vague ideals to the status of eternal truths. By contrast liberalism and the society it promoted were frankly capitalistic and bourgeois, and hence provided the ground for the development of socialism.

However, Gramsci changed his ideas on these matters in response to two crucial sets of events, the Russian revolutions of February and October 1917, and the experience of the factory councils and wave of working-class action which culminated in the workers' takeover of the Turin factories in 1920. With regard to the Russian revolutions, notably the Bolshevik Revolution of October 1917, Gramsci stressed the need for leadership, and the need for discipline and order to be provided by a revolutionary state. Whereas his earlier stance had been to some degree an anti-statist one, in following events in Russia in and after 1917 he came to argue that 'society cannot live without the state', and he stressed the creative role of a revolutionary minority leading the masses, saluting Lenin as 'the greatest statesman of contemporary Europe'. Gone was his critique of Jacobinism seen as a tactic of minority revolution typical of bourgeois revolutions, to be replaced by a new emphasis on the need for a proletarian state, of a highly disciplined kind: the need for 'a very strong socialist state' (*uno*

stato socialista saldissimo), with a necessarily military character
(Rapone 2011, 405). Gone too was his earlier more positive attitude
to liberalism, which Gramsci now saw as in fundamental and
possibly terminal crisis, at any rate irrelevant to the challenge of
building a new proletarian order which he thought had been put
on the agenda by the Bolshevik Revolution – and which was of
immediate relevance to Italy. The Russian Revolution showed the
need for a new type of state, the dictatorship of the proletariat,
and had indicated the institutional framework for realizing that
state – the organs of the soviets, councils of workers, soldiers and
peasants. In the course of his engagement with the factory councils
which had briefly taken over control of the factories in Turin in
August 1920, Gramsci came to develop his idea of a new type of
state, with the factory councils (or internal commissions) as the
organs of both anti-capitalist struggle and the nucleus of a form of
state distinct from that of parliamentary democracy. The impact
of these two events, Bolshevik Revolution and the *biennio rosso* of
1919–20, changed Gramsci's perspective on liberalism, democracy
and Jacobinism. Liberalism was now seen as irrelevant and outmoded rather than a factor of capitalist development. Democracy
was no longer seen as the worst enemy, but as something which
could be realized, not in the form of parliamentary democracy but
in a new type of state whose organs at the base were the factory
councils, supplemented by organs of popular power in the locality,
culminating in a 'National Congress of delegates of workers and
peasants'. This system of representation was based on the unit of
production, and as Rapone says this meant that 'in place of the
generic citizen, bearer of equal rights, the point of reference was man
as worker [*l'uomo quale specifico soggetto lavoratore*], so that economic
function coincided with political capacity' (Rapone 2011, 402).
Finally, Gramsci's earlier anti-Jacobinism was replaced by a new
concern with the importance of political leadership, as manifested
by the Bolsheviks, showing the need for a political party to
organize and discipline the mass movement which had arisen in
the Russian Revolution and more widely in the crisis of post-war
Europe. Through the control of production and mass mobilization
witnessed in the red two years the working masses were developing
the new culture and confidence which Gramsci saw as necessary

for a socialist society. But this needed to be complemented by political leadership and organization of the mass movement, through the agency of the political party. These were all themes which the *Prison Notebooks* deal with in a wider historical and also philosophical perspective, but the later discussion cannot be understood without some knowledge of Gramsci's practical and political experiences prior to his imprisonment.

It was through his engagement in the factory councils movement of the *biennio rosso* of 1919–20, and through his membership, and then leadership, of the newly formed (in January 1921, at the Livorno Congress) PCd'I (Partito Comunista d'Italia) that Gramsci acquired the political experience and knowledge on which he reflected in the *Prison Notebooks*, so that both of these episodes and formative experiences need at least a brief explanation in order to understand the themes of the *Prison Notebooks*. The red two years of 1919–20 were years of worker militancy, marked by strikes and occupation of the factories, notably in Turin, which Gramsci himself had previously described as the city in which 'the proletariat has reached a point of development which is one of the highest, if not the very highest, in Italy' (article of 18 December 1917, quoted in Giasi 2008a, 154), where 'within an area of a few thousand square metres there were concentrated tens and tens of thousands of workers' as he wrote in that article. The factory council movement developed in Turin towards the end of 1919, and it was in Turin that a general strike broke out in April 1920, the so-called 'clock-hands strike', provoked by a dispute over the adoption of daylight saving time. In September 1920 the occupation of the factories in Turin began, and 'shortly thereafter nearly all Italian heavy industry was taken over' (Cammett 1967, 113). Gramsci and his colleagues on *L'Ordine Nuovo* were actively involved in the workers' occupation of the factory, but above all sought in the pages of that journal, which in November 1920 became a daily newspaper, to theorize the movement of the factory councils and explain its significance. In Gramsci's articles of the time he explains that the factory councils were institutions different from the socialist political party and from the official trade unions, as indeed they were. The factory councils were open to all workers in the plant or factory, they elected committees which were charged with the running of the factories, defying the employers' attempts to shut the factories down and stop production. The *ordinovisti*, in particular Gramsci, saw the factory councils as the manifestation of the workers' capacity to organize and maintain industrial production, thus showing that the employers were superfluous, and production could go ahead without them. But Gramsci's analysis of these factory councils went further: his articles of the time argue that these councils were organizations of worker power which were, at least potentially, basic institutions of a new proletarian state. They were genuinely original institutions organized at the point of production through which the working class could affirm its power and its autonomy. Since this present text focuses on the *Prison Notebooks*, there is not space to discuss fully Gramsci's views, but some quotations can illustrate the core of his ideas. The factory councils movement was part of the general militancy of workers throughout Europe in the period after the War and the Russian Revolution, inspired by the idea of soviets (councils of workers, peasants and soldiers) to create a model of council communism, the direct rule of the producers.

In his articles in *L'Ordine Nuovo* on the factory councils Gramsci argued that the councils were institutions of a different type from the traditional institutions of working-class politics, party and union: 'Revolutionary organisations (the political party and the trade union) grow up on the terrain of political liberty and bourgeois democracy', Gramsci wrote, but 'we say that the present period is revolutionary', since the working class was 'beginning with all its energies (despite the errors, hesitations and setbacks only natural in an oppressed class, with no historical experience behind it, which has to do everything for itself, from scratch) to generate working-class institutions of a new type' (PPW 165). The factory councils were the basis of a new type of state: 'institutions devised to take over the role of the capitalist, in administrating and running industry; and to guarantee the autonomy of the producer in the factory, on the shop-floor' (PPW 113). Gramsci's articles during the *biennio rosso* expressed the belief that proletarian revolution was imminent, indeed actually occurring, and that the factory councils could be the institutions of a new type of state, based directly on the producers. He wrote of 'a determination on the part of the proletarian masses to introduce proletarian order into the factory, to make the factory the basic unit of the new State and to build the new State in a way that reflects the industrial relations of the factory system' (PPW 170). Against the reluctance of the PSI, the Italian Socialist Party, to give effective leadership to the factory council movement, and against the fear by union leaders that the factory councils were undermining union power, Gramsci saw the factory council as 'the most appropriate organ for mutual education and for fostering the new social spirit that the proletariat has managed to distil out of its fruitful, living experience in the community of labour' (PPW 118).

However, the factory council movement ended in defeat, though this was masked by an agreement in September 1920 which spoke of workers' control, though this was never realized, and two years after the return to work came the March on Rome of October 1922, which brought Mussolini and the fascists to power. As John Cammett, one of the first historians to bring Gramsci's work to an English-speaking public, writes, 'The industrialists had lost their faith in the "liberal state", and had become receptive to political expedients of quite a different order ... The hour of fascism was at hand' (Cammett 1967, 121). Gramsci's *Prison Notebooks* contain some allusions to the Turin movements and to *L'Ordine Nuovo* discussions, for example in the passage where Gramsci discusses the need for a new type of intellectual, 'closely bound to industrial labour': he writes that 'on this basis the weekly *Ordine Nuovo* worked to develop certain forms of new intellectualism and to determine its new concepts, and this was not the least of the reasons for its success' (SPN 9; Q12, §3, 1551). It would not be correct to oppose the 'early' Gramsci with his stress on factory councils to the 'later' Gramsci of the *Prison Notebooks* where the role of the political party is given much greater attention. Gramsci's criticisms of the political party in the early writings were directed to the PSI because of its failure to see the potential of the factory council movement. In his writings on Gramsci, Palmiro Togliatti insisted on the fact that Gramsci's writings on the factory councils did not mean that he neglected or ignored the need for a political party (Togliatti 2001, 207). Indeed it was Gramsci's critique of the failure of the PSI to play a decisive role in the years of the factory council movement that led him to call for the 'renewal' of the PSI, in an article of 8 May 1920, and to take part in the Congress of Livorno of January 1921 in which the Italian Communist Party was formed (the PCd'I, Partito Comunista d'Italia – it changed its name in 1944 to PCI, Partito Comunista Italiano). Nevertheless, one of the core themes of the *Prison Notebooks* is the reflection on the defeat of the working-class movement and the subsequent victory of fascism, and the implications of both for political action and the need for a new type of political party (the modern Prince – see Chapter 5 below).

The PCd'I formed in January 1921 was in its initial years marked by a radical intransigence and sectarianism, under the leadership of Amadeo Bordiga. Bordiga's stance was one of hostility to parliamentary politics, a form of 'ultra-leftism' which meant that he was opposed to the politics of the United Front which the Comintern proclaimed from 1921 on, when it first became clear that the wave of revolution stimulated by the Bolshevik Revolution had receded and that revolution in western Europe was no longer a realistic possibility. Here we can only give a brief outline of Gramsci's political thought and activity in the years from 1921 to his arrest in November 1926, highlighting those points important for understanding the issues handled in the *Prison Notebooks*. From being in many respects a political ally of Bordiga, Gramsci changed to acceptance of the policy of the United Front, which was an attempt, carried out with varying degrees of enthusiasm by the parties of the Communist International (Comintern), to form alliances with the socialist parties of their respective countries in an attempt to stave off the wave of reaction which in Italy took the form of fascism. Gramsci supported the policy of the 'Bolshevization' of communist parties, namely the insistence that communist parties everywhere had to accept the Bolshevik model of democratic centralism and the ban on factions, which the Bolshevik party itself had adopted after 1921. From 1922 to 1923 Gramsci was in Moscow, as the delegate of the PCd'I to the Comintern. He left Turin in May 1922 and once in Russia had to spend some time (indeed six months) in a sanatorium on the outskirts of Moscow (*Serebranyi Bor*, or Silver Wood) to recover from nervous exhaustion, and it was there that he met Julia Schucht, who was to become his wife. Recent research has suggested that before meeting Julia,

Gramsci had come into contact with her elder sister Eugenia, who had been a patient in the sanatorium for almost three years when Gramsci arrived there in July 1922. It seems that Gramsci had an amorous relationship with Eugenia, and that several emotionally charged letters which previous researchers thought directed to Julia were in fact addressed to Eugenia, though this was not evident since the letters were addressed to 'Dear Comrade' or 'Dearest' (*Carissima*) (Righi 2011). The latest research suggests that Gramsci transferred his affections from Eugenia to her younger sister Julia in the autumn of 1923, shortly before Gramsci left Moscow for Vienna. Their first child, Delio, was born on 10 August 1924.

Gramsci was present in Moscow for the Fourth Congress of the Comintern (held in November–December 1922). This Congress, as E. H. Carr says, 'marked an important point in the transformation and consolidation of Soviet policy. It was the end of the dramatic period of the Communist International' and this Congress 'was driven still further along the road of retreat' (Carr 1966, 437). It urged that the PCd'I should fuse with the PSI (Italian Socialist Party) in order to implement the policy of the United Front (though this fusion was never carried out). In June 1923 the Comintern decided to create a new Executive Committee for the PCd'I, and Bordiga resigned from the leadership of the party. In September 1923 Gramsci, who had been expecting to return to Italy, was ordered initially to go to Berlin, but this was changed to Vienna, in the wake of arrests by the fascist police in Italy of the leaders of the PCd'I, so that Gramsci was effectively leader (in exile) of the Italian party. He arrived in Vienna on 3 December 1923, remaining there until April 1924 when he was able to return to Italy, having been elected as deputy (member of parliament) for the region of Veneto, and thus protected, or so it seemed, by parliamentary immunity.

From Vienna Gramsci sought to combat Bordiga's rejection of the United Front policy, which led the latter to propose that the PCd'I leave the Third International. In opposition to this stance Gramsci built up the nucleus of a new leading group of the party with a clear commitment to the policy of the United Front (Fiori 1970, 167). One of the letters he wrote from Vienna to other leaders of the party (9 February 1924) deserves mention, because this letter develops ideas of the difference of the conditions under which the Bolsheviks came to power in Russia from conditions in the West, an idea fundamental to the Notebooks. Criticizing Bordiga's ('Amadeo's') view that 'the over-riding task must be the organisation of the party as an end in itself', and that once a Bolshevik party had been formed in Italy the masses would rise up, Gramsci wrote as follows:

> I think that the situation is quite different. ... The determination, which in Russia was direct and drove the masses onto the streets for a revolutionary uprising, in central and Western Europe is complicated by all these political super-structures, created by the greater development of capitalism. This makes the action of the masses slower and more prudent, and therefore requires of the revolutionary party a strategy and tactics altogether more complex and long-term than those which were necessary for the Bolsheviks in the period between March and November 1917.
>
> (SPW 199)

This suggests that Gramsci was developing an idea of socialism as a process, not as a sudden upheaval, and this letter anticipates the idea of 'war of position' which is a key theme of the *Notebooks* (Vacca in Daniele 1999, 139). In the Italian parliamentary elections of April 1924 Gramsci was elected as PCd'I parliamentary deputy for the region of Veneto, and was thus protected by his parliamentary immunity from arrest by the fascists, and so was able to return to Italy in May 1924. In August 1924 Gramsci was made secretary general of the PCd'I, a post he held until his arrest in 1926. His task was to change the sectarian Bordigan policy of the party to one of full acceptance of the idea of the United Front, in the face of the growing dominance of fascism following the March on Rome of October 1922. The murder of the socialist deputy Matteotti in June 1924 marked a turning point for the fascist regime. The anti-fascist parties (including the PCd'I) left the Italian Parliament in protest against the murder of Matteotti by fascist thugs, and took up their place in the so-called Aventine parliament, but this grouping of anti-fascist parties failed to work out a coherent plan of opposition to fascism (Lyttelton 2004, ch. 10). In November 1924 the PCd'I left the Aventine counter-parliament and took up their place in the Italian Chamber of Deputies, and it was there that Gramsci made his first (and only) parliamentary speech, on the subject of Freemasonery. The Matteotti crisis had not led to the weakening of the fascist regime. On the contrary, fascism was able to intimidate the opposition parties, and make the PCd'I illegal. The remainder of Gramsci's political activity was as leader of a party under conditions of repression by the fascist state. Fascism had been able to establish its hegemony, in the first instance through coercion and intimidation, but also through gaining support from a variety of social groups – and it was on this fact of fascist hegemony, and how to challenge it, that Gramsci was to reflect in his notes written in prison.

Gramsci was thus the secretary general of a revolutionary communist party operating in a fascist state, and also the leader of a party which was itself a section of the Third International, increasingly under Soviet control. As E. H. Carr states, given the failure of communist revolution to spread to western Europe, the task of the Comintern was 'to take refuge in the defensive until the time was once more ripe for an advance; and this meant to fortify Soviet Russia as the one present mainstay and future hope of the proletarian revolution' (Carr 1966, 438). At the same time, developments in Russia involved the member parties of the Comintern. Those developments involved the bitter disputes within the Russian Communist Party (RCP) on the building of socialism in Russia. These disputes involved Trotsky's idea of 'permanent revolution' in opposition to Stalin's concept of 'socialism in one country', and here again these are themes which are referred to in the *Prison Notebooks*, in the context of wider reflections on constructing a new type of society in Russian conditions, distinct from those of countries like Italy and western Europe generally. The conflicts of 1926 within the RCP and their international repercussions are significant for understanding Gramsci's political perspectives, and hence for grasping some of the themes of the *Prison Notebooks*.

In January 1926 the Third Congress of the PCd'I had taken place, outside Italy, in the French city of Lyons, and this was the only party congress held while Gramsci was the secretary general.

In the eyes of some students of the period it is this Congress which can be considered the real foundation congress of the PCd'I, and the Gramsci scholar Antonio Santucci observes that it was after that Congress that the party would succeed in taking a political path 'in the short term harsh in battles and sacrifices but rich in experiences and future developments' (Santucci 2005, 104). In preparation for that congress Gramsci had worked together with Togliatti to draw up the famous 'Lyons theses', which presented a profound analysis of the Italian political situation and the nature of fascism. But as Santucci says, the central theme of the theses, to be presented to the Congress, was the topic of alliances, the idea that 'the motive forces of the Italian revolution were the working class and the peasantry, and the peasants of the South and the islands and the peasants of other parts of Italy' (Santucci 2005, 103). At the Lyons Congress the new leading group of the party headed by Gramsci gained overwhelming support from the delegates, with 90.8 per cent of the votes over 9.2 per cent for the Bordiga faction, thus accepting the line of the United Front (Spriano 1967, ch. 30). This line itself was open to different interpretations in the Italian party as well as in the international communist movement, depending on whether the emphasis was on 'United Front from above' (alliance of parties and their leaders) or 'United Front from below' (i.e. attempts to win over the members of socialist parties and trade unions to form mass organizations, which indeed could be seen as an attempt to destroy the hold of 'reformist' parties and unions over their members). However, the guiding line of Gramsci's analysis was one of a United Front understood in terms of the working class forming an alliance with the peasantry, since as Gramsci stated in a meeting of the party's political bureau of 20 January 1926, 'in no country is the proletariat in a position to gain power and hold power through its own strength: it must therefore gain allies, and so must carry out a political line which allows it to place itself at the head of other classes which have anti-capitalist interests and lead them in the struggle for the overthrow of bourgeois society'. Gramsci went on to say that this was particularly true of Italy, 'where the proletariat is a minority of the working population and is geographically placed in such a way that it cannot presume to lead a victorious struggle for power without having first resolved the problem of its relationship with the class of peasants (agricultural workers)' (quoted in Santucci 2005, 103). This insistence on the idea of a class leading other classes and forming alliances to gain hegemony is also a theme developed much further in the *Prison Notebooks*. The idea of a link between workers and peasants in Italy as a condition for gaining hegemony, and more generally the problem of leadership of allied classes, were explored further in Gramsci's essay on the southern question, to be examined shortly.

In 1926 the conflicts within the RCP had come out into the open and the parties of the Comintern were dragged into the issues raised about the development of socialism in the Soviet Union and, by implication, issues of international revolution. While before 1926 Trotsky had been bitterly opposed by Kamenev and Zinoviev, in June 1926 the former enemies came together to form the United Opposition, in open conflict with Stalin and Bukharin who were at this stage (until the 'left turn' of 1928/29) allies defending the New Economic Policy, which in Bukharin's view meant 'riding to socialism on the peasant's nag'. The international dimension of this conflict opposed Trotsky's idea of permanent revolution to Stalin's policy of socialism in one country, and the issue was given immediacy by debates about the British General Strike of 1926, and Trotsky's proposal to break off relations with the Anglo-Soviet Trade Union Council. This was indeed what Trotsky's biographer Isaac Deutscher calls 'the decisive contest' between the Left Opposition and the duumvirate of Stalin and Bukharin (Deutscher 1959, ch. 5). From the Italian perspective, the conflict was witnessed at first-hand by Togliatti, the Italian delegate to the Comintern, who was present at some of the decisive meetings, notably the meeting of the Central Committee of the RCP in July 1926, at which Togliatti was present and on which he reported to the Italian party's Central Committee in a long despatch of 26 July. At that meeting Trotsky read a declaration which was, as Togliatti reported to his Italian comrades, 'without doubt the most important political event of the Plenum, and is an event destined to have consequences for the life of the Russian Communist Party which for the moment are incalculable but certainly quite serious' (Daniele 1999, 362). In the course of the coming weeks Togliatti reported to his Italian comrades on the defeat of the Left Opposition and the victory of the Stalin/ Bukharin majority in the RCP. His message, at least implicit, was that the Left Opposition had been routed, and that the PCd'I should line up with the majority and accept the Comintern line, all the more so as the Italian party had long been suspected of a dangerous 'leftism' because of its Bordigan beginnings.

The crucial document here is the letter, drawn up by Gramsci, of 14 October 1926, in the name of the Politburo of the PCd'I, and addressed to the Central Committee of the RCP, and sent by Gramsci to Togliatti with a request that he should look over it, amend it if necessary, and forward it to the Russian Central Committee. This letter, while declaring that 'we consider basically correct the political line of the majority of the Central Committee of the CPSU [Communist Party of the Soviet Union]', contained a powerful critique of the Stalin/Bukharin majority: 'But today you are destroying your work', this letter read. 'You are degrading, and run the risk of annihilating, the leading function which the CPSU won through Lenin's contribution. It seems to us that the violent passion of Russian affairs is causing you to lose sight of the international aspects of Russian affairs themselves; is causing you to forget that your duties as Russian militants can and must be carried out only within the framework of the interests of the international proletariat' (SPW 430). While supporting the line of the Bolshevik majority and calling for 'a firm unity and a firm discipline within the party which governs the workers' state', Gramsci's letter (written in the name of the Central Committee of the Italian party) stated that 'the unity and discipline in this case cannot be mechanical and enforced. They must be loyal and due to conviction, and not those of an enemy unit imprisoned or besieged, whose only thought is of escape or an unexpected sortie'. In its final paragraph the letter stated that 'Comrades Zinoviev, Trotsky, Kamenev have contributed powerfully to educating us for the revolution', and contained a fairly explicit critique of the measures used by Stalin and Bukharin to crush the United Opposition: 'we like to feel certain that the majority of the Central Committee of the USSR does not intend to win a crushing victory in the struggle, and is disposed to avoid excessive measures' (SPW 432), a statement which implied that while the Italian party might 'like to feel certain' that excessive measures would not be used, such certainty was not at present justified.

Togliatti's reaction on receiving this letter was to send immediately a telegram to the Politburo of the PCd'I followed up by a letter in which he tried to convince the Italian comrades that their view of the Russian conflicts, as expressed in the letter of 14 October 1926, did not grasp the reality of the situation in which the Left Opposition had capitulated, and warning the Italian party that they ran the risk of appearing to support the Left Opposition, stating that 'such a result would be most damaging' (Daniele 1999, 416). So for that reason he proposed not to forward the letter to the Central Committee of the CPSU as he had been asked to do. In his introduction to the documentation of this exchange of letters between Togliatti in Moscow and Gramsci (and the other leaders of the PCd'I) in Rome Giuseppe Vacca convincingly disposes of the interpretation that Togliatti on his own initiative did not forward the letter of 14 October. What happened was that Gramsci and the PCd'I leadership agreed that the letter should not be forwarded, and that the matter would be further debated at the upcoming meeting of the Italian party's Central Committee to be held in November 1926, where an emissary of the Comintern (Jules Humbert-Droz) would be present to update the Italian comrades on the current situation in the Soviet Union. In his letter to the PCd'I of 18 October 1926 Togliatti advised against forwarding the letter of 14 October, since in his view that letter could be used by 'oppositional groups which exist or are being formed in other parties of the Communist International', and the implication was clear – this could put the Italian party in a bad light with the majority of the Russian party, and possibly imperil its existence. He ended his letter with a postscript saying that he did not agree with the content of the letter of 14 October, 'for reasons of a general kind and for more particular reasons which I will explain in a letter to Comrade Antonio' (i.e. Gramsci), and this he did in a letter to Gramsci of 18 October, to which Gramsci replied in a letter of 26 October, and on both sides of this correspondence the tone was rather sharp. Togliatti's letter accused Gramsci of failing to make a distinction between the majority of the RCP and the Opposition, and the tone of Togliatti's letter implied that the main task was to rally behind the Stalin/Bukharin majority, given that, as he put it, 'probably, from now on, the unity of the Leninist old guard will no longer be – or will be only with difficulty – realised in a continuous manner' (SPW 433).

Gramsci's reply is significant in showing the political perspectives which he held in the weeks before his arrest on 8 November 1926, and on which he reflected (and which he revised) in the course of writing his *Notebooks* after his arrest. His reply to Togliatti suggested that 'your letter seems to me too abstract and too schematic in its manner of reasoning' (SPW 437). Gramsci rejected the idea that his letter of 14 October could be taken to weaken the position of the majority in the Russian party's Central Committee. The nub of Gramsci's reply lay in its stress on the importance of the unity of the Russian party, with the implication that the struggle against the Left Opposition should not be taken to extremes, as was to happen later with the Stalinist terror – which of course could not be anticipated in 1926. He wrote that Togliatti's line of reasoning was 'tainted by bureaucratism'. For Gramsci the crucial point was that the masses, on an international level, had to be convinced, nine years after the Bolsheviks had taken power, that 'the proletariat, once power has been taken, *can construct socialism*' (emphasis in original), and this belief could be instilled in the broad masses not by 'the methods of school pedagogy, but only by those of revolutionary pedagogy, i.e. only by the *political fact* that the Russian Party as a whole is convinced of it, and is fighting in a united fashion'. Gramsci's letter closed with an expression of regret that 'our letter was not understood by you, first of all, and that you did not in any case, in view of my personal note, try to understand better', all the more so as the letter of 14 October was 'a *whole* indictment of the opposition' (i.e. of the Russian opposition) (SPW 440).

This letter was written less than two weeks before Gramsci's arrest. The Italian party leadership had agreed to Togliatti's suggestion that the letter of 14 October 1926 should not be forwarded to the Russian Central Committee, but that the matter should be further discussed at a meeting of the Italian party's Central Committee to be held at Valpolcevera, near Genoa, on 1 November 1926, at which

Gramsci was to be present. The delegate of the Comintern, Jules Humbert-Droz, would be at this meeting and give those present an updated view of the situation in the Soviet Union. In the event, Gramsci did not attend this secret meeting. On his way to Genoa he was warned off by a police agent that there was a danger of his arrest if he proceeded on his journey, and so he turned back to Rome, where he was arrested on 8 November. It seems that the hope of Togliatti was that the secret meeting at Valpolcevera would result in the PCd'I leadership moderating or withdrawing its critique of the Russian party, as expressed in the letter of 14 October, but at that meeting no final resolution was taken. Reporting to Togliatti on the meeting the acting leader Grieco stated that the PCd'I agreed with the RCP majority, but that the question of 'socialism in one country' had been discussed, with some comrades hesitant with regard to Trotsky's position. This somewhat half-hearted endorsement of the Russian majority position may well not have been what Togliatti was hoping for.

How then can one sum up Gramsci's political position in the immediate period before his arrest? This constitutes the starting point for the *Prison Notebooks* – though as we shall see his later analysis went well beyond his positions of 1926. Clearly the Italian party, and Gramsci as its secretary general, was grappling theoretically and practically with the analysis of fascism and how to combat it. In a document of August 1926, 'A Study of the Italian Situation', Gramsci developed an analysis of the international situation which distinguished between 'the advanced capitalist countries' and what he called 'the typical peripheral states, like Italy, Poland, Spain or Portugal'. Gramsci wrote that 'in the advanced capitalist countries, the ruling class possesses political and organisational reserves which it did not possess, for instance, in Russia. This means that even the most serious economic crises do not have immediate repercussions in the political sphere' (SPW 408).

This was a perspective that was to be explored further in the *Notebooks*, since it was those 'political and organisational reserves' which constituted a powerful obstacle to the working class and its allies developing their hegemony. But in this period just before his arrest, Gramsci placed Italy (along with those other countries mentioned) in the category of 'typical peripheral states' where 'the state forces are less efficient'. It was an important characteristic of those 'peripheral states' that 'a broad stratum of intermediate classes stretches between the proletariat and capitalism'. Gramsci's 'study of the Italian situation' in August 1926 drew the conclusion that there was in Italy, and in the other countries of 'peripheral capitalism', 'a regroupment of the middle classes on the left', indeed what he called 'a molecular process' which had started in 1923, 'through which the most active elements of the middle classes moved over from the reactionary fascist camp to the camp of the Aventine opposition'. In turn this was 'accompanied by a parallel phenomenon of regroupment of the revolutionary forces around our party.' He drew the conclusion that the fundamental problem was 'the transition from the united front tactic, understood in a general sense, to a specific tactic which confronts the concrete problems of national life and operates on the basis of the popular forces as they are historically determined' (SPW 410). This seems in many ways a less pessimistic analysis than that of Togliatti: the latter seemed to be saying that in the present worldwide situation of 'capitalist stabilization' the only possible policy was to accept and fully endorse the decisions of the Russian party majority (Stalin/Bukharin), and to avoid anything that could be construed as support for the United Opposition in Russia (which had now surrendered to the majority) or in the Comintern as a whole. Gramsci's position was that at least in the countries of the 'capitalist periphery' there was the possibility of moving on from the United Front to a different tactic, in the light of the move of the intermediate classes to the left, as he saw it. Yet this revolutionary optimism was not born out, and Gramsci's arrest along with that of other communist leaders was to be a sign of fascist supremacy and its strength. However, it is essential to have some understanding of Gramsci's political position and his political analysis in 1926, because this furnished exactly the material and the problems which were handled in the *Prison Notebooks*, and provided the starting point from which he was to develop an entirely new vocabulary, and a new understanding, of politics, with correspondingly new concepts. Indeed, one expert on Gramsci, the British scholar Richard Bellamy, argues that it is Gramsci's 'analysis of peripheral capitalist states rather than his attempts to build a

Communist Party that will continue to absorb our attention', and that what emerges from Gramsci's early writings 'is a Gramsci as much concerned with the creation of a modern nation State as with its overthrow' (Bellamy 2014, 175). Certainly the question of forging a modern national consciousness is a crucial one in the *Prison Notebooks*. So too does Gramsci treat the limitations of the nation-state and of nationalism in an age of global capitalism.

One element which looms large in his *Prison Notebooks* is the question of alliances between social classes, and the way in which hegemony entails one social group (class) leading another and establishing its directing or leading role both intellectually and politically over allied groups. In the Italian case (and in other countries of the 'capitalist periphery') this meant in concrete terms an alliance of working class and peasantry, and a breaking of the hold of intellectuals like Croce and Fortunato over the peasantry of the south of Italy, in other words a confrontation with 'the southern question'. This was the point of view of the extended essay on the topic which Gramsci completed just before his arrest, which eventually was published in 1930, and which deserves a necessarily brief analysis here because important themes appear in this essay which were developed and extended in the *Prison Notebooks*. In a speech of 1949 on Gramsci as 'Thinker and Man of Action' Togliatti stated that Gramsci's essay on the southern question would, on its own, have been sufficient to put him 'among the leading political thinkers of contemporary Italy' (Togliatti 2001, 134). The essay on the southern question was the only extended piece of Gramsci's writing that was published in his lifetime, and it is an essay in which one of the fundamental topics of the *Prison Notebooks* is dealt with, namely the role of intellectuals and the need for the working class to develop its own stratum of intellectuals: 'This formation of intellectuals is needed if we are to see an alliance between the proletariat and the peasant masses', Gramsci wrote, adding 'even more so, an alliance between the proletariat and the peasant masses of the South'. The working class had to form its own stratum of intellectuals, since 'the proletariat, as a class, is short of organising elements; it does not have its own layer of intellectuals and it will only be able to form such a stratum, very slowly and laboriously, after the conquest of state power' (PPW 336). The essay on the southern question was written in 1926, though only published for the first time in January 1930 in the pages of *Stato Operaio* (Workers' state), the journal of the PCd'I in exile. Gramsci argued in that essay that 'the Southern peasant is linked to the great landowners through the mediation of the intellectual', in particular through intellectuals like Fortunato and Croce, in particular the latter, with whose ideas Gramsci was to engage in the *Prison Notebooks* at great length (PPW 330). Croce had (so Gramsci wrote) 'detached the radical intellectuals of the South from the peasant masses and made them participate in national and European culture'. It had been the task of *L'Ordine Nuovo* and the Turin communists, in Gramsci's words, to 'represent at the same time a complete break with that tradition and the beginning of a new development which has already borne fruit and will continue to do so' (PPW 334). The theme of the working class as 'leading' (*dirigente*) the peasantry, and the need for a class alliance between these two groups was clearly sounded in this essay. So too, in another theme to be developed in the *Prison Notebooks*, was the idea not just of the working class developing its own stratum of intellectuals, but the need for a new form of intellectual, one who could express the needs and problems of an advanced industrial society: 'Industry has introduced a new model of intellectual: the technical organiser, the specialist in applied science' (PPW 328). And equally the essay on the southern question introduces the theme of getting beyond the economic-corporate level, since Gramsci enjoined 'the metal-worker, the joiner, the builder, etc.' that 'they must think as workers who are members of a class that aims to lead the peasants and the intellectuals' (PPW 322). Here the theme of hegemony was explicitly sounded: 'The Turin communists had raised, in concrete terms, the question of the "hegemony of the proletariat": in other words, the question of the social basis of the proletarian dictatorship and the workers' State' (PPW 316). It was on these themes that Gramsci developed his ideas in the course of writing the *Prison Notebooks*. In his reaction to the two events of the Russian Revolution and the occupation of the factories and in his consideration of class alliances and the working class becoming hegemonic, Gramsci laid down the bases for his meditations in the *Prison Notebooks*.

We can now see Gramsci as above all a political actor, situated in the milieu of the Italian and international communist movement, and grappling with problems of how to organize the working-class movement in a period of capitalist reaction, which had taken particular vicious features in the shape of fascism in Italy. It is those themes of the nature of the historical epoch, its crises and the way in which subordinate groups could establish their intellectual and political hegemony which constitute the core ideas of the *Prison Notebooks* and led Gramsci to develop a new understanding of politics in the conditions of complex societies in the twentieth century.

SUGGESTIONS FOR FURTHER READING

There are two important books which represent the latest research on Gramsci's early writings and on the writings comprising the *Prison Notebooks*, and these two books have been heavily drawn on for this chapter. Unfortunately neither has as yet been translated into English. They are the study by Leonardo Rapone, *Cinque anni che paiono secoli: Antonio Gramsci dal socialismo al comunismo (1914–1919)* (Rome: Carocci, 2011), and Giuseppe Vacca, *Vita e pensieri di Antonio Gramsci 1926–1937* (Turin: Einaudi, 2012). The general perspective taken in this chapter on the *Prison Notebooks* owes much to the writings by Giuseppe Vacca cited in the bibliography, and on the insights given by Togliatti's views on Gramsci, which are collected in a new edition, edited by Guido Liguori: Palmiro Togliatti, *Scritti su Gramsci* (Rome: Editori Riuniti, 2001). Some of Togliatti's lectures and articles on Gramsci are available in English: Palmiro Togliatti, *On Gramsci, and Other Writings,* edited and translated by Donald Sassoon (London: Lawrence & Wishart, 1979). A short book by Antonio Santucci, *Antonio Gramsci 1891–1937* (Palermo: Sellerio, 2005), provides a very good overview of Gramsci's life, political activity and writings, and this has been translated into English: Antonio Santucci, *Antonio Gramsci* (New York: Monthly Review Press, 2010).

In English the best and most accessible overall biography remains that by Giuseppe Fiori, *Antonio Gramsci: Life of a Revolutionary* (London: New Left Books, 1970). Other useful sources on

Gramsci's biography are the books by Alastair Davidson, *Antonio Gramsci: Towards an Intellectual Biography* (London: Merlin Press, 1977), and Dante Germino, *Antonio Gramsci: Architect of a New Politics* (Baton Rouge: Louisiana State University Press, 1990).

Gramsci's pre-prison writings are available in a volume edited by Richard Bellamy, *Gramsci: Pre-Prison Writings* (Cambridge: Cambridge University Press, 1994), which contains a useful introduction, which is reproduced, along with some important essays on Gramsci and Croce, in Richard Bellamy, *Croce, Gramsci, Bobbio and the Italian Political Tradition* (Colchester: ECPR Press, 2014). The early political writings are also available in two volumes selected and edited by Quintin Hoare: *Selections from Political Writings 1910–1920* (London: Lawrence & Wishart, 1977), and *Selections from Political Writings 1921–1926* (London: Lawrence & Wishart, 1978).

For Gramsci's political activity before the period of his imprisonment, the book by John Cammett, *Antonio Gramsci and the Origins of Italian Communism* (Stanford: Stanford University Press, 1967), remains valuable and stimulating. For the period of the factory councils, the important works are those by Paolo Spriano, *The Occupation of the Factories: Italy 1920* (London: Pluto Press, 1975), and by Gwyn Williams, *Proletarian Order* (London: Pluto Press, 1975).

An indispensable source is Gramsci's *Prison Letters*, which are available in a full and very well-edited translation, edited by Frank Rosengarten and translated by Raymond Rosenthal, *Letters from Prison*, 2 vols (New York: Columbia University Press, 1994).

The historical and political background to Gramsci's political activity before and during his incarceration is covered in Adrian Lyttelton (ed.), *Liberal and Fascist Italy 1900–1945* (Oxford: Oxford University, 2002), and in much more detail in his *The Seizure of Power: Fascism in Italy 1919–1929* (London: Routledge, 2004).

2

THE NATURE AND GENESIS OF GRAMSCI'S *PRISON NOTEBOOKS*

KEY THEMES AND ORIGINALITY OF THE *PRISON NOTEBOOKS*

In order to understand Gramsci's *Prison Notebooks*, it is necessary to have some knowledge of the core themes which are developed in Gramsci's reflections on politics, on history, on culture and on philosophy. The *Prison Notebooks* seem at first glance to be an uncoordinated assemblage of very diverse reflections on all of those subjects, but in the light of recent scholarship it is possible to grasp the basic unity of thought which runs through the twenty-nine notebooks, and which also emerges in the English-language *Selections from the Prison Notebooks* (SPN), which is the text to which the present volume is designed to serve as a guide.

The *Prison Notebooks* have to be understood (at least in the perspective taken in the present book) as a fundamentally *political* text, if politics is understood in the broadest terms as the understanding of a historical epoch and an analysis of the forces acting to preserve and to change the nature of a political and social order. The complete version of the *Prison Notebooks* opens with an initial heading: 'First Notebook (8 February 1929)', followed by the words '*Notes and jottings*', and then by a list of sixteen 'main topics', ranging from the first one, '*Theory of history and of historiography*' and including, to give some selective illustrations, number 3, '*Formation of Italian intellectual groups*: development, attitudes', number 11, '*Americanism and Fordism*', and number 15, '*Neo-grammarians and neo-linguists* ("this round table is square")', with the phrase in brackets referring to an essay by a figure who looms large in the *Notebooks*, the Italian philosopher Benedetto Croce. The last in the list, number 16, is 'Father Bresciani's progeny', referring to a reactionary Jesuit writer who was prolific in his attacks on liberalism (QE1, 99; Q1, 5; the italicized words are those underlined by Gramsci himself). This list of topics, with the dating of 8 February 1929, heads the first of over 2,300 pages of notes, arranged in paragraphs of varying length, which range over a vast field of topics in politics, culture, history and philosophy. But their guiding thread can be seen as a political reflection on the defeat of the wave of revolution in Europe sparked off by the First World War and the Bolshevik Revolution of October 1917, and the attempt to explain that defeat by understanding the nature of the world order of twentieth-century Europe. In particular, Gramsci's *Prison Notebooks* should be seen as the attempt to develop a new theory of politics appropriate to the features of that historical epoch, and also as a wide-ranging reflection on the nature of politics and political action, as well as the search for a new philosophy of politics, based on Marxism but in some respects going well beyond classical Marxism, and certainly challenging the ways in which Marxism was interpreted by classical social democracy and (after 1917) by the communist movement of which Gramsci himself was a leader, as one of the founding members of the Italian Communist Party (Partito Comunista d'Italia, PCd'I) in 1921. In that search for a new political strategy Gramsci in the *Prison Notebooks* reveals himself as an extremely creative and innovative political thinker, sketching out not just a different perspective on politics and political action in modern society but offering an analysis of the ways in which hitherto subordinate groups can overcome their subaltern position and achieve *hegemony*, to use the term for which Gramsci has become famous and which is indeed the core concept of his reflections on political life and action.

The *Prison Notebooks* thus should be approached as an attempt, however fragmentary and cryptic in places, to understand the historical epoch opened up by the First World War and the Bolshevik Revolution and the enduring crisis of the society of that epoch, understood on a global level. This attempt at analysis of the nature of that historical epoch and its critical points is at the same time the exploration of a new form of political knowledge and strategy appropriate to that epoch, rejecting forms of political action and analysis which have no bearing on modern society in its most developed form. In turn such a new political understanding depends, in Gramsci's perspective, on the working-class movement developing its own autonomous and independent philosophy of politics, and indeed a philosophy in the broader sense encompassing ideas of will and creative action, seen as a necessary condition for any subordinate group to become in its turn hegemonic and leading. These are some of the key ideas which Gramsci develops in his *Prison Notebooks*, and which are to be explained in the present text. Given the nature of the endeavour which Gramsci set himself, the task of developing the understanding of the new historical epoch, and of the politics and philosophy appropriate to it, it is not surprising that such an endeavour requires a new language of politics, a different political lexicon of terms and concepts through which the new political knowledge and the corresponding political strategy could be expressed and analysed. For this reason the reader coming to the *Prison Notebooks* discovers a new vocabulary for analysing politics and society. Some of these new concepts (including the idea of hegemony) have become very well-known, sometimes with the result that they are detached from any explicitly Gramscian use and employed in a loose and watered-down way. Any reader of the *Prison Notebooks* will be struck by the deployment of certain key terms, which play a pivotal role in the theorization of politics which those *Notebooks* develop. Some, indeed most, of these concepts are ones whose names were not invented by Gramsci but used in earlier political theory, whether Marxist or not. This is true of the 'master concept' of *hegemony*, and of *civil society*, and of course the concept of *the state*, or the Hegelian idea of *ethical state*. In these cases, as we will show in the course of our exposition, Gramsci is taking familiar terms of political and social theory and giving them a new use and definition, filling them with a different content, employing an old language of politics in radically innovative ways, a case of 'new wine in old bottles'. The same is true of other key terms employed in the Gramscian analysis of politics, such as *passive revolution, Americanism and Fordism*, and what seems to be his own invention, *war of position* as opposed to *war of movement* or *war of manoeuvre*, to describe different forms of political strategy, the former the one appropriate to the political world after 1870. Other Gramscian conceptual innovations are related to his radical reworking of Marxism, and notably his use of the term 'the philosophy of praxis' to refer to Marxism, a term of crucial importance for his whole approach to politics and philosophy. This term was not employed merely (or even primarily) as a means of avoiding drawing the attention of the censor whose suspicions might have been aroused by use of the word 'Marxism'. It is a term which came to replace 'historical materialism' in the course of the writing of the *Notebooks* (see Cospito 2011a), and suggests the way in which Gramsci's version of Marxism went way beyond the economistic determinism which he saw as characteristic of both the Marxism of the Second International (1889–1914) and equally of Marxism– Leninism in its orthodox communist or Third International form, as exemplified in a text frequently referred to by Gramsci, Bukharin's book *Historical Materialism*.

This is to say, then, that reading the *Prison Notebooks* and understanding them entails encountering a vocabulary of often familiar terms which are used in new ways to provide a distinctly original conceptual apparatus of politics. Even if some of the terms (like state and civil society) are themselves established terms in the political vocabulary, they are used by Gramsci with radically original meanings, which open up what one leading expert on Gramsci (and present director of the Istituto Gramsci in Rome), Giuseppe Vacca, calls a 'new conception of politics' (Vacca 1991, 7). Vacca also observes that 'the *Notebooks* aim to develop fully a gnoseology of politics', a knowledge of politics and the exploration of political action seen as a creative field of human action not determined rigidly or immediately by economic factors (Vacca 1991, 25). In that way Gramsci took Marxist theory in new and creative directions, through his vehement and extended critique of 'economism', the idea that the economic base determines directly the political and ideological superstructure. Indeed, as will be more fully shown below, while frequently taking as his starting point Marx's famous and classic summary of his doctrine in the 1859 Preface to *A Contribution to the Critique of Political Economy*, Gramsci came to reject what one commentator (Cospito 2011a) calls the 'architectural metaphor' of base and superstructure, replacing that couplet with the entirely new idea of a 'historic bloc'. The *Prison Notebooks* focus on the role of intellectuals and the political party (seen as 'the modern Prince') as the chief agents of a transformation of consciousness and ideology. Such a transformation is seen as indispensable for any social grouping seeking to overcome its situation of subordination and intellectual dependency, in other words aiming to achieve hegemony. The *Prison Notebooks* therefore open up an original and novel intellectual world, with radically new ideas developed as tools for understanding the politics and society of the twentieth century. These are concepts also needed to comprehend the epoch in which we live today. This new intellectual world, and the concepts that go with it, certainly take their inspiration and starting point from Marxism, and are illustrated with references to certain core Marxist texts (the nature of Gramsci's Marxism is explored further below). Yet the Gramscian understanding of politics both extends and in a way transcends, or at the very least develops, the categories of Marxism, not least by recasting the terms of the classical base/superstructure distinction, and laying the emphasis on what Marx's 1859 Preface called the 'ideological forms in which men become conscious of this conflict and fight it out', the 'conflict' here being between productive forces of society and the property relations or existing relations of production (Marx 1973a, 426). Gramsci's distinct stance on these matters is well expressed in some of the many passages of the *Prison Notebooks* devoted to the critique of the ideas of the philosopher Benedetto Croce, with whom much of the *Prison Notebooks* is a form of critical dialogue (see Chapter 6). Gramsci writes that 'for the philosophy of praxis the superstructures are an objective and operative reality (or they become such when they are not pure individual machinations)' (FSPN 395; Q10 II, §41, 1319). So while Gramsci is certainly a Marxist in the sense of basing his thought on Marxism, which he sees as a totalistic and autonomous philosophy which both includes and goes beyond all previous movements of thought, Gramsci in some respects transcends Marxism or rethinks it in radically new directions, changing its emphasis from what he sees as the distortions of an economistic view to a much more open and creative one, emphasizing will and creative human action, expressed in another frequently used term, that of 'collective will', and exploring the processes through which such a collective will can be formed.

The *Prison Notebooks* thus constitute a classic text of twentieth-century political thought. As the editor of the first full-length text of the *Prison Notebooks* (Valentino Gerratana) put it, 'if a "classic" is an interpreter of their *own time* who remains topical for any age ... and if a "classic" is an author whom it is worthwhile to re-read and re-interpret in the light of new demands and of new problems, one can say that Gramsci today deserves the title of a classic author' (quoted in Liguori 2012, 310). One translator of Dante's *Divine Comedy*, the author Dorothy L. Sayers, wrote that 'the whole of the Middle Ages moves before us in Dante's thumb-nail sketches' (Dante 1949, 65). In the same way one could say that if not the whole, then at least many of the central episodes and themes of twentieth-century politics move before us in the *Prison Notebooks*, if sometimes in an allusive and coded way: the wave of strikes and factory seizures in Italy in the immediate post-war years (the so-called red two years 1919–20 or *biennio rosso*); their failure and the subsequent rise of fascism; reflections on Stalinism and fascism as political and social regimes; criticism of the erroneous (in Gramsci's view) policy followed after 1929 by the international communist movement (the so-called Third Period or class against class policy which proclaimed the imminent collapse of capitalism as a result of economic crisis); the significance of the crash of 1929; the nature of new methods of capitalist mass production; the attempt to create a new state and society in the Soviet

Union – these (among other episodes and processes) are all discussed in the *Prison Notebooks*. They are analysed in the context of a wide-ranging historical perspective, with references to the whole course of Italian and European history, from Roman Empire through the communes of the Middle Ages and comparisons of Renaissance and Reformation, with extended discussions of the Italian Risorgimento or movement of national independence, itself related to the development of ideas stemming from the French Revolution. The aim of such analysis is an intensely political one: to understand the nature of contemporary society and to use such understanding to develop a political strategy which could be suitable for that society, rejecting modes of political action which had led to defeat in the recent past and which failed to grasp the distinctive and complex characteristics of the modern age. In order to express such a new political strategy, a different vocabulary was necessary, and it is this which Gramsci develops through the pages of the *Prison Notebooks*, jettisoning what he sees as hindrances and obstacles to a clear view of contemporary reality. The *Notebooks* reveal a clear rejection of simplified and crude versions of Marxism (economism) and of political strategies (like that of Trotsky's 'permanent revolution' and the idea of a direct uprising against the state – 'war of manoeuvre') which are seen as outdated and irrelevant to the historical epoch of the contemporary world, whose salient features are analysed in Gramsci's notes.

One of the most important of the new concepts developed in the *Notebooks* is that of 'passive revolution', seen in a broad historical context as characteristic of much of the two periods opened up firstly by the French Revolution of 1789 and later by the First World War and the Bolshevik Revolution of 1917. Gramsci uses the term passive revolution in the first instance in the course of his analysis of the Italian Risorgimento, the movement to achieve the political independence and unity of the Italian nation. As with all the terms of his political analysis, this concept is not developed in an abstract way, but is formulated by Gramsci out of particular historical analyses, with reference to events and processes which he probes in detail, with close attention to leaders, parties, events, out of which a particular concept emerges, whether passive revolution or hegemony or other terms in his lexicon which are used to shed light on those events and processes, and more broadly to analyse the nature of a whole historical epoch. Passive revolution (the concept is analysed at greater length in Chapter 4 below) is a case in point. While Gramsci did not invent the term, he uses it primarily to analyse the Italian Risorgimento as a movement in which national unity and independence were achieved in ways which consolidated the domination of liberal and moderate groups, with results that shaped the nature of the Italian state and society after unification. But in the course of the *Prison Notebooks* the term is used with a wider significance, to characterize whole historical epochs, notably the period after 1815, in which liberalism and liberal parties established their intellectual and political dominance, and equally for the epoch following the revolutionary upsurge sparked off by the Bolshevik Revolution in Russia and the subsequent wave of working-class militancy and class struggle in Italy and elsewhere. Passive revolution is a term used by Gramsci to refer to attempts to contain popular pressure and adapt to modernity without fundamentally challenging the dominance of ruling groups. Gramsci calls this 'revolution without revolution', and sees both fascism and Americanism and Fordism as examples of passive revolution, in their different ways. Historically speaking, Gramsci saw passive revolution as characterizing both 'the period which followed the fall of Napoleon and that which followed the war of 1914–18' (SPN 106; Q15, §59, 1824). Gramsci characterizes the post-First World War period as constituting a decisive break which opened up a new historic period: 'And yet, everybody recognises that a whole series of questions which piled up individually before 1914 have precisely formed a "mound", modifying the general structure of the previous process'. Gramsci cites a whole range of problems as characterizing this period, listing them as 'parliamentarism, industrial organisation, democracy, liberalism, etc.', but he lays his emphasis on 'the fact that a new social force has been constituted, and has a weight which can no longer be ignored, etc.' (SPN 106; Q15, §59, 1824). The core theme of the *Prison Notebooks* is how this 'new social force' could put an end to the passive revolution and achieve the opposite, namely a complete or active revolution, even if neither of those adjectives is used by Gramsci to refer to a revolution that is not a passive one.

This new social force is that of the masses, the working class and peasantry, in general the mass of the subordinated or subaltern groups whose cultural and political emancipation involves a radical transformation, a revolution.

The *Prison Notebooks* should thus be seen as an ambitious attempt, written in the highly limiting conditions of a prison cell, to make sense of the modern world; that is, of the conditions of political action subsequent to the coming to power of fascism, first in Italy in 1922 and later in Germany in 1933, by which time Gramsci had been in prison already for seven years. Through the new conceptual apparatus deployed in the *Notebooks* (even if using familiar terms, but with different and innovative meanings) the aim is to explain the features of twentieth-century modernity, and to sketch out forms of political strategy through which hitherto subordinate groups could achieve hegemony, a form of intellectual and political leadership which educates and transforms the members of those groups, the 'new social force' referred to in the quotation just given. Gramsci thus is seeking a way forward that goes beyond the passive revolutions of fascism and liberalism, and indeed of what he calls 'Americanism and Fordism', the attempt to employ modern means of mass production without changing the structure of class relations. In philosophical as well as political terms (and for Gramsci the two cannot be separated – for him Marxism, or 'the philosophy of praxis', is 'a philosophy which is also politics, and a politics which is also philosophy'; SPN 395; Q16, §9, 1860), this means a perspective which rejects forms of determinism which see political action as determined directly and simplistically by the economic structure of society. His fundamental argument in the *Prison Notebooks* is to investigate the process through which a collective will could emerge, a collective will formed by hitherto subordinate groups aiming to transform the conditions of their subaltern situation. In Gramsci's own words, we have to investigate 'the problem of the formation of a collective will. In order to analyse critically what the proposition means, it is necessary to study precisely how permanent collective wills are formed, and how such wills set themselves concrete short-term and long-term ends – i.e. a line of collective action' (SPN 194; Q8, §195, 1057).

NATURE AND WRITING OF THE *PRISON NOTEBOOKS*

We now have to explain exactly the nature of the text of the *Prison Notebooks*, how they were written and how the text has come down to us in its present form. The matter is complicated, and raises a number of questions which do not have to be confronted in other 'great books' whose genesis and publication were far more straightforward. In the first place, it is necessary to explain the nature of the *Prison Notebooks* as a whole, before showing how the English *Selections from the Prison Notebooks* (the Hoare/Nowell-Smith edition) relate to the complete text of the *Prison Notebooks*.

Gramsci was arrested on 8 November 1926, at 10.30 in the evening. This was an arrest illegal even under the existing fascist laws, since at the time of his arrest Gramsci was a member of parliament and thus enjoyed the privilege of parliamentary immunity from arrest (Canfora 2012, 17). The privilege of parliamentary immunity was withdrawn from the communist members of parliament and from those socialists who had formed the Aventine opposition in protest against the murder of the socialist deputy Matteotti (123 deputies in all), but the law ratifying this withdrawal of parliamentary privilege only passed through the Chamber of Deputies on 9 November, the day after the arrest had been made. Initially held in prison in Rome, Gramsci was then sent as a prisoner, along with fellow communist deputies, to the island of Ustica, off the coast of Sicily, where he remained from the end of November 1926 until 20 January 1927, when he was transported to Milan, where he was questioned by the investigating judge drawing up the prosecution case, Macis. After more than a year in detention in Milan Gramsci was sent for what amounted to a show trial before the Special Tribunal in Rome, and this was the infamous occasion where the prosecutor said 'we have to stop this brain working for twenty years'. Gramsci was sentenced to prison for twenty years, four months and five days, and on 8 July 1928 was transferred for the long journey to the prison of Turi, in the south of Italy, arriving there on 19 July 1928. The most recent research divides Gramsci's time in prison into three phases (Daniele 2011). The first runs from his arrest in

November 1926 to February 1928, when he was held in the Milan prison of San Vittore. The second phase covers his detention in the penal establishment of Turi di Bari, from July 1928 until a severe health crisis in March 1933, when Gramsci had to be looked after continually day and night, by three comrades who took it in turns to be with him in twelve-hour shifts. In the early months of 1933 Gramsci envisaged the possibility of some agreement between fascist Italy and Soviet Russia which would lead to his liberation. There were hopes that the fascist government would celebrate its tenth anniversary in power by some humanitarian gesture, as long as this was not seen as arising from pressure by the PCd'I or as a result of the international campaign carried on to demand the release of Gramsci from prison. Yet this plan of what his sister-in-law Tania (Tatiana) called the 'big attempt' (*tentativo grande*) came to nothing. The final phase of Gramsci's imprisonment started in March 1933, when Gramsci was examined by Dr Arcangeli, who confirmed the chronically bad state of Gramsci's health. On 19 November 1933 Gramsci left the prison of Turi, and after a temporary stay in a prison in Civitavecchia he was transferred to the Cusumano clinic in Formia, but still under penal conditions of detention and surveillance. In August 1935 he was allowed to move to a clinic (the Quisisana) in Rome, suffering from extreme ill-health caused by the years of prison. After June 1935 the writing of the *Notebooks* stopped – Gramsci was unable to continue working on them, and thus the period he spent in Rome at the Quisisana clinic was one in which no more of the *Notebooks* were written. In what turned out to be the last months of his life Gramsci urged his wife to make the journey from Russia to Italy. He also considered the possibility of moving back to Sardinia, though in the end Gramsci agreed to make a request to be allowed to go into exile in the Soviet Union to be with his family and because of his own serious health condition. Such a request was drafted by his friend Piero Sraffa, but this was not finally submitted because of Gramsci's death, which none of his friends and family had expected, the result of a stroke on 27 April 1937.

What exactly are the *Prison Notebooks*, and how did they come to be written in such dire conditions of surveillance and imprisonment? As a result of the careful philological work carried out by Gianni

Francioni, it has been possible to establish in some detail the chronology of the *Notebooks* and to understand the way in which Gramsci worked on them. The following account is based on Francioni's studies, in particular his article 'Come lavorava Gramsci' (How Gramsci worked), which stands as a preface to the *edizione anastatica* of the *Notebooks* – an edition which is the photocopy of the notebooks in their original form. We first have to understand the hindrances to Gramsci being able to write and study at all while in prison. It was on 19 March 1927 that he wrote to his sister-in-law Tatiana Schucht to tell her of the scheme of study which he had proposed for himself. In this famous letter Gramsci wrote that 'my life still goes by always with the same monotony. Studying too is much more difficult than it might seem' (LP1, 83). At the time of this letter Gramsci was in prison in Milan, awaiting trial, and able to receive books, but it was not until nearly two years later, when he had been at Turi for more than seven months that he was given permission to write. In this letter of 19 March 1927 Gramsci wrote: 'I am obsessed (this is a phenomenon typical of people in jail, I think) by this idea: that I should do something *für ewig* ... I would like to concentrate intensely and systematically on some subject that would absorb and provide a centre to my inner life.' He went on to list four subjects for his proposed investigations: 'a study of the formation of the public spirit in Italy during the past century; in other words, a study of Italian intellectuals, their origins, their groupings in accordance with cultural currents, and their various ways of thinking, etc. etc.' The second topic was 'a study of comparative linguistics', and the third was 'a study of Pirandello's theatre and of the transformation of Italian theatrical taste that Pirandello represented and helped to form', while his final subject was 'an essay on the serial novel and popular taste in literature'. Gramsci wrote that there was 'a certain homogeneity among these four subjects: the creative spirit of the people in its diverse stages and degrees of development' (LP1, 83–84). As we shall see, Gramsci subsequently modified (on more than one occasion) his plan of study and of writing, and of the four topics listed in this letter it is only the first of them (the study of intellectuals, Italian and others) that is prominent in the *Notebooks*.

However, it was to be nearly two more years before Gramsci received permission to write in his prison confinement. Permission had been refused in March 1927, and this permission was only granted in January 1929, when he was in Turi, and then under stringent and repressive conditions. He was allowed only four books in his cell at any one time, and it seems the same limit was imposed on the notebooks in which he was allowed to write. These notebooks, which were given to him after having been stamped and signed by the prison governor, were school notebooks, obtained for him by his sister-in-law Tania. Here it is necessary to explain the form of the *Prison Notebooks* in their original edition, since none of this is obvious from the form in which they appear in the SPN. The *Quaderni del carcere*, or *Prison Notebooks*, consist of thirty-three such school notebooks, in which Gramsci wrote his notes and thoughts on a huge variety of topics. Of these thirty-three notebooks, four are ones in which Gramsci made translations from English, German and Russian. As he wrote to Tania once he had received permission to write in his cell, 'Do you know? I'm already writing in my cell. For the time being I'm only doing translations to limber up: and in the meantime I'm putting my thoughts in order' (LP1, 245). Gramsci wrote these notebooks over a period of six of his eleven years of incarceration, with the first notebook having as its first line the date of 8 February 1929, and the writing of the notebooks ceasing in the middle of 1935 as a result of the collapse of Gramsci's health. These notebooks consist of over 2,300 pages of notes as printed in the Gerratana edition, sometimes short paragraphs (on occasion of one or two sentences with a quote from a book or article which is summarized or commented upon in the note), and often of much longer sections devoted to particular themes. Each section (with a very few exceptions) is headed by a paragraph sign §, a number, and by a rubric or short phrase describing or summarizing the paragraph or section in question. Some of these rubrics recur frequently throughout the text of the *Prison Notebooks*, for example 'Formation of the Italian Intellectual Class', and (taking this as a random example), a typical entry in the *Prison Notebooks*, would start in the following way, as is the case with this one, paragraph 137 of Notebook 3:

§ (137). *The formation of the Italian intellectual class.* The effect of the socialist workers' movement on the creation of important sectors of the ruling class. The phenomenon in Italy is objectively different from that in other countries in this respect ...

(QE2, 114)

The paragraph number and the rubric (above in italics) are placed by Gramsci at the beginning of each of the 2,300 and more printed pages of notes that together constitute the *Prison Notebooks*. From what has been said it should be clear that the reader who is coming to the *Prison Notebooks* with their first port of call being the SPN will be presented with a text which in physical appearance and indeed in its coherence is quite different from the original version of the notebooks, which have a much more fragmentary look, divided as they are by these sections, each with its number and heading, and varying very much in length and in content. Some sections, as noted already, are just summaries of books or articles, with a sentence or two adding Gramsci's own observations. Other sections are much longer and coherent, dealing at length with such themes as the role of intellectuals, the critique of the ideas of Benedetto Croce, the history of the Italian Risorgimento, or problems of philosophy. The English SPN is therefore a much more tidied-up text, which brings together sections from different notebooks under headings such as 'State and Civil Society' or 'The Modern Prince' which are indeed themes that Gramsci discusses, but in the full version of the *Notebooks* they are discussed and presented in a much more fragmentary way.

For these reasons, the *Prison Notebooks* are a classic text like no other, especially when one takes into account the conditions under which they were written, and the political as well as the personal context of the notes which Gramsci penned in the twenty-nine notebooks (plus the four translation ones) which constitute the work. The letters which Gramsci wrote from prison, mainly to his sister-in-law Tatiana Schucht, as well as to his wife Julia Schucht, are an indispensable aid to understanding Gramsci's personal and intellectual preoccupations during the eleven years of his imprisonment. Giuseppe Vacca is right to point out, in his study of Gramsci's life and thoughts, that 'the correspondence forms an important key to help in the reading of the notebooks: in some cases they summarize the contents of the notebooks, in others they follow the development or anticipate the lines of research in the notebooks' (Vacca 2012, xv). As Gramsci wrote to Julia in a letter of 25 January 1936, written after he had been released from the prison in Turi, and was in a clinic in Rome, though still under police supervision and control, ' ... since 1926, immediately after my arrest, when my existence was abruptly and with not a little brutality impelled in a direction determined by external forces ... the limits of my freedom have been restricted to my inner life and my will has merely become the will to resist' (LP2, 353). In the same letter, describing his train journey to the clinic in Rome, and urging Julia to make the journey from the Soviet Union to Italy (which in the end she did not make), Gramsci wrote that 'after such a long time, after so many events, whose real meaning has perhaps in great part eluded me, after so many years of a wretched, compressed life, swathed in darkness and petty misfortunes ... I have changed a great deal'. As he explained, 'I have been cut off from the world for ten years (what a terrifying experience I had in the train, after six years of seeing only the same roofs, the same walls, the same grim faces, when I saw that during this time the vast world had continued to exist with its meadows, its woods, the common people, swarms of children, certain trees, certain vegetable gardens, but especially how struck I was at seeing myself in a mirror after so much time; I immediately returned to the carabinieri's side)' (LP2, 354).

Despite what he wrote in this letter about events whose real meaning had perhaps in great part escaped him, the *Prison Notebooks* are not an abstract text containing meditations on politics and philosophy with no reference to current developments or to the epochal transformations occurring at the time. In one sense they can be read as an analysis of the defeat of revolutionary aspirations in Italy and in Europe more generally in the period after the First World War and the Bolshevik Revolution. Gramsci sought to explain the victory of fascism in Italy and the failure of the working-class movement to oppose its seizure of power and political victory. The *Prison Notebooks* are in part an attempt to work through the implications of this defeat and to sketch out an alternative political strategy for the working-class movement in the broadest sense, in the light of the structure of modern liberal-democratic societies with their complex range of practices and institutions (civil society) so different from the society in which the Bolshevik Revolution had taken place in Russia. Yet the *Prison Notebooks* contain also, in a cryptic and Aesopian sense, a critique of Stalinism and authoritarian communism of the Bolshevik type, and Gramsci's political development, even under prison conditions, was to lead him to distance himself from the model of revolution imposed by the RCP (Russian Communist Party) on communist parties throughout Europe and the world. In a letter of 27 February 1933, again to his sister-in-law Tatiana, Gramsci reflected on the tribunal which had sentenced him and on the conditions of his imprisonment, and very strangely included his wife Julia ('Julca' in this letter) among those who in a sense had contributed to his incarceration:

> I was sentenced on June 4, 1928, by the Special Tribunal, that is, by a specific collegium of men, which could nominally be indicated by name, address, and profession in civilian life. But this is a mistake. Those who sentenced me belong to a much vaster organism, of which the Special Tribunal was only the external and material expression, which compiled the legal documents for the sentence. I must say that among these 'sentencers' was also Julca. I believe, indeed I'm firmly convinced she was there unconsciously, and then there is a series of less unconscious people.
>
> (LP2, 276)

This has led some authors to write of 'Gramsci's two prisons', the obvious fascist one to which he was condemned by the Special Tribunal acting as agents for the fascist state, with the personal intervention of Mussolini, the Duce or Capo of that state, and the other more metaphorical prison of the international communist movement. This theme is pursued in the book by the scholar Franco Lo Piparo (2012).

Gramsci's main correspondent in prison was Tatiana Schucht, his sister-in-law, but she in turn was in close communication with the eminent economist and close friend of Gramsci, Piero

Sraffa, based in Cambridge (England), who received from Tania copies of Gramsci's letters, which he then forwarded to Togliatti, who became leader of the PCd'I in exile and head of its foreign centre in Paris (Daniele 2011). Gramsci was aware of this, and realized that his dissent in prison from the political line which the communist movement (including the Italian party) took after 1929 was known through Sraffa to Togliatti and to the Comintern leaders in Moscow. This implies that his language in his letters (known to the Italian party centre in exile) and in his *Notebooks* (which of course were not known to them at the time they were being written) had to be doubly cryptic or Aesopian. Not only were his letters subject to fascist prison censorship, but were also being copied (by Tania) and forwarded to Sraffa and via him to the Italian party centre in exile. As for the *Notebooks*, the conditions under which they were written and the constant fear of their being impounded and censored imposed also limits on what could be written directly and openly, causing them to be written in a sort of coded language. While it may be true as some scholars argue that Gramsci's term for Marxism, the philosophy of praxis, did express his activist and non-deterministic concept of Marxism (this is discussed in Chapter 6 below), it was also a term used to avoid any explicit mention of Marxism, and has to be explained at least partially by a wish to avoid penalties imposed by the censor.

How then did Gramsci write the *Prison Notebooks*, and how were they structured and written under the rigorous and repressive conditions of fascist imprisonment? Following Francioni's work, it seems that Gramsci was only allowed three or at the most four notebooks in which to write in his cell at any one time (Francioni 1984). Francioni argues that in order to maximize the space available in which to write the notes, he would make a division of each notebook into two halves, starting a particular set of notes halfway through each notebook, and writing notes in more than one notebook at any one time. In this way each notebook could contain two sets of reflections and themes, which could be pursued simultaneously across more than one notebook, so that a topic written on in one notebook is then continued in another notebook. For example, 'Appunti di filosofia' ('Notes on Philosophy'), starts in Notebook 4, and occupies the second half of the original notebook. Then 'Notes on Philosophy II' continues this strand of thought in Notebook 7, again starting halfway through the actual notebook, with further 'Notes on Philosophy', the third block, coming in Notebook 8, also starting at the halfway point of that notebook, so that there is a continuing series of reflections on this theme which appear in the full printed version of the notebooks in three different sections but represent a continuous thread of thought even though physically separated in the notebooks, because of the prison restrictions which forced Gramsci to write that way and maximize the writing space and pages available to him. None of this is evident to the reader of the English language edition of the SPN, but needs to be kept in mind in order to appreciate the nature and compositional methods of the original text.

We also need to be aware of two other features of the text of the *Prison Notebooks*, both of which are also 'hidden' from the reader of the English-language selections. Gramsci wrote several notes and blocks of notes. These notes he then copied out again, in many cases adding and extending the original material, and these revised and developed versions constituted the 'special notebooks', a term coined by him to distinguish these notebooks from the 'miscellaneous' ones. The earlier versions were then crossed out, while leaving the text perfectly legible through the lines deleting the text. This is the second feature of the *Notebooks* which is not evident from the English-language selections, the distinction between the special notebooks, each of which is dedicated to a particular theme, and which comprise revisions of notes written in their original form at an earlier stage, from the miscellaneous notebooks, which contain notes and remarks of a very diverse nature, juxtaposed with no regard to thematic continuity. In the Italian edition of the complete text, and also in the as yet incomplete English translation of the full text, a distinction is made between A, B and C texts. The A texts are those notes which Gramsci recopied and (in many cases) revised and developed for the later special notebooks, crossing out the earlier versions (the A texts), while the fuller revised notes are called the C texts. The notes which fall in the category of B notes are those which Gramsci did not cross out and revise for the special notebooks. In both the Italian (1975) and the English (as yet incomplete) versions of the full text of the *Notebooks*, the A notes are printed in a smaller typeface, to make it clear that they reappear in a fuller version at some other point in the *Notebooks*, with reference given to the place of their later reappearance. Hence in the full version of the *Prison Notebooks* there is a considerable amount of repetition, given that Gramsci repeats and extends many of his earlier notes, reassembling them into the special notebooks which are dedicated to particular themes and in that way distinguished from the miscellaneous notebooks. Gramsci started the special notebooks in 1932, three years after having written the heading for the first ('miscellaneous') notebook in February 1929. Of the thirty-three notebooks, excluding from that total the four given over to translation exercises, seventeen are special ones, sometimes given a title by Gramsci to indicate the themes treated in those notebooks, and these special notebooks start with number 10, devoted to 'The Philosophy of Benedetto Croce', number 11 with the title (this one not given by Gramsci himself) 'Introduction to the Study of Philosophy', followed by number 12, 'Notes and Scattered Thoughts for a Group of Essays on the History of Intellectuals'. This notebook was followed by number 13, a substantial discussion of the politics of Machiavelli, which is also the subject of the much shorter Notebook 18. Two of the specials are devoted to the topic of culture (Notebooks 16 and 26), to which could be added the short Notebook 21 on 'Problems of Italian National Culture: 1 – Popular Literature'. The substantial Notebook 19 deals with problems of the Italian Risorgimento (though this one was not given that title by Gramsci), and Notebook 22 is devoted to the theme of Americanism and Fordism. The final special notebooks were written in the years 1934 to 1935, when Gramsci's health was giving out, and these are much shorter notebooks, concluding with the brief Notebook 29, 'Notes for an Introduction to the Study of Grammar', in which Gramsci went back to the philological studies of his student years.

From what has been said so far about the *Notebooks*, a number of things should be evident, the first of which is the enormous range of topics discussed in them, in both the miscellaneous and the special notebooks. These topics range from a discussion of Canto 10 of Dante's *Divine Comedy* (this is in the fourth notebook) through a thorough critique of the philosophy of Croce, the history and historiography of the Italian Risorgimento, as well as analyses of the structure of modern society under the heading of 'Americanism and Fordism', and the politics and significance of Machiavelli. Another important topic is the nature of culture and the significance of popular culture, while another crucial theme is the role of intellectuals and their significance not only in Italian history but more generally their role in both preserving and opposing the existing order (the distinction between 'traditional' and 'organic' intellectuals, discussed in Chapter 3 below). And this variety of topics listed so far does not include the diverse topics discussed in the miscellaneous notebooks, under such recurring rubrics as 'Past and Present' and 'Types of Journal'. While the *Prison Notebooks* therefore are certainly a classic of political theory, it is clear that they form a classic very different in nature, in form and structure, from other classics in the canon of political theory, from Plato's *Republic* to Hobbes's *Leviathan* or Rousseau's *Social Contract*, to name but a few. The reader confronting the *Prison Notebooks* for the first time is faced with a maze of seemingly disparate topics, and it is not surprising that words like 'labyrinth' and 'archipelago' have been used to describe the text and the problems facing the reader. As Francioni points out, the *Prison Notebooks* 'are not a systematic work: while the substance of their theoretical and conceptual foundation is profoundly unitary, the notebooks nevertheless have in great part the form of an ensemble of fragments' (Francioni 1984, 22). This fragmentary character is less evident from the English-language *Selections* (SPN) which piece together extracts from the various notebooks under headings given by their editors such as 'Notes on Italian History' and 'The Modern Prince'. This certainly has the advantage of imposing a certain unity on the text, and making it in some ways easier for the reader to read the *Prison Notebooks* as though they were a systematic treatment of issues of politics, history and philosophy. Indeed, the first Italian edition of the *Prison Notebooks* treated the text in this way, putting together parts of the Notebooks in a series of volumes each of which dealt with one particular theme. These volumes took notes from the full text and assembled them thematically, with reference to the topic signalled by the title of each volume, so that, for example, all of Gramsci's notes relating to the Italian Risorgimento appeared in the volume with that title. It was only in 1975 that the full edition of the *Prison Notebooks* was published, edited by Valentino Gerratana, and this reproduced the *Notebooks* not thematically but chronologically, following the text of each notebook in its entirety, and seeking to arrange the series of notebooks in the chronological order in which they were written. This edition has been up to now the definitive edition, though a new *edizione nazionale* is in the course of production, which makes a clearer distinction between the miscellaneous and the special notebooks, and includes the full text of the four containing Gramsci's translations from English, German and Russian. This new national edition of the *Notebooks* is in three parts, the first part consisting of the translation notebooks, the second part of the 'miscellaneous' ones, and the third devoted to the special notebooks, and with no difference in font between A texts and C texts (Cospito 2011b). The English language translation of the full text of the *Prison Notebooks* has so far only covered the first eight of the twenty-nine notebooks, and follows the Gerratana edition, with extremely full notes and scholarly apparatus provided by the editor Joseph Buttigieg (QE1, 2 and 3: 1992, 1996, 2007).

The approach to the *Prison Notebooks* thus presents problems distinct from those involved in other classic texts of political theory and from other great books. Instead of a text destined and prepared for publication, with a coherent argument deployed from beginning to end, as one could say was the case, for example, with Hobbes's *Leviathan*, we have a text which as Francioni says was written in a 'spiral' method (Francioni 1984, 22), with concepts introduced, revised, then repeated in a different way. For instance, one of the concepts for which Gramsci is best known is the idea of hegemony, yet there is in the *Prison Notebooks* no systematic exposition of this concept, which is introduced on several occasions by reference to particular historical and political examples, rather than in a general and abstract way. Francioni talks of Gramsci's method as that of an 'analogical model', in which Gramsci proceeds by 'isolating specific historical phenomena which offer similarities with contemporary reality that has to be interpreted' (Francioni 1984, 70). Francioni points out that, for example, the category of hegemony is developed in the *Notebooks* in this way – the concept is tested, so to speak, through Gramsci's analysis of the class relationships and struggles in the period of the Italian Risorgimento (Francioni 1984, 71). Nevertheless, despite the fragmentary and 'spiral' nature of the *Notebooks*, much more evident, as we have said, in the full edition of the *Notebooks* than in the 'reconstructed' English-language selections volume, there is a structure and certain basic themes, which were identified both by Gramsci himself and by later commentators like Francioni on the basis of their careful philological and textual investigations. We have seen that in his letter to Tania of 19 March 1927 Gramsci announced his intention to write something *für ewig*, something permanent or lasting, and the four central themes which he announced in that letter. Two years later, in a letter to Tania of 25 March 1929 Gramsci explained that he now wanted to focus on three principal topics. He wrote that he wanted no more books sent to him unless he specifically asked for them 'because only if I myself ask for them will the books fit into the intellectual plan I want to construct. I've decided to concern myself chiefly and take notes on these three subjects: (1) Italian history in the nineteenth century, with special attention to the formation and development of intellectual groups; (2) the theory of history and historiography; (3) Americanism and Fordism' (LP1, 257). This letter shows clearly Gramsci's focus on problems of history and historiography, as well as his principal concern with the role of intellectuals and intellectual groups, in Italian history as well as more generally, and the theme of Americanism and Fordism, as indicating his desire to make sense of modernity and the nature of economy and society in the contemporary world.

Yet after the letter of 1929 just quoted, Gramsci came again to revise and extend his scheme of work. Francioni notes that in Notebook 3 there is 'an extension of the field of research which breaks down and puts in crisis the programme of February' (Francioni 1984, 71). New rubrics appear in that third notebook, dealing with, among other topics, the history of the subaltern classes, the role of intellectuals in Germany, France and Italy, and popular literature in various countries. In Notebook 8 (discussed further below), there is a further list of topics given by Gramsci himself, under the heading 'Groupings of Subjects', and this list itself is preceded by two paragraphs which start by stating the 'provisional character – like memoranda – of these kind of notes and jottings', with Gramsci writing (to himself? to any future readers?) that such notes could result in 'independent essays, but not in a comprehensive organic work' (QE3, 231; Q8, 935). Gramsci insists in this paragraph that these notes often involve assertions which have not been verified, so that they are merely 'rough first drafts'. Further research, Gramsci wrote, might lead to these assertions being abandoned, and even being replaced by exactly contrary assertions (QE3, 231; Q8, 935). This suggests the hypothetical or provisional quality of the material contained in the *Notebooks*, which again affects the way in which we read this text, since the analysis developed by Gramsci is often, so to speak, him 'thinking aloud', or writing notes which reflect his grappling with a series of problems, rather than giving the considered definitive result of a conclusively meditated process of thought. This is one aspect rightly highlighted by a recent study of the *Notebooks*, by Fabio Frosini, who writes of 'the open and provisional dimension, at the limit hypothetical, of the thought that, almost surprised in the very act of its generation, we find in the Notebooks' (Frosini 2010, 16).

The *Notebooks*, then, are a text written under conditions of imprisonment in which Gramsci's access to books was restricted, in the sense that he could only have a limited number in his cell at any one time. Francioni offers a helpful periodization of the writing of these twenty-nine notebooks, plus the four used by Gramsci for translation exercises (Francioni 1984, 127–29). Francioni divides the process of writing the notebooks into four periods, the first of which started in February 1929 (as we have seen, over a year after Gramsci was given his prison sentence), and lasted until November 1930. This period involved work on four translation notebooks, and on eleven theoretical ones, of which two (Notebooks 1 and 3) were completed by November 1930, while others were either not filled or only just started. This first period ended in November/December 1930, with what Francioni calls a 'phase of transition' (Francioni 1984, 128), that is to say transition towards the reformulation and extension of Gramsci's initial project as sketched out in his letters to Tania of 19 March 1927 and 25 March 1929, quoted above.

This reformulation opens a second period of work on the *Notebooks*, covering the years from the end of 1930 to the spring (March/April) of 1932. This reformulation found expression in the early pages of Notebook 8, mentioned above, which opens with the heading 'Loose Notes and Jottings for a History of Italian Intellectuals', followed by a paragraph headed 'Principal Essays'. This list of essays starts with 'Development of Italian intellectuals up to 1870: different periods', and includes such topics as 'The medieval commune: the economic-corporative phase of the state', 'Cosmopolitan function of Italian intellectuals up to the 18th century', and ends with the topic 'Machiavelli as a technician of politics and as a complete politician or a politician in deed'. After that Gramsci added the words 'Appendices: Americanism and Fordism' (QE3, 231–32; Q8, 935–36). In turn this agenda for intellectual work is followed in Notebook 8 by the heading 'Groupings of Subjects', which gives a further list of ten areas of research. This list starts with '1. Intellectuals: Scholarly issues', followed by '2. Machiavelli', and includes as number 4 a theme which was treated extensively in a later notebook, namely 'Introduction to the study of philosophy and critical notes on a *Popular Manual of Sociology*'. As we shall see, this 'Popular Manual' was Gramsci's coded name for a text by the Russian Bolshevik leader Nicolai Bukharin on 'Historical Materialism', by reference to which Gramsci criticized Bukharin's mechanical and (as Gramsci saw it) deterministic form of Marxism. Francioni dates the writing of the first list (the 'Loose Notes and Jottings for a History of Italian Intellectuals') to a date between November and December 1930, while he suggests that the second list ('Groupings of Subjects') was written between March and April 1932, and has the character of a reflection or ordering of work already done, rather than a plan for work still to be embarked on. What is clear is indeed the reformulation of the initial plan of study, and a broadening out of Gramsci's work. Notebooks 5 and 6 fall in this period. If Notebook 5 is what Francioni calls 'the laboratory on the intellectuals', Notebook 6 is called by him 'the notebook on the State', in which Gramsci began his attempt to develop a new conception of the state. In a letter to Tania of 3 August 1931 Gramsci wrote that 'right now I no longer have a true programme of studies and work and of course this was bound to happen'. He explained that he had set himself 'the aim of reflecting on a particular series of problems, but it was inevitable that at a certain stage these reflections would of necessity move into a phase of documentation and then to a phase of work and elaboration that requires large libraries' (LP2, 51–52). Nevertheless, he continued, he was not 'completely wasting [his] time':

> One of the subjects that has interested me most during recent years has been that of delineating several characteristic moments in the history of Italian intellectuals. This interest was born on the one hand from the desire to delve more deeply into the concept of the State and, on the other to understand more fully certain aspects of the historical development of the Italian people.
>
> (LP2, 52)

This joint theme of the role of intellectuals and the need to redefine the nature of the state was taken up in another letter to Tania a few weeks later, when Gramsci wrote on 7 September 1931 that

> I greatly amplify the idea of what an intellectual is and do not confine myself to the current notion that refers only to the preeminent intellectuals. My study also leads to certain definitions of the concept of the State that is usually understood as a political Society (or dictatorship, or coercive apparatus meant to mould the popular mass in accordance with the type of production and economy at a given moment) and not as a balance between the political Society and the civil Society (or the hegemony of a social group over the entire national society, exercised through the so-called private organisations, such as the Church, the unions, the schools, etc.), and it is within the civil society that the intellectuals operate (Ben. Croce, for example, is a sort of lay pope and he is a very effective instrument of hegemony even if from time to time he comes into conflict with this or that government, etc.).
>
> (LP2, 67)

So it is evident that in this second period Gramsci had expanded his original plan even further, and that what was involved in the *Notebooks* was a rethinking of politics and the nature of the state, connected as always with his preoccupation with the role of intellectuals and the particular nature of Italian history. What Francioni calls the third period of the writing of the *Prison Notebooks* extended from the spring of 1932 to the end of 1933, by which time Gramsci had left the prison at Turi and (from August 1933) found himself, still under surveillance and prison-like conditions, in the slightly less repressive environment of the Clinica Cusumano in Formia. This period is the one which Francioni calls the most intense and the most demanding of the work Gramsci carried out in his notebooks. It was in that period that he abandoned his translation exercises and started on the first of the special notebooks, which (as explained above) were each designed to focus on a particular topic, and which in many cases saw Gramsci rewrite earlier notes (the so-called A texts) which he then crossed out when he had completed the later version. This period saw him working on ten notebooks, of which four were special notebooks, including Notebooks 10 and 11, the most philosophical ones, concerned respectively with the philosophy of Benedetto Croce, named by Gramsci in the letter of 7 September 1931 as a 'sort of lay pope', and with the theory of historical materialism as expounded by Bukharin in his book *Historical Materialism*, or as Gramsci refers to it 'the popular manual of sociology'. Francioni suggests that taken together with Notebook 11, and understood in the context of an overall vision of the philosophical work of 1932, Notebook 10 on Croce can be understood as 'the moment of greatest theoretical depth on the part of Gramsci, halfway through the journey of the *Prison Notebooks*' (Francioni 1984, 109). In the same year (1932) there were also some highly significant letters to Tania in which Gramsci explained his preoccupation with Croce's work, and his criticism of this most important thinker who for Gramsci represented the type of traditional intellectual who exercised a profound influence in Italy and well beyond.

The fourth and final period of the writing of the *Prison Notebooks* runs from the beginning of 1934, by which time Gramsci was already in Formia, to the summer of 1935, when his health was giving out after nine years in the fascist prisons. These two years saw Gramsci working on thirteen special notebooks and two 'miscellaneous' ones, but only Notebook 16 was completed. In March 1933 Gramsci underwent a severe crisis of health, described by him briefly in a letter to Tania of 14 March 1933: 'Precisely last Tuesday, early in the morning, as I was getting out of bed, I fell to the floor without being able to stand up by my own efforts. I've been in bed all these days, and very very weak. I spent the first day in a somewhat hallucinatory state, if I can put it that way, and I was unable to connect ideas with ideas and ideas with the appropriate words' (LP2, 281). A few days later (21 March 1933) he wrote to Tania again, describing some of the manifestations of what he had gone through: 'my body is traversed by twinges and by sudden ticks in the most various parts but especially in the legs and arms, and by distensions and contractions; I have the feeling of being "electrified", so to speak, and any abrupt or unexpected movement provokes a rapid sequence of twinges and upsurges of blood (my heart jumps into my throat, as the saying goes)' (LP2, 282). Francioni says that this last period of Gramsci's work on the *Notebooks* is marked by a greater fragmentation of the work, and by the fact that several of the special notebooks are unfinished, and often stop after a few pages. The reworking of the A texts in this period is limited to rather minor changes, compared with the more substantive changes which those texts underwent in the notebooks of the third period. Having said that, this last period saw Gramsci working on two substantive notebooks on the Italian Risorgimento (Notebook 19) and on Americanism and Fordism (Notebook 22) where he rewrote the A texts, the original version of his notes on these topics, even if without any substantive changes. The last of the notebooks, number 29, seems to have been written in April 1935, and Gramsci gave it the title 'Notes for an Introduction to the Study of Grammar'. This was a short notebook, and was the last text on which Gramsci was able to work.

In August 1935 Gramsci left the Cusumano clinic for the Clinica Quisisana in Rome, where he was to remain for the final months of his life, in which he sought permission to leave Italy to rejoin his family in the Soviet Union, or, if such permission was not granted, to be allowed to go to Sardinia. Yet neither the 'big project' of emigration to the USSR nor the plan to move to Sardinia came to anything. Gramsci had at one stage hoped that in the light of better relations between Italy and the Soviet Union his release could be agreed by diplomatic means between the two states, perhaps in terms of an exchange between him and some Italian prisoners held in Russia. Yet here again Gramsci was victim of the two prisons of fascism on the one hand, and Stalinism on the other, perhaps even three prisons if one adds the foreign centre of the PCd'I as a separate entity. Mussolini was reluctant to agree to Gramsci's release because it could be construed as a victory for the international campaign that had been launched to secure Gramsci's release. This campaign had been given renewed life by the publication of the report on Gramsci's health, which announced that it was unlikely his health could resist any more years of prison life. Gramsci remained insistent that he would not ask for pardon from Mussolini, and so the only way in which his release was acceptable was through a diplomatic arrangement between the two states. Yet for the Soviet regime and the Comintern, by now firmly subordinated to the foreign-policy requirements of the Soviet state, there was no real interest in pursuing negotiations for Gramsci's release, even in the context of the exchange with the Italian detainees held in the Soviet Union. This was the period of the start of the 'Popular Front' against fascism (announced at the Seventh Comintern Congress of 1935), so as relations between Italy and the USSR were cooling down, this meant that there was less chance of any negotiations between Italy and the Soviet Union. Finally, it seems that Togliatti, now leader of the PCd'I in exile, knew of Gramsci's reservations towards what had been up to 1935 the policy of the international communist movement, namely the sectarian policy of 'class against class', which treated social democracy as the left wing of fascism and therefore to be treated as an enemy rather than as a potential ally in the fight against fascism.

Indeed, while in prison in Turi Gramsci had come to open opposition with his party comrades who followed the PCd'I (and Comintern) line. It seems that news of this dissension on the part of Gramsci towards the party line had emerged and reached the foreign centre of the party in Paris. Of course at this stage no one knew what was in the *Prison Notebooks*. However, it was now clear that Gramsci was anything but an 'orthodox' communist, since he had developed his idea (and shared it with his fellow communist prisoners) that the aim of communist and socialist politics must be for a Constituent Assembly, in other ways the restoration or achievement of democracy, rather than the Comintern line (certainly up to 1935) that revolution and the dictatorship of the proletariat were the goals to be fought for (on this see Vacca 2012, ch. 8). While in prison in Turi, Gramsci had discussed with his fellow prisoners the strategy to be adopted in the struggle against fascism, and had articulated his dissent from the prevailing Comintern line, which the PCd'I had accepted. Up to 1935, this was the so-called 'class against class' line which combined a belief in the imminent collapse of the capitalist system with a sectarian hostility to social democracy, seen as an agent of capitalism with which there could be no thought of alliance or joint action against fascism. This changed after 1935 with the coming of the Popular Front strategy, which completely transformed the political line of the international communist movement, laying the stress on a broad popular alliance with social democrats (and others) to fight fascism. It seems that Gramsci's political analysis in prison was critical of both 'class against class' and, to a lesser extent, of the Popular Front. Gramsci's slogan of the need for a Constituent Assembly has to be interpreted, so argues Vacca, in terms of the general political analysis developed in the *Prison Notebooks* (Vacca 2012). This dissent from the party line led to hostility to Gramsci on the part of other communist prisoners in Turi, and news of Gramsci's 'heterodoxy', or 'revisionism', as Vacca calls it, was communicated to the PCd'I in exile. Terracini, one of those sentenced along with Gramsci by the Special Tribunal in 1928, wrote to the party centre in exile on 2 March 1931 that 'the rumour that Antonio radically disagrees with the line of the party is current and growing stronger in our groups in prison, with repercussions you can imagine' (quoted in Spriano 1979, 71).

In opposition to the Comintern (and PCd'I) line of the Third Period (before the switch to the Popular Front strategy) that fascism was weakening and that the expected crisis of the capitalist system put the idea of a proletarian revolution on the agenda as the goal to be fought for, Gramsci's analysis pointed to the relative success of fascism in Italy in implanting itself and the possibility that through its corporatism it could achieve both industrial and agrarian reform. Gramsci in his notebooks envisaged the possibility that 'if the state were proposing to impose an economic direction by which the production of savings ceased to be a "function" of a parasitic class and became a function of the productive organism itself, such a hypothetical development would be progressive, and could have its part in a vast plan of integral rationalisation' (SPN 315; Q22, §14, 2176; see Vacca 2012, 144). Hence expectations of the imminent collapse of fascism and the possibility of proletarian revolution against the capitalist system were based on a false analysis. The call for a Constituent Assembly fitted in with the broader political analysis developed in the *Prison Notebooks*, based on key ideas of a war of position, a broad struggle to achieve hegemony, to develop an anti-fascist movement of industrial and agricultural workers, as opposed to the war of manoeuvre, the idea of a sudden anti-capitalist (and anti-fascist) offensive with the objective of the immediate transition to proletarian revolution. These key concepts of Gramscian political analysis will be explained fully in the following chapters. It is clear that in his discussions with his fellow prisoners Gramsci explained his idea that the Communist Party should put forward the slogan of a Constituent Assembly, and that this meant a broad alliance fighting in the immediate period not for proletarian revolution but for the restoration of democracy. This was seen as a demand not for the period after the defeat of fascism but as an integral element in the struggle against fascism. It might be thought that this demand for a Constituent Assembly was quite in line with the new (after 1935) line of the Popular Front, and in a letter to Togliatti (leader of the PCd'I) written on 27 April 1937, two days after Gramsci's death, a fellow communist Mario Montagnana reported that 'the friend [i.e. Gramsci] said that "in Italy the Popular Front is the Constituent Assembly"' (quoted in Vacca 2012, 156). However it seems that Gramsci thought that the Popular Front strategy in its orthodox implementation was too much a defensive strategy or perspective. The Popular Front was for him not just a slogan for the transitional period between the fall of fascism and an expected or hoped-for proletarian revolution, but represented an aspiration to a new form of popular political action, rooted in the mass of the Italian people, bringing together industrial and agricultural workers. In his *Prison Notebooks* Gramsci had developed an entirely new concept of democracy and political action, quite different from orthodox communism and critical of the form which that had taken in the Soviet Union.

These matters are still the subject of lively debate among specialists and historians, and there are differences between them on the topic of the extent of Gramsci's disagreements with the official party line and whether it led to his ostracism by his fellow communist prisoners and to Gramsci's withdrawal from the political discussions he had had with them while in prison in Turi. Paolo Spriano puts it well when he admits that 'the discussion in any case is still open', while insisting on the 'wholly convincing' nature of 'his [Gramsci's] criticism of the hasty preparation of an insurrectional coup which would have no likelihood of coming to pass.' However, because of the deep divisions caused by his criticisms of the party line, Gramsci 'found himself virtually isolated, left on one side, by the majority of the members of the communist group in Turi' (Spriano 1979, 70). It is clear then that the *Prison Notebooks*, despite their necessarily fragmented form, have a series of coherent themes and that their subject matter is not an abstract political treatise but one concerned with intensely practical and topical questions. Gramsci was reflecting on the implications for political struggle of the defeat of the revolutionary wave of post-First World War Europe, and developing an entirely original set of political concepts to analyse the possibility of democratic and radical politics in modern complex societies. Understanding the labyrinth of the *Prison Notebooks* thus has to involve some under-standing of the political context in which they were written and the themes, however cryptic, which Gramsci addressed in the course of his political analysis. Of course, the wide scope of the *Notebooks* goes beyond a narrow concept of politics to tackle pro-blems of culture, philosophy and history, as well as the topic of revolutionary political action in the context of states and complex societies totally different from that in which the Bolsheviks had come to power in 1917. But to see the *Prison Notebooks* as an abstract theoretical text divorced from the problems of the day would be a distorted and limited perspective through which to analyse the concepts developed in them.

As we have seen, in August 1935 Gramsci was in the Quisisana clinic in Rome, in deteriorating health as a result of nearly ten years of incarceration, and still under strict police supervision, even in the clinic. In the words of Spriano, 'At the Quisisana clinic, too, the surveillance was continuous and watchful to a degree which might seem almost unbelievable, were it not that irreproachable witnesses have recalled it' (Spriano 1979, 106). Work on the *Notebooks* stopped in 1935, and it seems that initially Gramsci's plan was to move to Sardinia on completion of his prison sentence, which was to come on 20 April 1937. Seen as an enemy, obviously, by the fascist regime which had put him in prison, and seen as expendable or at least not a priority by the Soviet regime, then at the high (or low) point of Stalinism, and viewed as dangerously heterodox and as a critic of the party line by his party comrades and the leaders of the party in exile, Gramsci could not count on diplomatic forces or party support for his struggle to be at the least left free to go to Sardinia, or in the optimal context to be allowed to go to the Soviet Union to join his wife and children. On 25 March 1937 his friend (and crucial intermediary between Gramsci's sister-in-law Tania and the party centre in exile in Paris) Piero Sraffa visited Gramsci in the clinic in Rome, and this was to be their last meeting. After this meeting Sraffa then drew up the draft of a request to Mussolini to give authorization that Gramsci be allowed to move to Russia to rejoin his wife and children, since, in the words of the draft, the state of the applicant (Gramsci) 'is such as to prevent him doing any useful work, even of an exclusively intellectual nature, and to make any form of social life intolerable, except with relatives brought in to help him' (Spriano 1979, 179). This draft was dated 18 April 1937. On 25 April 1937 Gramsci received notice that the surveillance to which he was subject would be suspended, but on that very day he suffered a stroke from which he died two days later, at 4.10 in the morning of 27 April 1937.

How then did his *Notebooks* get saved and preserved, to constitute the text of one of the classics of twentieth-century political thought? They were removed from the clinic by Tania, to whom Sraffa wrote urging her to put them in a 'safe place', which Vacca says was the Soviet embassy in Rome, where they were placed by Tania no later than 5 May 1937. This account is challenged by another scholar, Franco Lo Piparo, who claims that the safe place was not in fact the Soviet embassy but the safe of the Banca Commerciale in Milan, and Lo Piparo suggests that the manuscripts of the *Notebooks* found their way to the Comintern archives in Moscow in April 1941, after having been first in the hands of Gramsci's wife Giulia (Julia) in Moscow, where they arrived in December 1938. Before that, according to Lo Piparo, the *Notebooks* had been 'for nearly a year and a half in places not clearly identifiable between Italy and Russia' (Lo Piparo 2013, 44). He suggests that before his death Gramsci had been concerned that the notebooks should not fall into the hands of Togliatti, of whom Gramsci had become mistrustful, blaming him for a letter (signed by Grieco) received in 1928, which exposed Gramsci to the risk of a longer prison sentence because of its indiscreet revelations. Nevertheless, again following Lo Piparo, it seems rather that Togliatti and Sraffa together kept tabs on the manuscripts of the *Notebooks* in the sense that they were keen that the communist authorities in Moscow did not scrutinize the *Notebooks*, because of their heterodox nature and the fact that, as Lo Piparo puts it, they contained passages 'all too clearly not in harmony with Soviet communism of those years or with the political line of the PCd'I' (Lo Piparo 2013, 108). Lo Piparo even thinks there is a missing notebook to be added to the ones currently known, though it seems this hypothesis is not supported by other scholars.

From Russia, where from the house of Julia Schucht the manuscripts were transferred in 1941 to the Comintern archives, the *Notebooks* made the return journey to Italy in 1945, again through the agency of Togliatti. But it took several years before the *Notebooks* were published in Italy, and, as already noted, their first appearance was not in their totality, arranged in the chronological order in which they had been written, but in a series which arranged the notebooks in six separate thematic volumes. These volumes appeared in the years 1948 to 1951, starting with the first on *Historical Materialism and the Philosophy of Benedetto Croce*, followed in 1949 by three volumes on *The Risorgimento, The Intellectuals and the Organization of Culture* and *Notes on Machiavelli, on Politics and on the Modern State*, concluding with *Literature and National Life* (1950) and finally with *Past and Present* in 1951. It was not until 1975 that the full edition of the *Notebooks* appeared, edited by Valentino Gerratana, who attempted to reconstruct the chronology of the *Notebooks* and to reproduce them as they were written, with full editorial apparatus tracing the references to the books and articles which Gramsci used, or referred to, in the course of writing. The Gerratana edition also makes a clear distinction between the A texts, those which Gramsci revised and rewrote into C texts, and then crossing out (but leaving perfectly legible) the original A text, and those texts labelled B texts which were left in their original form and not revised or extended. This has remained the standard text up to now, and has been used for the as yet incomplete Buttigieg English translation of the full text of the *Prison Notebooks*, which at the time of writing has covered the first eight of the twenty-nine notebooks (leaving aside the four translation notebooks, and neglecting the hypothesis put forward by Lo Piparo that there could be an as yet undiscovered notebook). This Gerratana edition is now being complemented, or perhaps replaced, by a new *edizione nazionale* of the *Notebooks*, currently in the course of production, and this new edition includes the four notebooks which Gramsci filled with translations.

Thus we can conclude with a few observations to summarize the nature of this classic text which the present study will be attempting to elucidate in the chapters that follow. In one sense it is a miracle that the *Prison Notebooks* have come down to us at all, given the dire conditions in which they were written, the oppressive surveillance which pressed on Gramsci while he was compiling them, and the heroic and sustained physical and mental efforts required to sustain coherent and original thought under such conditions, not to mention the more distant and perhaps metaphorical prison or disciplinary structure of orthodox communism in its more rigid Stalinized form which dominated the communist movement for nearly all the period of the composition of the *Notebooks*. The *Notebooks* were taken by Gramsci from Turi to Formia only because some of his fellow prisoners distracted the prison warders so that he could slip the notebooks into his suitcase. It could easily have been the case that they were confiscated and destroyed during the period of his imprisonment. Similar observations could be made about the journey of the *Notebooks* from Italy (taken from the Quisisana clinic by Tania immediately after Gramsci's death) to the Soviet Union, but it seems that their 'heterodox' character was not known by the Comintern guardians, perhaps because of Togliatti's intervention or protection, despite Gramsci's suspicions of Togliatti and his (Gramsci's) divergence from the official communist line to which Togliatti had to adhere. These *Notebooks* could so easily have been buried, or destroyed, in the Comintern archive. Even after their post-war return to Italy, it took several years for the *Notebooks* to see the light of day in a form accessible to a wider public, and even longer for the complete Gerratana edition to appear in 1975, nearly fifty years after the date of 8 February 1929 posted by Gramsci at the beginning of the first notebook. Not only are the *Prison Notebooks* a posthumous text, not seen or perhaps intended for publication by the author, at least in the form in which they have come down to us, but they constitute a text which took a long time to see the light of day.

Gramsci himself, in the pages of the *Prison Notebooks*, offered some reflections on how to study a text which the author himself had not revised for publication. This paragraph of the *Notebooks* is headed 'Questions of Method' (SPN 382–86; Q16, §2, 1840–44), and evidently it deals with how to study the work of Marx, and also with the question of the relationship between Marx and Engels. Gramsci wrote that if one wishes to study 'the birth of a conception of the world which has never been systematically expounded by its founder', then some preliminary detailed philological work has to be done. It would be necessary first of all to 'carry out as a preliminary a meticulous philological work, carried out with the most scrupulous accuracy, scientific honesty and intellectual loyalty and without any preconceptions, apriorism or *parti pris.*' He also insisted on the need to distinguish between those works which the author had completed and published, and those 'which remain unpublished, because incomplete, and those which were published by a friend or disciple, not without revisions, rewritings, cuts, etc., or in other words not without the active intervention of a publisher or editor'. Gramsci warned that 'the content of post-humous works has to be taken with great discretion and caution' and must not be seen as definitive, 'but only as material still being elaborated and still provisional'. Gramsci insisted that in studying a thinker, especially one whose conception of the world lacked a systematic exposition, the 'search for the *leitmotif*, for the rhythm of the thought as it develops, should be more important than that for single casual affirmations and isolated aphorisms' (SPN 384; Q16, §2, 1841–42). While Gramsci was referring explicitly to the works of Marx he was probably thinking also of his own writings, and this suggestion is reinforced by the fact that on several occasions in the course of his *Notebooks* he explicitly emphasized their provisional character, the idea that they were notes developed in the absence of a proper library and that they might need to be modified and even abandoned in the light of further research which was not possible in his present conditions. Hence we are dealing, in the pages that follow, with a text that is in many respects unique, not just because of the circumstances in which it was written and composed, but because of the labyrinthine and spiral nature of Gramsci's meditations on politics, history, culture, literature, religion, education and a whole host of other disparate topics. The guiding leitmotif, to follow Gramsci's own injunction, has to be discovered and analysed. Certainly one such leitmotif is the reflection on the defeat of the working-class movement after the First World War and the rise and hegemony of fascism, and the nature of the historic (and organic) crisis of twentieth-century Europe to which fascism provided one answer, if only temporary and contradictory. How could a new form of politics be developed, one adequate to the conditions of modernity evident in the twentieth-century? And in what ways was a new culture necessary for such a form of politics, and how too could that be fostered and developed? These are some of the themes which Gramsci analysed in his *Notebooks*, and which need to be clarified in the exposition of the following chapters. In addition, one question has to be posed in the course of the exposition and analysis: given that the world has changed fundamentally since the period in which the *Prison Notebooks* were written, what do the concepts developed in that text have to say to those of us living in the twenty-first century?

Taking, then, the SPN as the entry point for the study of Gramsci's *Prison Notebooks*, while recognizing the particular and in some ways limited nature of those selections, the following exposition seeks firstly to explain and clarify the key concepts of Gramsci's *Prison Notebooks*, secondly to place them in some kind of historical context and to develop a critical analysis of the material, to show the originality and new perspectives on politics, culture, philosophy, opened up by Gramsci's thought, and finally, in the light of new scholarship, Italian and international, to assess in what ways this classic text speaks to the conditions of twenty-first-century politics, a world far removed from that of the 1920s and 1930s in whose harsh circumstances the *Prison Notebooks* were composed.

SUGGESTIONS FOR FURTHER READING

There is a very useful guide to the terminology and concepts of the *Prison Notebooks* in the *Dizionario gramsciano: 1926–37*, edited by Guido Liguori and Pasquale Voza (Rome: Carocci, 2009). The most detailed researches on the way in which Gramsci wrote the *Notebooks* and the dating of the *Notebooks* are those by the Italian scholar Gianni Francioni in his book *L'Officina gramsciana: Ipotesi sulla struttura dei 'Quaderni del carcere'* (Naples: Bibliopolis, 1984), followed up by his article of 1992, 'Il bauletto inglese: Appunti per una storia dei "Quaderni" di Gramsci', *Studi Storici* 33, no. 4 (1992): 713–41, and his introduction to the *edizione anastatica* (photocopy of the original manuscripts of the *Notebooks*), *Come lavorava Gramsci* (Rome: Biblioteca Treccani, 2009). None of this material seems to be available as yet in English or summarized in the English-language literature. The ongoing work on the *edizione nazionale* of the *Prison Notebooks* is summarized in the article of Giuseppe Cospito, 'Verso l'edizione critica e integrale dei "Quaderni del carcere"', *Studi Storici* 52, no. 4 (2011): 881–904, and this whole issue of *Studi Storici* is given over to articles dealing with the new 'national edition' and its significance for Gramsci studies. The articles by Maria Luisa Righi on 'Gramsci a Mosca tra amori e politica (1922–23)' and Chiara Daniele on Gramsci's *Prison Letters*, as well as the other articles in this issue, are important. The most important recent study of Gramsci's life and thought in the period during which he wrote the *Prison Notebooks* is that by Giuseppe Vacca, *Vita e pensieri di Antonio Gramsci 1926–1937* (Turin: Einaudi, 2012).

In English, the book by Paolo Spriano, *Gramsci: The Prison Years* (London: Lawrence & Wishart, 1979), remains important for its account of Gramsci's incarceration. Gramsci's *Prison Letters*, in the full two-volume edition edited by Frank Rosengarten (New York: Columbia University Press, 1994) is the best accompaniment to reading the *Prison Notebooks* themselves, which are available in the *Selections from the Prison Notebooks*, edited by Quintin Hoare and Geoffrey Nowell-Smith, which provides the framework for the analysis in the present book. Those who wish to go beyond the *Selections* can turn to Derek Boothman's edition of *Further Selections from the Prison Notebooks* (London: Lawrence & Wishart, 1995), and to the complete English translation of Antonio Gramsci, *Prison Notebooks*, by Joseph Buttigieg, though at present the three volumes of this translation, with very full notes and introduction (New York: Columbia University Press, 1992, 1996, 2007) only cover the first eight of the twenty-nine notebooks. There is also a very good, if brief, discussion of the *Prison Letters* and the *Notebooks* in the book by Antonio Santucci, *Antonio Gramsci,* which is available in English translation (New York: Monthly Review Press, 2010).

3

INTELLECTUALS AND EDUCATION

THE PROBLEM OF INTELLECTUALS

As explained in the previous chapter, the analysis of Gramsci's *Prison Notebooks* developed in this guidebook follows the structure and chapter headings of the English-language *Selections from the Prison Notebooks*, abbreviated as SPN. References to the *Selections* will be complemented by references to the complete Italian edition of the *Prison Notebooks* as well as to other available English translations, including the as yet incomplete English translation of the full text of the *Notebooks*. At the time of writing this only covers the first eight out of the twenty-nine notebooks.

Focusing on the SPN, then, this opens with Part I headed 'Problems of History and Culture', with the first two chapters of that part dealing with Gramsci's views on intellectuals and on education respectively. The pages of the SPN dealing with intellectuals and education are taken from one of Gramsci's 'special' notebooks, in this case Notebook 12, written in 1932, some three years after the first notebook was started, and given the title by Gramsci himself of 'Appunti e note sparse per un gruppo di saggi sulla storia degli intellettuali' ('Jottings and Scattered Notes for a

Group of Essays on the History of Intellectuals'). It is worth noting the somewhat tentative and provisional character which Gramsci gives to his reflections on intellectuals. Here, as elsewhere in the *Notebooks*, he emphasizes that these are thoughts which would need to be refined and revised in the light of further research and bibliographical sources, which were not available to him in the conditions under which the *Notebooks* were written. Gramsci's comparative survey of the role of intellectuals in different countries carries with it his proviso that 'these observations require to be controlled and examined in more depth' (SPN 17; Q12, §1, 1524), emphasizing their exploratory character. We should also note that while the pages in the SPN are taken from the special Notebook 12, this notebook itself is the rewriting of several extended notes which appear in their first version in the earlier Notebook 4 (which was written between 1930 and 1932), notably in its paragraphs 49 (given the rubric by Gramsci 'The Intellectuals') and 50 ('The Common School'), as well as paragraph 55 on 'The Educational Principle in Elementary and Secondary School'. So the text of the pages of the SPN is taken from a notebook which itself was the second version of earlier reflections by Gramsci on the topics dealt with.

If the SPN text thus begins with extracts from Notebook 4, revised and repeated in Notebook 12, there are good reasons for starting its selections with Gramsci's reflections on a topic fundamental to the arguments developed throughout the *Notebooks* as a whole. The first of the twenty-nine notebooks, given the precise date of 8 February 1929, begins with a listing by Gramsci of 'main topics', of which the third is 'Formation of Italian intellectual groups: development, attitudes'. We have already quoted from the famous letter to his sister-in-law Tatiana (Tania) of 19 March 1927 where he announced that he felt he should do something *'für ewig'* (for ever), focusing on four subjects, of which the first was 'a study of the formation of the public spirit in Italy during the past century; in other words, a study of Italian intellectuals, their origins, their groupings in accordance with cultural currents, and their various ways of thinking, etc., etc.', a topic which Gramsci added was 'highly suggestive, which naturally I could only sketch in broad outline, considering the absolute impossibility of having at my disposal the immense volume of material that would be necessary' (LP1, 83). In another letter to Tania, dated 17 November 1930, Gramsci wrote that he had been taking notes 'on the subjects that interest me most'. He wrote that 'I've focused on three or four principal subjects, one of them being the cosmopolitan role played by Italian intellectuals until the end of the eighteenth century, which in turn is split into several sections: the Renaissance and Machiavelli, etc.' (LP1, 360). Indeed Gramsci suggested in this letter that 'if I had the possibility of consulting the necessary material I believe that there is a really interesting book to be written that does not yet exist', though he went on to say that 'I say book, meaning only the introduction to a number of monographs, because the subject presents itself differently in different epochs and in my opinion one would have to go back to the times of the Roman empire' (LP1, 360).

From these indications in his letters it is clear that the question of intellectuals was one with which Gramsci was deeply engaged, as it comes high on the list of subjects he envisaged that would constitute the main topics of the *Notebooks*. His references to this theme in his letters and the historical research he thought was required for an adequate treatment of the topic bear out this primary place which the role of intellectuals occupied in his mind. The quotations given here from his letters refer to the role of *Italian* intellectuals, and the way in which Gramsci thought they had played a cosmopolitan role rather than linking up in Italy with the mass of the population. However, his concern with intellectuals and with education was a broader one, going beyond the specifically Italian role of intellectuals. Gramsci's notes on intellectuals illustrate his broader concern with the ways in which he envisaged hitherto subaltern groups emerging from their subordinate position and becoming hegemonic, playing a leading or directive (*dirigente*) role in society. In order for that to happen, such subordinate groups had to develop and create their own organic intellectuals and move above a limited, 'economic-corporate' level of consciousness. In this process the role of intellectuals was of crucial importance, and it could be said that Gramsci's reflections on intellectuals are among the most innovative in Marxist theory, and indeed in social theory generally. It was not that this topic had been neglected by previous Marxists, starting with Marx, Engels and Lenin themselves. It was Lenin, in his pamphlet *What Is to Be Done?*, who insisted that 'without revolutionary theory there can be no revolutionary movement' (Lenin 1973 [1902], 28), and who argued that revolutionary theory had to be brought to the working-class movement 'from without', meaning by that through the agency of the intelligentsia. In *What Is to Be Done?* Lenin argued that 'the doctrine of socialism, however, grew out of the philosophic, historical and economic theories elaborated by educated representatives of the propertied classes, by intellectuals', and placed Marx and Engels evidently in the category of intellectuals: 'By their social status, the founders of modern scientific socialism, Marx and Engels, themselves belonged to the bourgeois intelligentsia' (Lenin 1973, 38). Gramsci was thus contributing to a debate central to socialist and Marxist movements of his time, focusing on the question of how the theory necessary to a revolutionary movement was to be developed by the agents of that movement, and the function of intellectuals, not themselves necessarily, or usually, workers, in that process. But Gramsci's theorization of intellectuals and his analysis of their role are both much wider and more penetrating than anything on the topic carried out previously by socialist theorists.

It is also worth observing that the very term 'intellectual' itself was a recent modern creation, a neologism coined in the heat of the debates about the Dreyfus case in France. Indeed in the minds of those who initially used the term, 'intellectual' was rather a term of abuse, indicating those who were guilty of abstract reasoning and a false universalism which neglected the specific concrete needs of society and social cohesion. Such at least was the view of the French nationalist writer Maurice Barrès who gave a contemptuous definition of the intellectual as someone who saw society in abstract universal terms. For Barrès the intellectual was typified by the defenders of Dreyfus, people who were willing to sacrifice the interests of the French army and of the cohesion of the French nation for abstract Kantian ideas of universalism. They were therefore 'déracinés', uprooted or rootless people who lived in a world of speculation remote from the needs of a particular society at a specific moment in time (McClelland 1970, 175). The word intellectual thus came into the world paradoxically introduced by those who thought of it as a term of abuse, referring to a stratum of people divorced from real life. It is ironical that while Gramsci's theory of intellectuals takes the opposite line, he also acknowledged that the problem of intellectuals in Italy was that historically they had been separate from the mass of the people because of their cosmopolitan function, as opposed to a truly national role. It is clear then that in his thoughts on intellectuals Gramsci was contributing to a key debate of modern politics on the significance of a new phenomenon, the intellectual, someone who lived on and for ideas, whether that was seen by people like Barrès as a symptom of social disaggregation or by Marxists like Lenin as a necessary element in a revolutionary movement.

DEFINING THE INTELLECTUAL

There is therefore a good case for putting Gramsci's notes on intellectuals as the first section of the selections in SPN, given the central importance of this topic to his thought as a whole. The first point to keep in mind when reading his thoughts on this matter is the guideline Gramsci himself provides, in a letter of Tatiana of 7 September 1931, in which he writes that 'the research I have done on the intellectuals is very broad', and significantly he stated that: 'At any rate, I greatly amplify the idea of what an intellectual is and do not confine myself to the current notion that refers only to the preeminent intellectuals' (LP2, 67). While the pages of the *Prison Notebooks* are full of references to preeminent intellectuals, and notably to the one whom Gramsci saw as the most significant Italian intellectual of his day, namely Benedetto Croce, it is clear that his extension of the concept of intellectual broadens the scope of the term well beyond reference to great thinkers and to those conventionally thought of, in our day, as intellectuals, such as Sartre or Hayek, for example. In one sense, Gramsci extends the concept of intellectual to include everyone, at least in the way in which he insists that all human activity involves thought and is therefore an intellectual practice: 'There is no human activity from which every form of intellectual participation can be excluded ... *homo faber* cannot be separated from *homo sapiens*', with the corollary that 'all men are intellectuals, one could therefore say: but not all men have in society the function of intellectuals' (SPN 9; Q12, §1, 1516). Gramsci insists that one cannot define intellectuals as those who use their intellect, or as we might say live through the exercise of brain rather than brawn, since all human activity is in part an intellectual one: 'one cannot speak of non-intellectuals, because non-intellectuals do not exist' (SPN 9; Q12, §3, 1550). But if all human beings were in that sense intellectuals since any form of labour or human activity is in part cerebral, there were in any society some individuals who practised a specialized form of intellectual activity. These people exercised the function of intellectuals. Everyone, according to Gramsci, can fry an egg or sew up a ripped jacket, without that making them into a cook or a tailor. Similarly, while everyone exercises in some way their brain, that has to be distinguished from those who constitute 'specialised categories for the exercise of the intellectual function' (SPN 10; Q12, §1, 1516).

But what exactly was that function? Gramsci defines intellectuals in a specialized sense as the agents of legitimation of the existing order. They operate as the functionaries of the superstructure. Gramsci's ideas here are both complex and condensed. He states that 'the relationship between the intellectuals and the world of production is not as direct as it is with the fundamental social groups but is, in varying degrees, "mediated" by the whole fabric of society and by the complex of superstructures, of which the intellectuals are, precisely, the "functionaries"' (SPN 12; Q12, §1, 1518). Shortly after this sentence, comes a further description of the function of intellectuals, this time defined as follows: 'The intellectuals are the dominant group's "deputies" exercising the subaltern functions of social hegemony and political government' (SPN 12; Q12, §1, 1518–19). The Italian word here translated as 'deputies' is *commessi*, which usually means a shop assistant or errand boy. The activity of intellectuals is therefore carried out in the sphere of the superstructure, in 'the complex of superstructures', within which Gramsci defines two levels: the first 'level' is that of civil society, 'the ensemble of organisms commonly called "private"', contrasted with the level of political society or the state. In this passage Gramsci relates hegemony to the plane of civil society, whereas the state and what he calls '"juridical" government' is the sphere of '"direct domination" or command' (*'dominio diretto' o di comando*; SPN 12; Q12, §1, 1518). So the argument is that intellectuals are active in both spheres, the sphere of hegemony and that of direct domination or coercion exercised by the state. Gramsci expands on the distinction between these two spheres, explaining that 'social hegemony' involves 'the "spontaneous" consent given by the great masses of the population to the general direction imposed on social life by the dominant fundamental group'. 'Dominant fundamental group' is clearly a means of referring to an economically dominant ruling class, and the consent of the mass of the population stems from, in Gramsci's words, 'the prestige (and consequent confidence) which the dominant group enjoys because of its position and function in the world of production'. The hegemony of such a group is secured by the consent given by the mass of the population, but this consent is complemented by, in Gramsci's words, 'the apparatus of state coercive power which "legally" enforces discipline on those groups who do not "consent" either actively or passively'. Gramsci adds that this coercive apparatus is 'constituted for the whole of society in anticipation of moments of crisis of command and direction when spontaneous consent has failed' (SPN 12; Q12, §1, 1519).

Intellectuals therefore constitute the personnel of these two levels of the superstructure (civil society and state), but there is, according to Gramsci, a whole range of positions and ranks of the intellectuals. These range from the highest level where are to be found what he calls 'the creators of the various sciences, philosophy, art, etc.', contrasted with the lower levels peopled by 'humble "administrators" and divulgators of pre-existing, traditional, accumulated intellectual wealth' (SPN 13; Q12, §1, 1519), who presumably just pass on the ideas of the first-rank 'premier league' (not Gramsci's term) intellectuals like Croce. Gramsci also points out not only that his analysis of intellectuals 'has as a result a considerable extension of the concept of intellectual' (SPN 12), but that 'in the modern world the category of intellectuals, understood in this sense, has undergone an unprecedented expansion' (SPN 12–13; Q12, §1, 1519–20). In words which seem very relevant today, he talks of the standardization of qualifications for intellectual tasks, and the resultant 'competition which makes necessary organisations for the defence of professions, unemployment, over-production in the schools, emigration, etc.' (SPN 14; Q12, §1, 1520). However, the most exciting part of Gramsci's discussion of intellectuals comes in his (partly historical) analysis of the relation of intellectuals to the whole class structure of society, 'the ensemble of the system of relations in which these activities (and therefore the intellectual groups who personify them) have their place within the general complex of social relations' (SPN 8; Q12, §1, 1516).

Gramsci's analysis starts with a general distinction between organic and traditional intellectuals, before developing a more specific analysis of the historical development of intellectuals in particular countries. It is important to keep in mind his extended notion of intellectuals, broadening the concept well beyond the conventional association of the term with academic or purely scholarly activity. Gramsci explains that every rising and ruling class has developed its own stratum of intellectuals, who give that class consciousness of its function, not just in the economic field but more generally: 'Every social group, coming into existence on the original terrain of an essential function in the world of economic production, creates together with itself, organically, one or more strata [ceti] of intellectuals which give it homogeneity and an awareness of its own function not only in the economic but also in the social and political fields.' 'Social group' in this sentence obviously refers to a social class in the Marxist sense, and in particular the bourgeoisie, as is made clear by the following sentence, referring to 'the capitalist entrepreneur' who 'creates alongside himself the industrial technician, the specialist in political economy, the organisers of a new culture, of a new legal system, etc.' (SPN 5; Q12, §1, 1513). These presumably constitute the intellectuals who are the 'deputies' (commessi), who establish and maintain the hegemony of the bourgeoisie. The crucial implication for Gramsci is that the proletariat, as part of its struggle for hegemony, would similarly have to establish its own stratum of intellectuals who would give the working class awareness of its ability to emerge from subalternity. This would involve extending its horizons above and beyond the economic-corporate level. How this could be done, the agencies and problems for the creation of such organic intellectuals of the working class is one of the central preoccupations of Gramsci in the *Prison Notebooks*.

Intellectuals then, at least the organic type, are those linked to a (rising) class, who give it the consciousness needed to be hegemonic, and whose existence and activity are a vital and necessary part of the process of achieving hegemony. But Gramsci distinguishes such organic intellectuals from the traditional intellectuals, who constitute, or think they do, a separate stratum removed from the world of production and class struggle. Any rising class, creating its own organic intellectuals (and evidently Gramsci is thinking of the bourgeoisie here) will, as he says, encounter 'categories of intellectuals already in existence', groups 'which seemed indeed to represent an historical continuity uninterrupted even by the most complicated and radical changes in political and social forms'. Such traditional intellectuals are formed over a long historical period. Gramsci cites as the typical example 'the ecclesiastics, who for a long time (for a long phase of history, which is partly characterised by this very monopoly) held a monopoly of a number of important services: religious ideology, that is the philosophy and science of the age, together with schools, education, morality, justice, charity, good works, etc.' Such traditional intellectuals do indeed 'put themselves forward as autonomous and independent of the dominant social group', so they appear to be in a position of Olympian detachment from the class structure: 'the intellectuals think of themselves as "independent", autonomous, endowed with a character of their own, etc.' (SPN 7–8; Q12, §1, 1514–15). Yet Gramsci rejects any idea of what some years later the sociologist Karl Mannheim, in his book *Ideology and Utopia*, would call the *freischwebende Intelligenz* or 'free-floating intelligentsia' (Mannheim 1936). The traditional intellectuals might think of themselves as autonomous, and be organized in groups with their own traditions. Gramsci indicates that this independence is not really the case, and suggests that even the traditional intellectuals of his day, such as Croce and Gentile, realize this: 'Croce in particular feels himself closely linked to Aristotle and Plato, but he does not conceal, on the other hand, his links with senators Agnelli and Benni, and it is precisely here that one can discern the most significant character of Croce's philosophy' (SPN 8; Q12, §1, 1515). Agnelli was the head of Fiat, and Benni the head of a vast chemicals firm (Montecatini). The success of a rising class depends also on its ability to absorb into its own ranks and indeed to conquer the traditional intellectuals, a capacity in part dependent on the extent to which it has formed its own organic intellectuals. Gramsci observes that 'one of the most important characteristics of any group that is developing towards dominance is its struggle to assimilate and to conquer "ideologically" the traditional intellectuals', and in his view 'this assimilation and conquest is made quicker and more efficacious the more the group in question succeeds in simultaneously elaborating its own organic intellectuals' (SPN 10; Q12, §1, 1517). If this is not done, then Gramsci suggests that the traditional intellectuals will remain an obstacle to the reshaping of society in the interests of the new class. The further implication seems to be that the organic intellectuals of the bourgeoisie of yesterday have become the traditional intellectuals of today, and seek to maintain an intellectual hegemony which has to be challenged by the new organic intellectuals of the working class.

While for Gramsci the paradigm case of traditional intellectuals was represented, historically by the ecclesiastics, by the Church, in his own time he saw Benedetto Croce, the Italian philosopher, as the prime example of a traditional intellectual. Croce's name appears many times in the *Prison Notebooks*, and hence in the present guide to the *Notebooks*, since Gramsci constantly engages with his ideas on history, philosophy, culture and indeed on politics. There is an interesting paragraph in Notebook 6, §10, in which Gramsci indicates that the role of the traditional intellectual is no longer possible in modern times, under the conditions of mass politics. In the course of a discussion of Croce's criticism of works of popular history (which Croce called 'belletristic history') Gramsci wrote that 'the role of the great intellectuals, even if it has remained intact, is much more difficult to affirm and develop in the present milieu: the great intellectual, too, must take the plunge into practical life and become an organiser of the practical aspects of culture, if he wants to remain a leader; he must democratize himself, be more in touch with the times. Renaissance man is no longer possible in the modern world, at a time when increasingly large masses of humans are participating actively and directly in history' (QE3, 7; Q6, §10, 689). Later in this same paragraph Gramsci writes that 'the traditional intellectuals are detaching themselves from the social grouping to which they have hitherto given the highest, most comprehensive form and hence the most extensive and complete consciousness of the modern state', and this detachment meant that 'they are signalling and sanctioning the crisis of the state in its decisive form' (QE3, 9; Q6, §10, 690–91). Presumably this means that the traditional intellectuals such as Croce were no longer linked to the state, since Croce had distanced himself from the fascist state. But this separation of intellectuals from the state apparatus and from practical political concerns was a sign of 'a phenomenon similar to the split between the "spiritual" and the "temporal" in the Middle Ages, a phenomenon that is more complex now than it was then, to the extent that modern life has become more complex' (QE3, 8; Q6, §10, 690). The traditional intellectuals of his day, Gramsci seems to be saying, are unable to perform any constructive tasks or provide genuine intellectual leadership in the conditions of modern mass politics. Similarly, the organic intellectuals of the bourgeoisie had been unable to link up with the masses and develop a popular implantation. This left the way open to the organic intellectuals of the working class, but they had first to be created. How then could the working class form its own stratum of organic intellectuals, a task necessary in order to achieve power? As part of the answer to this problem, Gramsci presents a short survey comparing the history in different countries of the process of formation of intellectuals, and the ways in which the bourgeoisie managed or failed to construct a stratum of organic intellectuals. This comparative historical exercise has important implications for the task of forming organic intellectuals of the working class, in Italy as elsewhere.

   One of Gramsci's constantly repeated themes is that Italian intellectuals in the past had failed to develop links with the popular masses, and that they were so to speak seduced into a cosmopolitan mindset through the institutions first of the Roman Empire and then of the Catholic Church. It is not clear whether here he is talking of organic or traditional intellectuals, and in fact the distinction seems to get rather blurred. What is however clear is that he often notes that in Italy there was a separation between the intellectuals and the broad mass of the population: 'as far as Italy is concerned the central fact is precisely the international or cosmopolitan function of its intellectuals, which is both cause and effect of the state of disintegration in which the peninsula remained from the fall of the Roman Empire up to 1870' (SPN 17; Q12, §1, 1524). The weight of the Papacy in Italy meant that the Church provided the pole of attraction for the intellectuals. Gramsci compares the situation in Italy with that in other countries, in which the organic intellectuals of the bourgeoisie were able to put themselves at the head of broad mass movements to achieve bourgeois hegemony within the framework of the nation-state. The classic case was that of France, which Gramsci described as offering 'the example of an accomplished form of harmonious development of the energies of the nation and of the intellectual categories in particular' (SPN 18; Q12, §1, 1524). Gramsci contrasted the French ideal type, where the intellectuals of the pre-Revolutionary period of 1789 had prepared the bourgeoisie adequately for its hegemony, with the historical development of England and Germany, where the power of traditional intellectuals of the landowning classes was much greater. In England, for example, 'the new social grouping that grew up on the basis of modern industrialism shows a remarkable economic-corporate development but advances only gropingly in the intellectual-political field', so that the 'old land-owning class ... loses its economic supremacy but maintains for a long time a politico-intellectual supremacy and is assimilated as "traditional intellectuals" and as directive [*dirigente*] group by the new group in power' (SPN 18; Q12, §1, 1526). Gramsci thus compared the process of the establishment of bourgeois hegemony in Italy, France, Germany and England, and the respective roles played by the organic intellectuals of the bourgeoisie. Only in France, according to his argument, had the organic intellectuals won intellectual supremacy, resulting in the intellectual dominance of French culture throughout Europe in the eighteenth and nineteenth centuries. The failure of intellectuals in Italy to root themselves in the life of the nation, because of their cosmopolitan allegiances (Roman Empire and Papacy) had meant that Italian national unification came late, and in the form of a crippled or passive revolution, and these ideas are analysed in the following chapter dealing with history and modernity. So in a sense the intellectuals in Italy had failed to become truly organic, to put themselves at the head of the productive elements of Italian society, so there was a big separation or gulf between Italian intellectuals and the mass of the nation, a gulf which was typified in Gramsci's own day by intellectuals like Croce who remained aloof from democratic strivings in a position of Olympian detachment. Gramsci often makes the comparison between Renaissance and Reformation (see Frosini 2012). The Renaissance, in his portrayal of it, was an elitist movement appealing to intellectuals like Erasmus. The Reformation, on the other hand, was a popular movement of intellectual and spiritual renewal and intellectual reform which involved the masses. Gramsci quoted Croce's reference to Erasmus saying that wherever Luther appeared culture went out of the window, expressing the distaste of the intellectual for mass culture: *ubicumque regnat lutheranismus, ibi literarum est interitus* ('wherever Lutheranism reigns, there is the death of letters'; SPN 394; Q16, §9, 1859; first version is in QE2, 142; Q4, §3, 423). This comparison had two implications for the politics of Gramsci's own time: he portrayed Croce as the traditional intellectual, a modern Erasmus, rather removed from any project of cultural renewal among the mass of the population. And furthermore, Marxism was the contemporary equivalent of the Reformation, aiming to spread a new mentality and culture among the masses hitherto excluded from elite culture. But this task of moral and intellectual reform required the formation of new organic intellectuals of the working class, leading Gramsci to discuss how this could be achieved.

As well as the comparison of the role of intellectuals in France, Italy, England and Germany, this section of the *Notebooks* makes a thinly veiled allusion to the Bolsheviks, in a paragraph discussing Russia. There Gramsci refers to earlier experiences of Russia, in which intellectual development was brought through the imitation of German and French experience, since in Russia 'national forces were inert, passive and receptive' (SPN 19; Q12, §1, 1525). But in more recent times, Gramsci noted, clearly referring to the Bolsheviks here, 'an elite consisting of some of the most active, energetic, enterprising and disciplined members of the society emigrates abroad and assimilates the culture and historical experiences of the most advanced countries of the West', yet did so 'without however losing the most essential characteristics of its own nationality'. So in that respect the Bolshevik intellectuals were the opposite of the Italian ones, since they had maintained a 'national-popular character'. This Bolshevik elite had assimilated the culture of the advanced West 'without breaking its sentimental and historical links with its own people' (SPN 20; Q12, §1, 1525). The modernizing process was different from that under Peter the Great, where the progressive element was imported from Germany, whereas the Bolsheviks were genuinely national-popular and represented an indigenous reaction to the historical weight of Russia's inertia. The general conclusion is thus clear: for a class to achieve hegemony, it has to create its own organic intellectuals who give that class consciousness of its role and educate it beyond the limited range of what Gramsci calls the 'economic-corporate level'. In Italy this process had not been carried out by the intellectuals who remained separate from popular culture. Gramsci's concern was with the process through which the working class could create its own intellectual stratum, and with the process through which the hitherto subaltern or subordinate class could establish its intellectual hegemony.

ORGANIC INTELLECTUALS AND THE POLITICAL PARTY

The reason for Gramsci's deep interest in the role of intellectuals is that the formation of an intellectual group (the organic intellectuals) was seen by him as a necessary and vital part of the process through which a rising class achieves and maintains its directing (*dirigente*) role in society. The bourgeoisie had managed to do this, classically in France, and with greater or lesser success in other countries, as Gramsci's historical survey revealed. But this was not just an historical or academic analysis, since, like all of Gramsci's historical investigations it contained clear lessons for present-day politics. How could the working class do what the bourgeoisie had, to varying degrees in varying countries, managed to do, namely to create a stratum of its own intellectuals which would give it, in Gramsci's words, 'homogeneity and an awareness of its own function not only in the economic but also in the social and political fields' (SPN 5; Q12, §1, 1513). Gramsci frequently uses the phrase, taken from the French thinker Ernest Renan, of 'moral and intellectual reform', to denote a cultural transformation which would give the hitherto subaltern classes (workers and peasants) a sense of their own worth and ability to transform, and direct, the economy and society in general. Another influence on Gramsci was that of the French thinker Georges Sorel, author of *Reflections on Violence*, a book which contains this sentence which seems to resonate with many of the notes in the *Prison Notebooks*. Chapter 7 of Sorel's book announces that 'the problem that we shall now try to solve is the most difficult of all those which a Socialist writer can touch upon'. This problem he presented as follows: 'We are about to ask how it is possible to conceive the transformation of the men of today into the free producers of tomorrow working in manufactories where there are no masters' (Sorel 1950, 237). Sorel's own answer to the question he posed was, as he summarized on the last page of his book, 'violence enlightened by the idea of the general strike', stating that 'it is to violence that Socialism owes those high ethical values by means of which it brings salvation to the modern world' (Sorel 1950, 249).

Gramsci's answer to the question was very different, though the idea of transforming the workers of today 'into the free producers of tomorrow' had been a constant theme of his political activity, notably in the factory council movement of 1919–20. Whereas Sorel had no faith in political parties, parliamentary politics, or, it seems, in traditional educational institutions, Gramsci's ideas of the intellectual transformation of the workers of today into the hegemonic class of tomorrow were focused on the role of the political party and the need to form a stratum of organic intellectuals, intellectuals of a new type, different from the intellectuals as known so far in Italian history and politics. Gramsci was under no illusions about the difficulties involved in creating such a stratum of organic intellectuals of the working class. In a passage which comes later in the SPN, in the section dealing with 'The Study of Philosophy' (this section is more fully analysed in Chapter 6 below) Gramsci wrote that 'the process of creating intellectuals is long, difficult, full of contradictions, advances and retreats, dispersals and regroupings, in which the loyalty of the masses is sorely tried'. Yet in this same passage he stated that 'critical self-consciousness means, historically and politically, the creation of an elite of intellectuals'. In a long and rather complex sentence, Gramsci argued for the necessity of such an elite of intellectuals, without which the masses could not be organized or gain any self-consciousness: 'A human mass does not "distinguish" itself, does not become independent in its own right without, in the widest sense, organising itself; and there is no organisation without intellectuals, that is without organisers and leaders [*dirigenti*], in other words, without the theoretical aspect of the theory–practice nexus being distinguished concretely by the existence of a group of people "specialised" in conceptual and philosophical elaboration of ideas' (SPN 334; Q11, §12, 1386). So the key question was the creation of such a group of intellectuals, who would develop in association with the working class as the stratum of its organic intellectuals.

Gramsci certainly saw the political party as an essential institution for the formation of this group of organic intellectuals. His view of the party as the modern Prince, one of the formulations for which Gramsci is famous, is discussed more fully in our Chapter 5 below, but in the section of the SPN dealing with intellectuals Gramsci observes that the party 'for some social groups is nothing other than their specific way of elaborating their own category of organic intellectuals directly in the political and philosophical field and not just in the field of productive technique' (SPN 15; Q12, §1, 1522). The implication here is clearly that the political party functions as an educational association through which the members of a particular social group (class) are able to transcend the purely economic-corporate level, and develop a different level of awareness. Gramsci makes clear the difference between a professional association and a political party. In the professional association (and this could well include a trade union) 'the economic-corporate activity of the tradesman, industrialist or peasant is most suitably promoted', whereas by contrast 'in the political party the elements of an economic social group get beyond that moment of their historical development and become agents of more general activities of a national and international character.' Equally importantly, the political party was the channel through which new leaders were formed, indeed that was the basic function of the political party, according to Gramsci. The party's task was one of taking 'those elements of a social group which have been born and developed as an "economic" group – and of turning them into qualified political intellectuals, leaders [*dirigenti*] and organisers of all the activities and functions inherent in the organic development of an integral society, both civil and political' (SPN 16; Q12, §1, 1523). The political party was responsible for 'welding together the organic intellectuals of a given group – the dominant one – and the traditional intellectuals' (SPN 15; Q12, §1, 1522). We saw earlier that for a class to be 'hegemonic' this absorption by the organic intellectuals of the remaining traditional intellectuals was seen by Gramsci as a necessary part of the process of becoming a ruling class. In the sentence just quoted, the process is described with reference to the dominant group, whose organic intellectuals are fused with the traditional ones, but one can assume that Gramsci is here talking of any group (social class) which aims to become dominant. It requires for this purpose a political party which turns its members from those of an economic group, with restricted horizons, into qualified political intellectuals.

In that sense Gramsci insists that all members of a political party are thus intellectuals. He observes that 'an intellectual who joins the political party of a particular social group is merged with the organic intellectuals of the group itself, and is linked tightly with the group' (SPN 16). Perhaps this could be a reflection on his own path of development, as a student or intellectual himself who joined a party (the Italian Socialist Party or PSI, Partito Socialista Italiano) and became closely connected with the working class of Turin and its struggles. But certainly Gramsci intends this to have more general significance, pointing to the political party as performing an essentially intellectual and educative function. Gramsci observes that the statement 'that all members of a political party should be regarded as intellectuals is an affirmation that can easily lend itself to mockery and caricature', but he insists that the function of the party, or rather of its members, was indeed 'directive and organisational, i.e. educative, i.e. intellectual'

(SPN 16; Q12, §1, 1523). The members of a political party were definitely intellectuals because, whatever their particular grade or level in the party, they had got beyond the economic-corporate level of consciousness and became educated to become aware of wider issues, precisely those 'of a national and international character', awareness of which was needed for groups to become hegemonic or leading. The political party was thus the essential vehicle for a group to rise above what Lenin in *What Is to Be Done?* called the level of trade-union consciousness, in which workers made demands merely of an economistic character, namely improving wages and conditions, rather than challenging the system as a whole. But while on one level it seems that Gramsci's view of the educational role of the party is similar to that of Lenin, in that both see the party as a necessary vehicle of developing a political education that gets beyond the economic level, Gramsci does not endorse Lenin's view of the party as bringing socialist consciousness to the workers from outside. In the passages which appear in this section of the SPN, the emphasis of Gramsci seems to be on the political party as transforming members of the working class into organic intellectuals, rather than an elite of intellectuals bringing the correct theoretical enlightenment to economistically inclined workers. This question of whether Gramsci is a Leninist in his view of the party is a complex one, and will be returned to in Chapter 5 below, in the context of Gramsci's concept of the party as the modern Prince. But certainly the party for Gramsci is seen as a crucial institution for the process of moral and intellectual reform. The party is the crucible through which the working class could form its group of organic intellectuals.

There is also discussion by Gramsci of the nature of the intellectual – what type of intellectual would be needed to fulfil the role of organic intellectual of the working class? Gramsci offers some ideas on what he calls 'the new type of intellectual' that is needed for this purpose, different from what he calls 'the traditional and vulgarised type of the intellectual', represented by 'the man of letters, the philosopher, the artist'. This new type of intellectual has to be someone, it is implied, who is closely bound up with the world of production, with industry and science, suggesting that these could be worker-intellectuals who are practical and experienced in the world of work as well as being able to reflect on broader issues and are not limited to an economic-corporate mode of thinking. Gramsci states that 'in the modern world, technical education, closely bound to industrial labour even at the most primitive and unqualified level, must form the basis of the new type of intellectual'. It is not surprising that in this context he refers again to the experiences of the factory councils and the journal *L'Ordine Nuovo* which reflected and expressed Gramsci's ideas of the factory council as the institution based at the point of production which could become the foundation of a new workers' state. In Notebook 12, devoted to 'Notes for a Group of Essays on the History of Intellectuals', Gramsci claims that 'the weekly *Ordine Nuovo* worked to develop forms of new intellectualism and to determine its new concepts' (SPN 9; Q12, §3, 1550). The contrast between this new intellectualism and the traditional mode of being of intellectuals seems to be between the rhetorical practices of the old-style intellectuals, and the fact that the new intellectuals are much more directly immersed in the real life of production and industry, rather than eloquence. Gramsci describes the 'mode of being of the new intellectual' as one of 'active participation in practical life, as constructor, organiser, "permanent persuader" and not just a simple orator'. The picture is one of an active organizer who develops 'from technique-as-work' to 'technique-as-science and to the humanistic conception of history, without which one remains "specialised" and does not become "directive" (specialised and political)' (SPN 10; Q12, §3, 1550). Clearly this picture of the new intellectual offers a contrast with traditional ideas of the intellectual, as perhaps exemplified by someone like Benedetto Croce, the philosopher in his study surveying all of past philosophy and history and culture from a position of Olympian detachment. The new intellectual as portrayed here is someone very different from Renaissance man, and (to echo the quote about 'Renaissance man' given earlier) is a person who has 'taken the plunge into practical life', or perhaps emerged as a worker-intellectual from practical life and been educated and transformed through engagement and activity in the political party. Indeed it seems that this figure of the new intellectual overlaps with that of the democratic philosopher, discussed in Chapter 6 below.

The key points remain the importance of the political party in forming this new intellectual stratum, and the ways in which this figure of the new intellectual makes up the body of organic intellectuals which the working class needs to form as part of its rise to hegemonic status. Two remarks can be made concerning Gramsci's portrayal of intellectuals, old and new, and the relevance of that portrayal today. The first is to wonder whether modern-day political parties do or can fulfil the educational role which Gramsci ascribes to them, as means of formation of intellectuals. The second remark concerns the portrayal of the new intellectual, a figure which seems a very demanding role to play. The political party is for Gramsci an essential institution in the process of forming the organic intellectuals of the working class. His concept of the intellectual is, as previously noted, a much broader category than denoted by the everyday use of the concept of intellectual, commonly regarded as someone removed from everyday life and productive activities, specialized in the analysis and production of ideas. It is true that Gramsci preserves something of this notion, when he distinguishes between the intellectual activity which everyone performs, whatever their role in society, and those who as he says perform the function of intellectuals, acting as deputies (*commessi*) of the dominant social group. The latter group would be those whose speciality is in handling of ideas and whose work is brain rather than brawn, intellectual rather than directly productive. If intellectuals of the dominant group are those who are the 'functionaries of the superstructures', as Gramsci also calls them, then he is clear that any group (social class) challenging the presently existing ruling class and its intellectual functionaries would have to develop its own body of organic intellectuals. In that process the political party plays a vital role. But if in the contemporary politics of our own day political parties have been somewhat hollowed out, and play a predominantly electoral role, getting out the vote at election times and acclaiming the party leader at party conferences, then it seems doubtful whether political parties are so important in forming the body of organic intellectuals needed for successful politics of counter-hegemony (see Mair 2013 on 'the hollowing of Western democracy').

Furthermore, the idea presented by Gramsci of the new kind of intellectual as a permanent persuader who is actively involved in practical life, which seems to involve a direct role in production as well as in mobilizing people and spreading a vision of society (contesting dominant structures of meaning), is one which would be hard to realize practically. It might be difficult to envisage anyone performing such a function in contemporary society, all the more so as the means of communication remain dominated by capitalist and market-oriented concerns, represented by figures like Rupert Murdoch and Silvio Berlusconi, whose economic power gives them great control over the media and the means of manipulating popular consciousness. This raises a point made by many commentators on Gramsci (Bellamy 2014, 154; Adamson 1980, 179; Karabel 1976) who question where there might be the spaces (in a metaphorical sense) needed to elaborate the organic intellectuals of an ever more complex society. If political parties have been hollowed out, if newspapers are increasingly controlled by press magnates and become the means of diffusing a chorus of very similar ideas, then the space for oppositional ideas and the institutions for nurturing organic intellectuals seems to be increasingly constrained. In his analysis of *The State in Capitalist Society*, Ralph Miliband wrote of the way in which 'whatever their endless differences of every kind, most newspapers in the capitalist world have one crucial characteristic in common, namely their strong, often their passionate hostility to anything further to the Left than the milder forms of social-democracy, and quite often to these milder forms as well' (Miliband 2009, 160). One may wonder whether much has changed in that respect since those lines were written, and whether there is any equivalent in contemporary society to the salons of the pre-1789 *ancien régime* which provided oppositional islands in which the critics of absolutism could formulate their ideas. Gramsci was well aware of these problems, as indicated by his statement quoted above that 'the process of creating intellectuals is long, difficult, full of contradictions, advances and retreats, dispersals and regroupings' (SPN 334; Q11, §12, 1386). In a society which is more complex and where knowledge becomes more fragmented and specialized, one may wonder whether the organic intellectual envisaged by Gramsci could emerge, and whether the picture of the intellectual he presents requires certain conditions (institutional spaces to develop such organic intellectuals) which are less likely to be present in contemporary market-driven society. Institutions of working-class education, like the Workers' Educational Association (WEA) in England, which formerly provided channels outside of the workplace for popular education, are less significant than they were, and this may be symptomatic of a society in which education becomes increasingly specialized and vocational. Studies of the history of popular education and workers' education may bear out this somewhat pessimistic picture (see Steele 2007).

ON EDUCATION

The section of the SPN headed 'On Education' contains Gramsci's thoughts on some of these issues. These pages of the SPN are also taken from Gramsci's Notebook 12, and follow on from his remarks on intellectuals. These pages address themselves to the educational reforms introduced in Italy by the fascist ideologue Giovanni Gentile as minister for education, who succeeded Croce in that role. The most important point which emerges from Gramsci's notes on this subject seems to be his critique of narrowly vocational education, which under the guise of being democratic has on the contrary the effect of orienting education to fix people in a particular role and in that way to harden rather than diminish class divisions. Gramsci notes that 'the multiplication of vocational schools which specialise increasingly from the very beginning of the child's educational career is one of the most notable manifestations of this tendency' (SPN 40; Q12, §2, 1547). If the political party was one channel through which the new kind of intellectual could emerge, Gramsci is also keenly interested in education in the usual sense of the word, the educational institutions through which citizens of a democratic order could be formed. He notes the 'unprecedented difficulties' which still have to be overcome 'if our aim is to produce a new stratum of intellectuals ... from a social group which has not traditionally developed the appropriate attitudes' (SPN 43; Q12, §2, 1550). His concern here is with the role of education in a class-divided society, where children from a particular social background have advantages stemming from that background in developing the capacity for sustained study, for what he calls the 'particular apprenticeship' and the 'psycho-physical adaptation' necessary for intellectual work. As Gramsci points out, 'the child of a traditionally intellectual family acquires this psycho-physical adaptation more easily. Before he ever enters the class-room he has numerous advantages over his comrades, and is already in possession of attitudes learnt from his family environment' (SPN 42; Q12, §2, 1549). It has to be said that Gramsci sets a demanding standard for intellectual activity and study, perhaps stemming from his own experience. His argument seems to be that the more romantic idea of education as self-expression and the opposition made by some educational theorists between instruction and education (to favour the latter) neglected the pedagogic and intellectual discipline which it was necessary to instil into students at an early age. Gramsci writes that 'in education one is dealing with children in whom one has to inculcate certain habits of diligence, precision, poise (even physical poise), ability to concentrate on specific subjects, which cannot be acquired without the mechanical repetition of disciplined and methodical acts'. The following sentence seems even more severe and demanding: 'Would a scholar at the age of forty be able to sit for sixteen hours on end at his work-table if he had not, as a child, compulsorily, through mechanical coercion, acquired the appropriate psycho-physical habits?' (SPN 37; Q12, §2, 1544). Another interesting aspect of Gramsci's views on education seems to be the insistence on the teacher and the school generally as combating what Gramsci called 'folklore' and traditional conceptions of the world. Gramsci argues that the primary school in Italy 'taught a more modern outlook based essentially on an awareness of the simple and fundamental fact that there exist objective, intractable natural laws to which man must adapt himself if he is to master them in his turn' (SPN 34; Q12, §2, 1540). Gramsci seems to be endorsing the school as the appropriate institution for such a task, even if there could be argument about the means of achieving such a modern form of instruction.

His concern in this section of the *Notebooks* is with education as a democratic force, and as a means of breaking down rather than reinforcing class divisions. Gramsci criticizes the increase in the number of vocational schools, which cement social divisions and perpetuate hierarchy. In opposition to such vocational schools, his proposal is for 'a single type of formative school (primary–secondary) which would take the child to the threshold of his choice of job, forming him during this time as a person capable of thinking, studying, and ruling – or controlling those who rule' (SPN 40; Q12, §2, 1547). In turn this criticism of vocational schools and the advocacy of a less vocational or instrumental form of education stems from Gramsci's idea of democracy, which in turn seems to invoke (though not explicitly) Aristotle's idea that 'all should share alike in a system of government under which they rule and are ruled by turns' (Aristotle 1958, 315). Gramsci's version of this idea applies specifically to democracy, seen as not a matter of increasing the particular skills of individuals in certain roles, but enabling them to form the capacity to rule and be ruled. Gramsci writes that 'democracy, by definition, cannot mean merely that an unskilled worker can become skilled. It must mean that every "citizen" can "govern" and that society places him, even if only abstractly, in a general condition to achieve this' (SPN 40). This must be the purpose of a democratic or citizen education, 'ensuring for each non-ruler a free training in the skills and general technical preparation necessary to that end' (SPN 40; Q12, §2, 1547–48). So a purely technical and vocational kind of education would not achieve that aim of equipping citizens or giving non-rulers the possibility of becoming rulers, or at least controlling the rulers. It seems that Gramsci is seeking to criticize a system of education which crystallizes class division and keeps those whom he calls the 'instrumental class' (those who are subordinate or subaltern) in such a role, by providing them with education confined to the narrow horizons of a particular function. In that respect Gramsci's critique of education seems to parallel his views on the necessity of the working class transcending an economic-corporate level. Such a level of consciousness, and a form of education which goes along with it, is an obstacle to the achievement of hegemony by hitherto subaltern groups. The ideas presented in Notebook 12 on intellectuals and education thus suggest the failure of intellectuals in Italy to develop a truly national-popular implantation in the wider society, and the need for a genuinely democratic system of education to go beyond the limits of a subaltern form of consciousness.

These ideas have to be connected to the wider analysis of the *Prison Notebooks* as a whole. Gramsci's reflections on intellectuals do not refer to a narrow stratum of great thinkers who preside over and above society, though clearly he was aware of the significance of dominant intellectuals like Croce, whose ideas were then vulgarized and spread throughout society by a whole range of lesser intellectuals. Gramsci points to the proliferation and spread of the number of intellectuals in modern society: 'In the modern world the category of intellectuals ... has undergone an unprecedented expansion' (SPN 13; Q12, §1, 1520). He points to the different ranks of intellectuals, and to the problems to which the expansion in the number of intellectuals gives rise: 'the possibility of vast crises of unemployment for the middle intellectual strata, and in all modern societies this actually takes place', as he writes (SPN 11; Q12, §1, 1520). One other feature of Gramsci's analysis is of the social origins and social functions of the intellectuals. In Italy as in other societies there are strata which traditionally 'produce' intellectuals, as he puts it – the petty bourgeoisie form the groups out of which many intellectuals are recruited. But the core point of his analysis is to focus on intellectuals as, on the one hand, agents of legitimation of the existing order, the deputies or functionaries of the superstructure, and on the other hand as potential critics of that existing order. This is not to say that in Gramsci's thought intellectual criticism on its own would be sufficient as a challenge to the existing order. The point is rather that unless and until the battle for intellectual supremacy is won, then no purely political challenge to the existing order could be effective. The undermining of the intellectual assumptions of the existing order is thus a task that has to be completed before any revolutionary change could take place. In the task of that intellectual critique of existing society, what could be called oppositional intellectuals, or in Gramsci's terms organic intellectuals of the working class, would be the most important element. The implication of this idea is that at least part of radical politics consists in the nurturing and formation of such a stratum, not as of a group apart from or over and above the mass of the population, but closely linked, precisely in an organic way, to people in their daily productive life – at least that seems to be suggested by the idea of the new intellectual as an active participant in practical life. The formation of such organic or counter-hegemonic intellectuals takes place by means of the political party, but also through the education system more generally, and the process of formation of intellectuals requires an approach to education different from narrowly vocational perspectives. Certainly Gramsci is unique in the Marxist tradition in giving such an important role to intellectuals, and seeing them not as bringing the truth to the workers from outside the working class, but in some sense being formed in and through the mass of the population and remaining in contact with them. Intellectual struggle was thus for Gramsci part of a sustained opposition to the existing order. Through intellectual activity in the broadest sense, primitive notions of folklore and common sense as acquiescence to the existing order could be transcended, and this was the necessary condition for radical political transformation.

The problem for our own times is to see where and how such intellectual contestation could be advanced, and where the institutions for such a process could be identified. Gramsci seems to be making an implicit comparison between the way in which the bourgeoisie in pre-Revolutionary France developed their critique of the absolutism of the *ancien régime*, and the possibilities for a similar critique of capitalist society. While in contemporary liberal-democratic societies there are certainly dissenting voices and critical intellectuals, figures like Noam Chomsky, to take one obvious example, one may wonder whether such people are isolated figures of dissent whose critical voices are drowned out by the mass media which reinforce a very different kind of common sense and create a climate of ideological hegemony which is very hard to oppose. The paradox seems to be one to which Gramsci's own thought draws attention. As we shall see in the chapter dealing with his ideas on civil society, one of the main ideas of the *Prison Notebooks* is his famous concept of hegemony, the idea that forms of social life are not maintained solely or primarily by force, but are supported by the diffusion of ideas which block off any alternative vision of society. The complexity of civil society today and the control over the media given by powerful economic interests make it more difficult for alternative ideas to be formulated, or at least once formulated then to achieve a mass audience. Many of the institutions which in the socialist movement did historically function as nurseries for the potential organic intellectuals of the working class have been eroded by the fragmentation of the working class and the decline of any alternative vision of society apart from the 'anything goes' inclinations of postmodern perspectives. It is therefore difficult to see how such organic intellectuals could be formed. In terms of educational institutions, schools and institutions of higher learning are increasingly disciplined to produce students and graduates who can find a job in an ever more competitive market place, and this too undermines the possibilities of intellectuals in Gramsci's sense being the agents of the intellectual and moral reform which he saw as a precondition for radical change. Finally one may wonder whether in such a fragmented society, disciplined by the necessities of neo-liberalism and its market-oriented philosophy, there is space for intellectual activity critical of the existing order. If universities, to take one example, are ever more dependent on funding from corporations and from governments eager for policy-oriented research, then that source of critical intellectual discussion is rather limited. The same seems to be true of political parties in which the educational aspect of their activity remains subordinate to much more practical tasks, concentrated more narrowly on winning elections and mobilizing support at election time rather than on the long-term horizon of educational and intellectual work. These are all problems of the gaining of hegemony, put in Gramsci's terms. They are best examined in the framework of his views on history and modernity, which form the subject matter of the next chapter.

SUGGESTIONS FOR FURTHER READING

There are useful articles on Gramsci's views on intellectuals in volume 3 of the four-volume collection of articles on Gramsci edited by James Martin, *Antonio Gramsci: Critical Assessments of Leading Political Philosophers* (London: Routledge, 2002). Volume 3 contains articles on 'Intellectuals, Culture and the Party', with its first section (part 10 of the whole four-volume set) containing valuable articles on 'The Theory of Intellectuals'. The articles by Karabel on 'Revolutionary Contradictions' and King on 'The Social Role of Intellectuals' (separately listed in the bibliography) are particularly valuable.

Gramsci's views on education are discussed in the collection edited by Carmel Borg *et al.*, *Gramsci and Education* (Lanham, MD: Rowman & Littlefield, 2002) and that edited by Peter Mayo, *Gramsci and Educational Thought* (Oxford: Blackwell, 2009), and in the monograph by Harold Entwistle, *Antonio Gramsci: Conservative Schooling for Radical Politics* (London: Routledge & Kegan Paul, 1979). There are some useful essays (by Entwistle, Simpson and Adamson) on Gramsci's educational theories in part 12 of the collection edited by James Martin, *Antonio Gramsci: Critical Assessments of Leading Political Philosophers*, vol. 3 (London: Routledge, 2002).

For more general reading on the topic of intellectuals, the following books are useful, though not all of them focus directly on Gramsci: Stefan Collini, *Absent Minds: Intellectuals in Britain* (Oxford: Oxford University Press, 2006); Zygmunt Bauman, *Legislators and Interpreters: On Modernity, Post-modernity and Intellectuals* (Cambridge: Polity, 1987); Janet Hart, 'Reading the Radical Subject: Gramsci, Glinos and Paralanguages of the Modern Nation; Strange Rhapsody', in R. Suny and M. D. Kennedy (eds), *Intellectuals and the Articulation of the Nation* (Ann Arbor, MI: University of Michigan Press, 1999); Amitai Etzioni and Alyssa Bowditch (eds), *Public Intellectuals: An Endangered Species?* (Lanham, MD: Rowman & Littlefield, 2006); Richard A. Posner, *Public Intellectuals: A Study of Decline* (Cambridge, MA: Harvard University Press, 2001); Christian Fleck, Andreas Hess and E. Stina Lyon (eds), *Intellectuals and Their Publics: Perspectives from the Social Sciences* (Farnham: Ashgate, 2009).

4

HISTORY AND MODERNITY

In one of his last letters to his son Delio, Gramsci wrote that 'I think you like history just as I did when I was your age, because it deals with human beings. And everything that deals with people, as many people as possible, all the people in the world as they join together in society and work and struggle and better themselves should please you more than anything else' (LP2, 383). In some ways Gramsci's views on history do provide the key to understanding the *Prison Notebooks*. Many of his most significant concepts, such as hegemony and passive revolution, are developed through the analysis of historical events and processes, rather than being presented in an abstract and ahistorical way. This chapter seeks to analyse and clarify two sections of the SPN, the one headed 'Notes on Italian History', which forms the third chapter of Part I ('Problems of History and Culture'), and 'Americanism and Fordism', which constitutes the third chapter of Part II ('Notes on Politics'). Chapters 1 and 2 of 'Notes on Politics' (dealing with, respectively, 'The Modern Prince', centred on Gramsci's view of the political party, and 'State and Civil Society') are discussed in our next chapter. The aim here is to clarify Gramsci's concepts of history and of modernity. How did he apply a Marxist concept of history to Italy (and indeed to the world beyond Italy), and what was his analysis of the features of contemporary society to which he gave the label of 'Americanism and Fordism'? It is clear that Gramsci's analysis of history had as its purpose to shed light on the present, on how society had come to be what it was, and what were the possibilities for the development of contemporary society. He criticizes much of the literature on the Italian Risorgimento as being dilettantish and superficial. Echoing Croce's view that 'all history is contemporary history', Gramsci writes that 'if writing history means making history of the present, a great book of history is one which in the present moment helps emerging forces to become more aware of themselves and hence more concretely active and energetic' (Q19, §5, 1983–84). So his view of history is that historical analysis has to be directed to the present, to identify tasks that had been inadequately carried out by the dominant groups which had ruled up to now. If the Italian Risorgimento had been, as Gramsci said, a passive revolution, then what were the lessons to be learned by those (like Gramsci) who wanted a revolution that was not passive and which involved the mass of the Italian people? And what were the features of the modern economy, of mass production as exemplified by contemporary American capitalism, which were unavoidable features of modern life that any such revolution had to take into account? And finally, as a question for those of us reading the *Prison Notebooks* in the conditions of the world of the twenty-first century, how much of Gramsci's analysis remains of relevance today?

Much of the material contained in the SPN chapter 'Notes on Italian History' deal with the Italian Risorgimento, the movement for Italian unification and independence from foreign rule. This was a complex and protracted process, which ended only in 1861 with the declaration of Victor Emmanuel as King of Italy. Even then, Venice and the Veneto were not yet part of the newly formed kingdom. That only happened in 1866, and it was not until 1870 that Rome was incorporated into the Kingdom of Italy and became its capital. Gramsci's discussion of the Risorgimento throws up many names and episodes unfamiliar to the English reader who is not a specialist on the process of Italian unification. Nevertheless, the main lines of Gramsci's analysis are clear enough, and so too are the implications he draws from his presentation of Italian history in the nineteenth century. One other preliminary point should be made: Gramsci's historical analysis pointed out lessons for the politics of his own time. He saw the process of the Risorgimento as a passive revolution, an important concept in Gramsci's political thought, and one which has to be explained further. His analysis of Italian history implied that the Risorgimento had left Italy with a defective legacy. It had been an incomplete revolution which it was the task of the working-class movement to bring to fruition and in that way complete the process of making Italy a truly modern nation. Much of Gramsci's analysis of Italian history focused on the ways in which the bourgeoisie in Italy (and the intellectuals associated with that class) had in some sense failed to achieve the task of making Italy a modern nation-state, and of integrating the mass of the population in that state. The implication was that Italy in the early twentieth century was in some sense backward, and that a particular set of historical circumstances had prevented the Italian middle class from being the agents of modernity. The bourgeoisie had failed to become a hegemonic class, and its intellectuals had not succeeded in creating a truly national-popular culture. Gramsci suggests that this was something which the socialist or communist movement would have to realize, so in that way they would accomplish the task of moral and intellectual reform which still needed to be carried out. These are all complex ideas, expressed as always in the *Prison Notebooks* in an allusive and condensed fashion, but through the historical analysis Gramsci developed important concepts of political theory which go beyond the particular cases (notably Italy) analysed through his historical discussion.

THE RISORGIMENTO: HEGEMONY AND SUBALTERNITY

How then can one clarify the 'Notes on Italian History' (pages 52 to 120 of SPN), the greater part of which is devoted to the topic of the Risorgimento? Much of this chapter of SPN derives from Notebook 19, written up in 1934–35, one of the special notebooks that brings together many of Gramsci's earlier notes, which were rewritten for this notebook. Gramsci's analysis focuses on the two broad parties (parties in the broadest of senses) that were the prime movers in the process of Italian unification. The two movements were those of the Moderates on the one hand, and the Action Party (Partito d'Azione) on the other, the former being led by Cavour and the forces of Piedmont, the latter having as its leading figures Mazzini and Garibaldi, whose ideas were democratic and republican. The difference between these two strands of the Risorgimento is stressed by one of the leading Italian historians of this movement, Alberto Banti. He writes that 'the political-constitutional hypotheses which the republicans or democrats had in mind were irreconcilable with those that were realized under the leadership of Cavour and of Victor Emmanuel' (Banti 2004, 119). The picture which Gramsci presents of the democratic and republican strand is highly critical of the so-called Action Party. According to his analysis, it was the party of the Moderates who directed the whole process of the Risorgimento, while the Action Party remained in tow and subordinate to the Moderates. Gramsci quotes and endorses the judgement of Victor Emmanuel that he controlled, if only indirectly, the Action Party: 'The assertion attributed to Victor Emmanuel II that he "had the Action Party in his pocket", or something of the kind, was in practice accurate – not only because of the King's personal contacts with Garibaldi, but because the Action Party was in fact "indirectly" led by Cavour and the King' (SPN 57; Q19, §24, 2010). The Moderates, in Gramsci's terminology, acted as the organic intellectuals of the ruling class, since they were closely linked to the upper classes. Indeed he seems to suggest that the political actors of the Moderate Party were the same people as the holders of economic power. Gramsci argues that 'the Moderates were a real, organic vanguard of the upper classes, to which economically they belonged. They were intellectuals and political organisers, and at the same time company bosses, rich farmers or estate managers, commercial and industrial entrepreneurs, etc.' (SPN 60; Q19, §24, 2012). In that way the party of the Moderates manifested the identity of representatives and represented. Such a 'condensation' or organic concentration made possible the hegemony or power of attraction which this grouping exercised on other sections of society, notably on the intellectuals of the subordinate or subaltern classes. In that way the subaltern sections of society were deprived of leaders or intellectuals who could possibly have articulated oppositional ideas, had they not been seduced or absorbed into the ranks of the intellectuals who supported the existing order. The power of the Moderates was then not an example of hegemony through 'domination' (*dominio* in Italian) but rather of hegemony through 'intellectual and moral leadership' (*direzione intellettuale e morale*) (SPN 57; Q19, §24, 2010).

Two crucial points emerge from Gramsci's portrayal of the Moderates in the Italian Risorgimento. The first is that power is exercised not only through coercion but equally importantly through intellectual leadership. Gramsci puts this very clearly, when he says that a social group (and clearly he means here classes in a Marxist sense) exercises its supremacy both as dominion (*dominio*) and as direction (*direzione*). The former is exercised over enemy groups (whom the ruling group intends to 'liquidate') and the latter over 'kindred and allied' groups who are attracted to and subordinated by the intellectual leadership of the ruling group. Indeed, according to Gramsci, the leading group 'decapitates', at least in a metaphorical sense, the subordinate class, by taking over its leaders and intellectuals who become absorbed into the ruling group. The reference here is to the Italian phenomenon of *trasformismo* or 'transformism', notably as practised by the Italian Prime Minister Giolitti, adept at enticing leaders of opposition parties into leading positions, neutralizing their oppositional stance. Gramsci talks of 'the gradual but continuous absorption, achieved by methods which varied in their effectiveness, of the active elements produced by allied groups – and even of those which came from antagonistic groups and seemed irreconcilably hostile' (SPN 59; Q19, §24, 2011). So that is part of the process by which dominant groups maintain their power, co-opting oppositional forces into their ranks, and securing power by the spread of their ideas. Significantly Gramsci talks (as a specific illustration of this general process) of the ways in which the Moderates did this: they stabilized the apparatus of their intellectual, moral and political hegemony 'through means which one could call "liberal", that is through means of individual initiative, which are "molecular" and "private"' (SPN 59; Q19, §24, 2011). So political and social power are secured through the channels of private initiative, in other words through the institutions of civil society, whose relationship with the state is developed further by Gramsci in his 'Notes on Politics' (examined in our next chapter).

The second crucial point relates to oppositional groups, or groups (social classes) which aspire in their turn to become hegemonic. Gramsci's famous words emphasize the need for such a social group to become leading (*dirigente*) *before* the conquest of governmental power. Indeed, as he says, this process of becoming leading (in an intellectual sense) is 'one of the principal conditions for the winning of such power' (SPN 57; Q19, §24, 2010). So the implication is that gaining intellectual dominance or primacy must happen before any attempt at seizing governmental power is made. Here, as so often in the *Prison Notebooks*, Gramsci is using a specific historical episode (the intellectual subordination of the democrats in the Italian Risorgimento) as the basis for a wider point of political analysis. Any group (social class) which wants to gain governmental power, whether in a revolutionary or non-revolutionary way, has therefore to exercise moral and intellectual leadership before it could have any chance of establishing itself in government, but how is this to be done? Clearly it implies the importance of an intellectual presence or weight in existing society, hence the necessity (as we saw in the previous chapter) for organic intellectuals of the rising class to formulate the claims to intellectual leadership, or to articulate the alternative ideas which will gain mass support. Such a process in turn presupposes the presence of institutions or arenas in which such ideas could be developed and the claims to intellectual and moral leadership (*direzione*) furthered. This forms part of what Gramsci called a war of position, a concept further analysed in the next chapter of this book. One problem with this idea of winning intellectual leadership before seizing governmental power is clearly identified by the English scholar Richard Bellamy in his writings. Bellamy argues that 'the "war of position" strategy, whereby hegemonic control of society can be won prior to an assault on the state, depends on the relative autonomy of civil society. Whereas this precondition largely prevailed in the case of the *ancien régime*, the same cannot be said of the states of modern industrial western nations'. Bellamy points out the greater power of such states to, as he puts it, 'block counter-hegemonic projects more effectively than under earlier regimes', and the fact that 'bourgeois democracy itself channels potential opposition into supporting and upholding the state, disarming radical demands for a new form of socialist state' (Bellamy 2014, 154). These points are well taken, and one could add to them that it is not just the power of the state which can 'block counter-hegemonic projects', but institutions of civil society like the media which are important in this regard. If popular tabloid newspapers, to mention only one example, have huge power to diffuse a particular conception of life and view of the world which sustains the existing order, then this too makes the task of achieving intellectual leadership before attaining governmental power a far more difficult one.

Bellamy's reference to the *ancien régime* is apposite, because it is clear that Gramsci was thinking of the French Revolution in his historical analysis of nineteenth-century Italy and the lessons to be drawn from it. In France, in the pre-Revolutionary period, the Enlightenment intellectuals and *philosophes* did articulate ideas of rationalism and the critique of absolutism which paved the way for the upheaval of 1789 (Cranston 1986). The task of presenting some kind of alternative model of society which could gain mass support is more problematic in the conditions of contemporary bourgeois democracy, as Bellamy suggests. Gramsci in his analysis of the contending parties in the Italian Risorgimento criticizes the Action Party by comparing them unfavourably with the Jacobins of the French Revolution. The passages in which Gramsci makes this comparison go back to Notebook 1, paragraph 44, taken up again and revised in Notebook 19 (SPN 55–90), so it is clear that Gramsci was concerned with these topics from the very earliest stages of the *Notebooks*. Gramsci states that there was nothing in the Action Party comparable to 'this Jacobin approach, this inflexible will to become the "leading" [*dirigente*] party' (SPN 80; Q19, §24, 2030). The Jacobins of the French Revolution had established links between town and country, and gained the support of the peasantry, and in that way had advanced the revolution, 'pushing the bourgeoisie forward through kicks in their backside', as Gramsci put it, since the Jacobins were 'an extremely energetic and resolute group of men' (Q19, §24, 2026). By contrast, the men of the Action Party, leaders like Mazzini and Garibaldi, had failed to support the peasants' demand for land, and had even repressed popular uprisings, as with the case of the Risorgimento leader Bixio in Sicily, an episode vividly analysed in the recent book by Lucy Riall, *Under the Volcano*, which deals with the uprising in the village of Bronte in Sicily. She writes that 'there is little doubt that Bixio's determination to contain the disturbances in Bronte reflected a shared resolve on the part of the democratic leadership at all costs to keep the Sicilian countryside under control' (Riall 2013, 135). Gramsci reproaches the leadership of the Action Party for not having linked up with the peasantry and been more positive in response to their demands. This was an example of their ideological and practical subordination to the party of the Moderates. He argues that in order for the Action Party to have become an autonomous force (rather than subordinated to the Moderates) and for them to have 'imprinted on the Risorgimento a markedly more popular and democratic character', they would have had to develop an 'organic programme of government'. Such a programme would have needed to reflect the demands of the popular masses, in particular those of the peasantry. That would have been the only way to oppose effectively the 'spontaneous attraction' exercised by the Moderates, through 'resistance and counter-offensive "organised" following a plan' (Q19, §24, 2013).

While it is easy to get somewhat lost in the details of Gramsci's historical discussion, it is clear that he saw the Italian Risorgimento as a passive revolution, or a revolution which was incomplete, in the sense of having failed to create a new state which incorporated the mass of the population. In Gramsci's famous words, which express his harsh view of the Risorgimento, his judgement on the leaders of the Risorgimento was that 'these men effectively did not know how to lead the people, they did not know how to arouse its enthusiasm and passion'. Nor had they achieved the ends they set for themselves: 'They said they were aiming at the creation of a modern state in Italy, and they in fact produced a bastard. They aimed at stimulating the formation of an extensive and energetic ruling class and they did not succeed; at integrating the people into the framework of the new State, and they did not succeed'

(SPN 90; Q19, §28, 2053). This idea of the Risorgimento as a passive revolution had wider implications for Gramsci's view of twentieth-century history and of modernity, and is important for understanding the significance of his thought today.

PASSIVE REVOLUTION

While the bulk of the 'Notes on Italian History' deals with the Risorgimento, they contain a broader analysis, both of the history of Italy in other periods, and of the wider trajectory of European history in general. In France the Jacobins had pushed the revolution to its limits, and had included wider sections of the population. The point of the analysis which Gramsci makes is to compare the ways in which, he argues, the bourgeoisie came to power in the various European countries – 'differences between France, Germany and Italy in the process by which the bourgeoisie took power (and in England)' (SPN 82; Q19, §24, 2032). This process had received its fullest development in France, but in Germany and England the line of historical development was more muddied. The rising class of the bourgeoisie had come to some accommodation with the old class of the aristocracy (the Junkers in Prussia). In England, even though those whom Gramsci called the 'English Jacobins', namely Oliver Cromwell and the Roundheads, had shown great zeal and energy, the old aristocracy remained as the governing stratum, even, says Gramsci in a rather contestable formulation, 'the intellectual stratum of the English bourgeoisie' (SPN 83; Q19, §24, 2033). In Italy the bourgeoisie had not proved itself a revolutionary class, and this was why the movement of the Risorgimento had proved itself a passive revolution, one which had not included the mass of the population. Gramsci suggests that in part this was because in the Europe of 1815 and thereafter, the spectre of popular power raised by memories of the French Revolution frightened the bourgeoisie. The Action Party shared this fear. That was why they had not mobilized the peasantry, and remained dominated by the party of the Moderates.

Gramsci was thus operating in the context of a Marxist view of history, of history as class struggle, of a process by which the bourgeoisie establishes its hegemony which then comes to be challenged by the rising class of the proletariat. In seeking to apply this to Italy, Gramsci understood that this bourgeois revolution had been incomplete or thwarted in Italy. In part this was because the middle classes were afraid that mobilizing the peasantry would lead to a more general attack on property, as had happened, albeit within limits, during the French Revolution. But Gramsci's analysis goes further, with emphasis on features which he suggests are deeply rooted in Italian history. Because of the legacy of the Roman Empire and the continuing importance of the Papacy, Italian intellectuals had never established a proper national-popular culture. They had remained separated from the mass of the people. From the times of the Roman Empire onwards, there had been a process of 'denationalization' of Rome. Italy had become a 'cosmopolitan terrain' (Q19, §1, 1960). Gramsci suggests that the movement of the cities in Italy, the communal movement (the movement of the *communi*), had never led the Italian middle class to transcend the economic-corporate level, in other words to the formation of a modern centralized nation-state. So in some senses the Italian bourgeoisie – for clearly explicable historical reasons – had not carried out the mission which in classical Marxist theory was ascribed to it, of being a revolutionary class. In the words of the *Communist Manifesto*, 'the bourgeoisie has at last, since the establishment of modern industry and of the world market, conquered for itself, in the modern representative state, exclusive political sway' (Marx 1973b, 69). Gramsci's historical analysis suggested that this process had been somehow distorted in the Italian case. The intellectuals of the bourgeoisie had been seduced by the cosmopolitan vocation of the Papacy, and had never therefore been tied in with the mass of the people. The bourgeoisie itself in the Italian case (in the period of the city-states and communes) had never got beyond a relatively limited horizon of economic-corporative interests. Later, in the nineteenth century, fear of peasant and proletarian revolution limited its political ambitions, so that the Italian state which emerged from the Risorgimento period was a 'bastard', in the sense of a political unit which did not command the loyalty of the mass of its population. The mass of the population did not share in the culture of the new state, which had been created by a 'passive revolution', a term which Gramsci uses often and which has been taken up by later commentators to give it a wider significance.

An important use of the term passive revolution comes in paragraph 24 of Notebook 19, itself a rewriting of paragraph 44 of Notebook 1. In the first version of this paragraph, Gramsci states that 'in order to exercise political leadership or hegemony one must not count solely on the power and material force that is given by government'. He argues that 'this truth is clearly demonstrated by the politics of the Moderates, and it is the solution of this problem that made the Risorgimento possible in the forms and within the limits in which it was accomplished as a revolution without revolution, or in V. Cuoco's words, as a passive revolution' (QE1 137; Q1, §44, 41). The reference here is to Vincenzo Cuoco and his essay on the revolution of 1799 in Naples, which established the Parthenopean Republic (Cuoco 1998). This short-lived episode was led by a group of Italian Jacobins, and the experiment was suppressed by a bloody counter-revolution led by Cardinal Ruffo and the mass of the Neapolitan *lazzaroni* or lumpenproletariat (Davis 2006, chs 4 and 5). What then did Gramsci really mean by the term passive revolution, and what is its significance for his thought in general? In an interesting discussion of 'Gramsci and the era of bourgeois revolution in Italy', the historian Paul Ginsborg suggests that Gramsci used the term with two meanings. The first meaning was of a transformation without the active participation of the masses. In the second sense of the term, it referred more to a process of molecular political transformation, in which oppositional movements were so to speak decapitated by having their leadership co-opted into the ranks of the ruling elite. This was precisely the process indicated by the Italian term of *trasformismo* or 'transformism', practised, as noted earlier, in a high degree by the Italian Prime Minister Giolitti. As for historical examples of passive revolution in the first sense, Gramsci refers to the Parthenopean Republic of 1799 as one example, in that the group of enlightened Jacobins who led this republic failed to gain the support of the peasantry and urban poor, who then rallied to the leadership of the clerical counter-revolution. But clearly the predominant example for him was that of the Italian Risorgimento, which was a passive revolution in that the Action Party had been too timid (in Gramsci's view) in linking up with the peasantry and trying to satisfy their demands. Thus the Risorgimento could be seen as a revolution without a revolution, a movement which had unified Italy but had not done so in such a way as to include the mass of the population in the newly formed state. Hence his phrase, quoted earlier, that the leaders of the Risorgimento 'said that they were aiming at the creation of a modern state in Italy, and they in fact produced a bastard' (SPN 90; Q19, §28, 2053).

A passive revolution then is a process which results in important political and social changes, but without involving the mass of the population. The opposite of a passive revolution would then presumably be an active revolution, though Gramsci himself never uses this term. One commentator, Walter Adamson, uses the term complete revolution, to indicate what Gramsci meant by a revolution which possessed the features lacking in passive revolutions (Adamson 1980, 164). While never using the terms active revolution or complete revolution, it is clear what Gramsci held up as an example of such a process, and that was the French Revolution of 1789, analysed by him through his discussion of Jacobinism. Gramsci paints a very positive picture of the role of the Jacobins, notably in their ability to link up with the rural masses and satisfy their demands. He uses the term Jacobinism more generally to indicate 'the particular methods of party and government activity which the French Jacobins displayed, characterised by extreme energy, decisiveness and resolution'. The latter definition could be used in a pejorative sense to mean a politician consumed by hatred of opposing forces and 'the sectarian element of the clique' (SPN 66; Q19, §24, 2017). For Gramsci, however, the Jacobins of the French Revolution were not characterized merely by their determination, but by their capacity to be leading (*dirigente*). The comparison he makes repeatedly is between the French Revolution and the action of the Jacobins, on the one hand, and the Risorgimento and the Action Party (and also the Moderates) on the other. In the former case, in Gramsci's reading, in the course of the development of the French Revolution 'a new elite was selected out which did not concern itself solely with "corporate" reforms, but tended to conceive of the bourgeoisie as the hegemonic group of all the popular forces' (SPN 77; Q19, §24, 2028). So the Jacobins had succeeded in the task of liquidating the enemy groups (the forces of the *ancien régime* and the party of the Girondins) as well as leading or directing allied forces, namely the peasantry, in that way achieving an alliance of rural poor and urban masses. So for Gramsci the Jacobins were not 'abstract dreamers', but 'they were convinced of the absolute truth of their slogans about equality, fraternity and liberty, and, what is more important, the great popular masses whom the Jacobins stirred up and drew into the struggle were also convinced of their truth' (SPN 78; Q19, §24, 2028). In that sense they were hegemonic, since they had succeeded in convincing the mass of the population of the validity of their ideas. It seems that Gramsci is using this historical analysis (here as in many other places in the *Notebooks*) to draw distinctly political lessons for the present. The implication is that this task of leading allied groups (notably, in Italy at least, the peasantry) is what a revolutionary party would have to achieve in contemporary conditions, so as to establish a historical bloc able to maintain its hegemony without the use of force or coercion. In the case of the Jacobins, the verdict of Gramsci was clear: 'They created the bourgeois State, made the bourgeoisie into the leading, hegemonic class of the nation, in other words gave the new State a permanent basis and created the compact modern French nation' (SPN 79; Q19, §24, 2029).

Neither the Moderates nor the Action Party had come up to the mark of a complete revolution in the course of the Risorgimento. The Action Party remained in subordination to the Moderates. Historically this was manifested by Garibaldi accepting the leadership of Victor Emmanuel, and by the surrender of his forces to the army of Piedmont after the Battle of Aspromonte in 1862. So Gramsci condemns the Action Party since in his view in that party 'there was nothing to be found which resembled this Jacobin approach, this inflexible will to become the "leading" [*dirigente*] party' (SPN 80; Q19, §24, 2030). But the Moderate Party do not fare much better in his judgement. They too failed to achieve a fully hegemonic role, even though they had conquered power. Their situation was one of 'dictatorship without hegemony', or domination without the function of leadership. Gramsci argues that in the Risorgimento the leading role had been taken by a state, namely Piedmont, rather than by a class. That state performed the role which should have been that of a class, and what resulted was what could be called (not a phrase Gramsci uses himself) a revolution from above, or a process imposed from above which failed to secure the support of the popular masses or the bulk of the country. The implication is thus that the Risorgimento was a failed or incomplete revolution. As Ginsborg writes, talking of the formation of the Italian nation-state, 'the reliance upon a monarchist army and subservience to a monarchist constitution, this *substitution* of a state for a class, was heavily reflected in the political ordering of the new nation state ... The supreme moment of bourgeois revolution in Italy was therefore a deeply flawed one.' Echoing Gramsci's analysis, Ginsborg notes that 'above all, the Italian revolutions failed to resolve the agrarian question' (Ginsborg 1979, 45). It seems that the picture which Gramsci presents of the Risorgimento is one in which a state (Piedmont) with its own structures imposed itself as the model for the Italian nation-state, and cut short any attempt to create a more democratic state responsive to the needs of its citizens. To quote Ginsborg again: 'Bourgeois democratic principles were henceforth always to be subordinate to the somewhat different political programme of Camillo Cavour' (Ginsborg 1979, 61). Gramsci's historical analysis takes this idea of passive revolution back in time, to the earlier failure of the Italian bourgeoisie to develop into a truly national class and to get beyond a narrowly economic-corporate level. Gramsci's analysis of the failure of the Risorgimento and of Italian history more generally rests on his idea of a historic bloc or alliance between northern industrialists and southern landowners, an alliance which curtailed hopes for democratic advance. In opposition to that bloc, a new democratic alliance had to be constructed, of workers and peasants. Those ideas were only hinted at in the *Prison Notebooks*, which viewed the problem from a more general historical perspective, seeing passive revolution as a feature of European history in the period after the French Revolution, as is clear from the final section of the 'Notes on Italian History', with the heading (added by the editors of SPN) of 'The History of Europe Seen as "Passive Revolution"' (SPN 118; Q10, §9, 1227). What were the broader implications of Gramsci's use of the concept of passive revolution, or revolution without revolution, and the significance for his wider theory of history? And what are the implications of passive revolution for the politics of our own time?

FROM RISORGIMENTO TO FASCISM, AND BEYOND

While the Risorgimento obviously provides for Gramsci the fullest example of a passive revolution, he presents the term in a wider perspective, proposing 'the thesis of the "passive revolution" as an interpretation of the Risorgimento period, and of every epoch characterised by complex upheavals' (SPN 114; Q15, §62, 1827). He seems to suggest that the term could serve as a way of explaining the whole sweep of European history in the post-1789 epoch, and that it relates to a whole strategy of containing or limiting popular pressure and democratic striving. Here again it is important to realize that Gramsci's historical analysis is carried out with the aim of shedding light on the present, and with the purpose of drawing political lessons for the present, explaining the conjuncture in which progressive forces find themselves. The final section of the 'Notes on Italian History' is significant in this respect. Gramsci here criticizes the historical work of the philosopher Benedetto Croce. Gramsci's fuller critique of Croce is dealt with in our Chapter 6 below, with respect to Croce's philosophical work. In the section under discussion here (SPN 118–20; Q10, §9, 1226–28), Gramsci focuses on Croce's *History of Europe in the Nineteenth Century* and his *History of Italy since 1871*. His critique of Croce is that in both cases Croce begins his historical narratives after the revolutionary upheavals of, respectively, the French Revolution and the Risorgimento, so that 'he excludes the moment of struggle' (SPN 119; Q10, §9, 1227). Gramsci presents Croce as the theorist or ideologist of passive revolution, of the period of European history in which the revolutionary impetus of the French Revolution was so to speak watered down, and pressure from below limited and contained. In Gramsci's words, Croce's 'book on the *History of Europe* is nothing but a fragment of history, the "passive" aspect of the great revolution which started in

France in 1789' (SPN 119; Q10, §9, 1227). Passive revolution is here presented not just with reference to the Risorgimento but more generally as characteristic of Europe after 1815, which Gramsci calls 'the period of restoration-revolution, in which the demands which in France found a Jacobin-Napoleonic expression were satisfied by small doses, legally, in a reformist manner', so that it was possible 'to avoid agrarian reform, and, especially, to avoid the popular masses going through a period of political experience such as occurred in France in the years of Jacobinism, in 1831, and in 1848' (SPN 119; Q10, §9, 1227). So here passive revolution is contrasted with the revolutionary upsurges not just of 1789 but of 1831 and 1848. Passive revolution seems here to indicate a political strategy of ruling groups aimed at averting revolutionary upheaval, or preventing an active or complete revolution.

Croce is here presented as theorizing or expressing such a perspective of restoration rather than revolution. Gramsci indicates that this attempt to keep the lid on revolutionary pressure was the task both of liberalism and of fascism, which in this respect was the heir to liberalism, though each acted in different historical conditions. This is indicated by the following sentence, which suggests that fascism can be added to the list of examples of passive revolution: 'But, in present conditions, is it not precisely the fascist movement which in fact corresponds to the movement of moderate and conservative liberalism in the last century?' (SPN 119; Q10, §9, 1228). Gramsci is arguing that liberalism (of a moderate and conservative type) and fascism were both seeking to develop the productive forces and go with the flow of modernity, while at the same time avoiding the involvement of the masses in that process, averting any possible radical challenge from below. In that limited sense fascism was progressive in that it developed and modernized the economic framework of Italian society while at the same time repressing the working-class movement and the popular classes more generally. So fascism, one could say, in some respects shared some features with the Risorgimento: both were modernizing phenomena but carried out such modernization almost at the expense of, or certainly without the active partici-pation of, the mass of society. So the suggestion is that passive revolution in the fascist case was also a revolution without a revolution. In Gramsci's words, 'The ideological hypothesis could be presented in the following terms: that there is a passive revolution involved in the fact that – through the legislative intervention of the State, and by means of the corporative organisation – relatively far-reaching modifications are being introduced into the country's economic structure in order to accentuate the "plan of production" element' (SPN 120; Q10, §9, 1228). But while 'socialisation and co-operation in the sphere of production are being increased', this was done 'without however touching (or at least not going beyond the regulation and control of) individual and group appropriation of profit' (SPN 120; Q10, §9, 1228). Fascism therefore sought to develop the productive forces of industry (Gramsci's phrase) while keeping those productive forces 'under the direction of the traditional ruling classes' (SPN 120; Q10, §9, 1228). Passive revolution is thus a strategy for averting a complete revolution. Gramsci then moves to the question of how such a strategy could be opposed. It is here that he introduces the concept of war of position, and again this has important implications for political strategy both in Gramsci's time and in ours. In the present context, Gramsci's idea of passive revolution indicates an attempt to promote modernity while at the same time preserving the features of an exploitative and class-divided society. As we shall see later on in this chapter, he develops a similar analysis in his discussion of Americanism and Fordism, asking whether Fordism (standardized mass production) is a strategy for developing modernity while reserving the fruits of modern production methods for a ruling class. This poses the question of how modernity could be developed in different ways, through the unfolding of a different kind of revolution, a complete revolution in which the mass of the population could be integrated into the economic, political and social structures of modernity and benefit from such a situation.

Gramsci poses the question of the relation of passive revolution to war of position. He writes in interrogative mode, 'Can the concept of "passive revolution", in the sense attributed by Vincenzo Cuoco to the first period of the Italian Risorgimento, be related to the concept of "war of position" in contrast to war of manoeuvre?' (SPN 108; Q15, §11, 1766). The idea of war of position is analysed more fully in the following chapter, but for the moment it can be defined as distinct from a frontal direct assault on state power (i.e. from a war of manoeuvre). Indeed the war of position can be seen precisely as the attempt to exercise a leading (*dirigente*) role in society and establish hegemony before taking over state power, in other words exactly the task that according to Gramsci both the Action Party and the Moderates failed to achieve in the course of the Risorgimento. Gramsci raises the question whether there is 'an absolute identity between war of position and passive revolution', and whether there exists 'an entire historical period in which the two concepts must be considered identical' (SPN 108; Q10, §9, 1227). He avoids giving a direct answer to his own questions, but the line of analysis seems clear. In a historical period in which ruling groups seek to modernize society while at the same time maintaining their power and averting radical change, such radical change could only come about once subaltern classes or oppositional groups had established hegemony, had themselves become *dirigenti*. At such a moment (though it obviously is a process rather than a particular moment or event) 'the war of position becomes a war of manoeuvre', only then would a revolution be possible in terms of a takeover of the state, though Gramsci does not put it in such a straightforward way. Gramsci seems to regard the volunteers rushing to join Garibaldi's expedition to Sicily (the Expedition of the Thousand) as a sign of weakness rather than of strength. While he notes that the course of events in the Risorgimento 'revealed the enormous importance of the "demagogic" mass movement, with its leaders thrown up by chance, improvised, etc.', Gramsci notes how this mass movement was 'taken over by the traditional organic forces – in other words, by the parties of long standing, with rationally-formed leaders, etc.' (SPN 112; Q15, §15, 1773). The implication is that in a period of passive revolution it is only a war of position which could build up the forces needed to challenge the structure of society. By war of position is indicated the opposite of a direct challenge to state power in the streets or on the barricades. It seems to indicate the taking over of positions in civil society, and the creation of organic forces rather than spontaneous upheaval or phenomena like those of the volunteers of the Risorgimento period and Garibaldi's Sicilian adventure, whose success depended in part on chance events and adventitious factors, such as the fact, noted by Gramsci, that 'the English fleet effectively protected the Marsala landing and the capture of Palermo, and neutralised the Bourbon fleet' (SPN 112; Q15, §15, 1773).

It is clear that Gramsci is using passive revolution not just as a term to analyse some particular historical episodes such as the Risorgimento or the Parthenopean Republic, but more broadly as characterizing a whole historical epoch, an epoch for which a different political strategy (war of position) is appropriate. The chapter in the SPN on 'Notes on Italian History' ends with such a broad-brush survey by Gramsci of the course of European history since the French Revolution, which paints the picture of alternate periods of war of movement and war of position. The first such period of 'movement' was that of the French Revolution itself, followed by what Gramsci calls 'a long war of position from 1815 to 1870' (SPN 120; Q10, §9, 1229), suggesting that much of the nineteenth century was a period of seeking to contain or limit the impact of the French Revolution and the pressures from below which that unleashed. Then the next period of war of movement was unleashed by the First World War and the Russian (Bolshevik) revolution, whose impact was felt in Italy by the movement of factory councils in which Gramsci took an active part (see Chapter 1 above). In his words, 'In the present epoch, the war of movement took place politically from March 1917 to March 1921; this was followed by a war of position whose representative – both practical (for Italy) and ideological (for Europe) – is fascism' (SPN 120; Q10, §9, 1229). Combining this sentence with the one previously quoted that it was 'the fascist movement which in fact corresponds to the movement of moderate and conservative liberalism in the last century' one could derive certain conclusions from Gramsci's analysis of Italian and European history, namely that fascism had succeeded in establishing its hegemony, or at least that the war of movement opened up by the war and the Russian Revolution had ended in the failure of socialist revolution. Fascism represented a passive revolution in that it pursued the development of the pro-ductive forces while at the same time suppressing any democratic and socialist politics based on the working class and its potential peasant allies. Hence a new political strategy was needed if passive revolution were to be succeeded by some more complete revolution. This new strategy, termed 'war of position', would entail the creation of a new political culture, to be achieved not through a direct uprising or frontal assault on the power of the state, but through the institutions of civil society, a term whose significance for Gramsci is explored in the next chapter. Only in that way could passive revolution be transcended and alternative forms of political activity be developed.

Some modern scholars, especially in the field of international political economy, interpret passive revolution very broadly, seeing it as crucial for understanding the formation of the modern state, and using the term to apply to a wide variety of cases in the contemporary world, ranging from Scotland to Mexico and Russia under perestroika and China (Morton 2010). Adam Morton defines passive revolution as 'a mode of class rule associated both with ruptural conditions of state development, ushering in the world of capitalist production, and class strategies linked to the continual furtherance of capitalism as a response to its crisis conditions of accumulation' (Morton 2010, 332). It is not clear whether such an extended use of the term 'passive revolution' represents a case of concept stretching or the overextension of a term used by Gramsci in a more limited sense, relevant only to Italy and then to Europe since the French Revolution, rather than to state development in general. One of the contributors to the *Capital and Class* special issue on 'Approaching Passive Revolution' (Callinicos 2010) suggests the dangers of such an overextension of the concept. The next task is to reflect more generally on Gramsci's view of history as it was deployed in his reflections on Italian and European history.

HISTORY AND MODERNITY

Before proceeding to analyse Gramsci's views of Americanism and Fordism as an analysis of modernity, it is worthwhile adding some reflections on the theory of history and modernity contained in this chapter ('Notes on Italian History') of the SPN, most of which was concerned with analysis of the Risorgimento as an example of stunted bourgeois revolution. Gramsci's long analysis of the Italian Risorgimento was set in the context of a quite succinct comparative historical analysis of what he called 'differences between France, Germany and Italy in the process by which the bourgeoisie took power (and England)' (SPN 82; Q19, §24, 2032). The process which Gramsci saw as having its clearest representation in France in 1789 was not repeated in such a classic fashion anywhere else. In other countries bourgeois revolutions were in a way stunted, so that the non-bourgeois classes retained a considerable degree of power, for example the Junkers in Prussia, and in England too, where Gramsci claims that 'the old aristocracy remained as a governing stratum, with certain privileges, and it too became the intellectual stratum of the English bourgeoisie' (SPN 83; Q19, §24, 2033). It is not clear why Gramsci attributed to the aristocracy in England and in Germany this intellectual function, implying that the bourgeoisie could not carry it out itself. In the German case Gramsci wrote that 'if these old classes kept so much importance in Germany and enjoyed so many privileges, they exercised a national function, became the "intellectuals" of the bourgeoisie, with a particular temperament conferred by their caste origin and by tradition' (SPN 83; Q19, §24, 2032). In Italy, as we have seen, the democratic impetus which the Jacobins in France had given to the revolutionary process was absent because of the failure of the Action Party to act in the same way as the Jacobins and to be responsive to the needs of the peasantry. Gramsci argues that this absence of a Jacobin equivalent in Italy had its historical reasons: 'If in Italy a Jacobin party was not formed, the reasons are to be sought in the economic field, which is to say in the relative weakness of the Italian bourgeoisie and in the different historical climate in Europe after 1815' (SPN 82; Q19, §24, 2032). Both factors were analysed at different stages in the *Prison Notebooks*. The relative weakness of the Italian bourgeoisie had long and deep historical roots, as manifested in its failure to get beyond an economic-corporate level during the medieval period of the city-states or communes. Its weakness was both cause and effect of its failure to develop its own intellectuals, since in Italy the intellectuals had been diverted by the supranational appeal of first Roman Empire and then of the Catholic Church, so that the Italian bourgeoisie had not developed a modern nation-state such as had developed in France and England (even if in England, according to Gramsci, the bourgeoisie had in some way fused with the aristocracy). The other factor was also evident. In the different historical climate in Europe after 1815, the economically dominant classes were aware of what had happened in France in and after 1789, and became wary of unleashing popular pressures from below. Hence Gramsci stated, as quoted above, that moderate and conservative liberalism practised the politics of passive revolution to contain and avert any revolutionary challenge.

What then are the key points which emerge from Gramsci's historical analysis of the Risorgimento and other historical episodes? Gramsci was operating within the framework of a Marxist view of history which saw classes and class struggle as the motor of history. In some important sense Italy was (in his view) a special case in which (compared with France) the bourgeoisie had failed to transcend the economic-corporate level. Gramsci's view is clearly expressed in a paragraph from Notebook 6 (not included in SPN), given the rubric 'The Commune as an Economic-Corporative Phase of the State'. There he argues that 'by the beginning of the fifteenth century, the spirit of initiative of Italian merchants had declined; people preferred to invest the wealth they had acquired in landed property and to have a secure income from agriculture rather than risk their money again in foreign expeditions and investments'. He poses the question of 'how did this happen?', and writes that 'the fundamental cause resided in the very structure of the commune, which was incapable of developing into a great territorial state' (QE3, 35; Q6, §43, 719). While Gramsci does not explicitly draw any lessons from the historical record, it seems legitimate to draw the inference that his analysis of the medieval communes (city-states) and of the Risorgimento paints the picture of a thwarted modernity, of a bourgeoisie which did not fully develop the power to create a modern nation-state until relatively late in the day (compared with France, England and Spain). And when such a nation-state was created, as we have seen it failed to meet the needs of the subaltern social strata, workers and peasants. A further implication seems to be that it was for the working class and its party to be the agent of the tasks which the bourgeoisie had left uncompleted, namely the advance to modernity, to the development of the productive forces and the achievement of modernity in both an economic productive sense and in a political sense as well. As we have noted, Gramsci saw fascism as in some senses a developmental force, in that it sought the modernization and development of the productive industrial basis of society, but it did so while repressing the working-class movement. One commentator on Gramsci, Walter Adamson, sums up his ideas as follows: 'Like many, though not all, passive revolutions, fascism was progressive in a defensive fashion, since it was designed to curb a still more progressive political force. Its peculiar feat was to have promoted the development of industrialism without the radical cataclysm of a proletarian revolution' (Adamson 1980, 201).

There are a number of questions raised by Gramsci's historical analysis as sketched out in the *Prison Notebooks*. First, primarily of concern to historians, is the question of the accuracy and validity of his view of the Risorgimento. Some later historians (e.g. Rosario Romeo) contest Gramsci's view that distribution of land to the peasants (which he criticizes the Action Party for not envisaging) would have been either feasible or economically progressive. One of the leading Italian contemporary historians of the Risorgimento suggests that partly as a result of this debate the themes of Gramsci's presentation of the Risorgimento are 'slowly losing interest' (Banti 2004, 142). A recent summary of the events of the Risorgimento and the historiographical debate on its significance by one of the British experts on the period, Lucy Riall, maintains that 'by emphasising class as the motor force of history, Gramsci ignores the crucial role played by politics in the transformation of society. Finally, his notion of "passive" revolution in Italy relies on a model of successful revolution in France that is highly questionable' (Riall 2009, 98). It seems unfair to accuse Gramsci of ignoring the crucial role played by politics, since much of his analysis focuses on the nature of political leadership offered by the respective parties of the Moderates and the Action Party, as our exposition has tried to show. It is certainly true that Gramsci uses as the standard for real revolutionary change the French Revolution of 1789, and he may well present a broad and too one-dimensional view of the Jacobins and their relationship to the rural masses. Paul Ginsborg in a sympathetic discussion of passive revolution suggests that 'the tendency to exaggerate the actual achievements of the French Revolution and render mythical its principal heroes is not one he [i.e. Gramsci] manages to avoid'. Ginsborg states that 'the picture of peasant consent constructed by Mathiez and adopted by Gramsci seems no more than half the truth', since as he says 'certain parts of the countryside, particularly those near the borders, responded enthusiastically to the demands of the *levée en masse* but others were lukewarm if not overtly hostile' (Ginsborg 1979, 54).

One Italian scholar, Giuseppe Galasso, in a valuable essay on 'Gramsci and the Problems of Italian History', makes some important points in his discussion of Gramsci's views on Italian history, which focus on Gramsci's view of the identity of history and politics. Galasso makes it clear that Gramsci was not putting the Risorgimento on trial, or denying that it was in certain respects progressive. Galasso suggests that Gramsci's historical analysis of the Risorgimento was not 'an authentic history to be opposed to the liberal tradition', but that Gramsci's analysis 'is and is intended to be a *political* one, his approach is one of an analysis of the dominating forces of Italian society and of the opposition to those forces'. Gramsci was concerned with 'a political strategy constructed scientifically, in other words based on the scientific critique of the whole of the past' (Galasso 1978, 153). So Gramsci was not necessarily saying that the Risorgimento should or perhaps even could have turned out differently from how it did, even though he has harsh criticisms of the Action Party. Galasso writes that 'Gramsci had not failed to recognize the creative and progressive character of the Risorgimento's achievement, rather he found in the history of a unified Italy a distortion, a hardening and a progressive running-down of that double creative and progressive impetus' (Galasso 1978, 167). So the point is not really that Gramsci was trying to give an alternative reading or provide a different history of the Risorgimento, but trying to explain how the present political situation had been formed by previous historical developments, since for him 'history was present-day politics in nuce'. We have already quoted Gramsci's view that 'a great historical work is one which in the present helps the developing forces [*le forze in isviluppo*] to become more aware of themselves and thus become concretely more active and creative [*attive e fattive*]' (Q19, §5, 1983–84). So his interpretation of past Italian history in the nineteenth century and indeed earlier was designed as part of a *political* project, to show how present-day class struggle and conflicting forces had been formed by previous developments, with the aim of showing more clearly the tasks which still needed to be achieved.

Leaving aside these debates about the historical and political significance of Gramsci's analysis of Italian history, there are two points which emerge from this chapter of the *Prison Notebooks* (the 'Notes on Italian History') which seem important for understanding the arguments of the *Notebooks* as a whole, and assessing their significance today. The first is the question of passive revolution or rather the ways in which Gramsci suggested that the passive revolution represented by fascism could be challenged, namely the war of position. The problem here is the one raised by Bellamy, quoted above to the effect that the modern state has the power to block counter-hegemonic projects much more effectively than the state of the *ancien régime* could do. This is what another expert on Gramsci, Walter Adamson, calls 'the paradox of civil society'. Adamson argues that 'the ability of the French and English bourgeoisies to gain an ascendency within civil society may simply reflect the weakness of civil society/political linkages in an earlier capitalism' (Adamson 1980, 221). One can question whether such opportunities would be available to the working-class movement, either in the period in which Gramsci was writing, or in our contemporary society. Adamson for his part maintains that 'unfortunately for Gramsci's political and cultural theory, there is no guarantee that the proletariat will have anything close to the same freedom of manoeuvre within contemporary civil society' (Adamson 1980, 221). He uses much the same idea as Bellamy when he writes that 'the ability of those controlling Western political societies to block the formation of an alternative hegemony was unprecedentedly high' (Adamson 1980, 221). For Adamson, the paradox consists in the fact that Gramsci suggests that the war of position has to be fought on through the institutions of civil society at the same time as arguing that the ability of the state to control and influence civil society is greater in the conditions of modernity than was the case in premodern society. There is an interesting passage in one of the last notebooks (number 25), with the title 'On the Margins of History (History of Subaltern Social Groups)', in which Gramsci discusses the nature of the medieval communes (or city-states). He explains that in those city-states the people were able to establish for themselves certain communal liberties: 'The people thus manages to dominate the commune, overcoming the previous ruling class, as in Siena after 1270, in Bologna with the "Sacrati" and "Sacratissimi" ordinances, in Florence with the "Ordinances of Justice" [*Ordinamenti di giustizia*]' (Q25, §4, 2286). But contrasting the state of the Middle Ages with the modern state, Gramsci goes on to write that 'the modern state substitutes for the mechanical block of social groups their subordination to the active hegemony of the directing and dominating group [*una loro subordinazione all'egemonia attiva del gruppo dirigente e dominante*], and thus abolishes some autonomies, which however are reborn in another form, as parties, unions, cultural associations' (Q25, §4, 2287). This presents a picture of a state which is more powerful in suppressing the development of counter-hegemony, even if the dominance of the ruling group can be challenged by parties, unions and other associations of civil society. In short, if the message of Gramsci's historical analysis is one of the failure of the parties of the bourgeoisie to establish a genuine hegemony, then it leaves open many problems of how the working-class movement could achieve this end and how it could develop the full modernity, economic and political, that was stunted in Italy for historical reasons analysed by Gramsci himself.

The second issue is also taken from this same commentator on Gramsci, Adamson, when he contrasts Gramsci's open-ended view of history (his denial of historical inevitability and of the mechanical view of historical progress presented in some versions of the Marxism of the Second International), with what Adamson calls 'the concept of a universal proletariat as historical actor' (Adamson 1980, 245). Of course, in the analysis of Italian history examined in this chapter there is little, if any, mention of the proletariat, for the obvious reason that in his discussion of the

Risorgimento Gramsci was concerned (primarily) with middle-class groups and parties and the way they established their hegemony (or failed to do so). But the implication of Gramsci's analysis seems to be that the tasks which the bourgeoisie had failed to carry out (or only carried out through the incomplete process of passive revolution) would have to be done by the proletariat, led by a political party (the modern Prince). Adamson suggests the need 'for close empirical analysis of class fragmentation and recomposition as an ongoing process within all advanced industrial societies' (Adamson 1980, 245). The phenomenon of class fragmentation is one which has only intensified over the last few years, with the undermining of Fordist methods of mass production and the decline of manufacturing industry in European and American society, replaced by the manufacture of the commodities of advanced modern, or postmodern, societies taking place in China, India and other newly industrializing countries (the BRICS, as they are sometimes known – Brazil, Russia, India, China and South Africa). This raises the very large question of whether the features of contemporary postmodern society include the presence of the coherent agency of change, the proletariat, which certainly Gramsci saw as the necessary bearer of progress. Ginsborg in his article on 'Gramsci and the era of bourgeois revolutions' draws attention to what he rightly calls 'one of his (Gramsci's) most provocative analogies', when Gramsci writes that 'what is needed, therefore, is an examination of the various "most advantageous" combinations for building a "train" to move forward through history as fast as possible'. This sentence follows a list of the various 'fundamental motor forces of Italian history', of which the first is presented by Gramsci as 'the Northern urban force' (SPN 98), of which Gramsci writes that 'the first of these forces retains its function of "locomotive" in any case' (SPN 98; Q19, §26, 2042). The question which follows is whether this idea of the urban force, more generally of the proletariat, as the 'locomotive' of the train of history is still valid. This also leads on to Gramsci's analysis of modernity, as expounded in his notes on Americanism and Fordism, the exposition and analysis of which forms the second half of the present chapter.

AMERICANISM AND FORDISM

Notebook 22 of Gramsci's *Prison Notebooks* is one of the special notebooks given over to one topic, in this case given the title by Gramsci himself of 'Americanism and Fordism'. Most of this notebook appears in the SPN as the third chapter of Part II, 'Notes on Politics', of which chapters 1 ('The Modern Prince') and 2 ('State and Civil Society') are discussed in the following chapter of this present volume. The reason why in this sole instance the arrangement of the SPN has not been followed in the present exposition is that in some respects Gramsci's reflections in the chapter on 'Americanism and Fordism' constitute a complement to the previously discussed notes on Italian history. In those notes the predominant theme was one of how the Risorgimento had been a passive revolution which had blocked off or hampered the development of Italy into a modern nation-state, and how the historical record showed the incomplete and somehow stunted nature of Italy's nation-state formation. The notes on Americanism and Fordism can be read as in some way a continuation of this theme. They show Gramsci grappling with the shape and nature of contemporary modern capitalism, and the way in which the American form of capitalist rationality challenged European society and posed problems for European capitalism. Gramsci also makes a connection with the theme of passive revolution, posing the question of 'whether Americanism can constitute an historical "epoch", that is, whether it can determine a gradual evolution of the same type as the "passive revolution" examined elsewhere and typical of the last century', the 'elsewhere' presumably referring to his analysis of the Risorgimento and of the course of Italian (and European) history since the French Revolution (SPN 279; Q22, §1, 2140). In other words, in the notebook on 'Americanism and Fordism' it seems that Gramsci is examining the mass standardized production typified by the Ford motor company, in order to explore the implications for contemporary Italian society and the political consequences of such new means of production. In comparison with some of the more philosophical sections of the *Notebooks*, this particular notebook seems more straightforward and less cryptic, even if some of Gramsci's reflections on fascism are slightly coded to refer to the phenomenon of 'corporativism', seen as characteristic of the fascist regime. Gramsci is thus examining industrial or capitalist modernity, as exemplified in its most advanced form by the mass production of American enterprise, and seeking to work out the social and political consequences of such methods of production.

The meaning Gramsci attributes to the terms Americanism and Fordism seems clear enough – the use of conveyer-belt techniques and more generally the rationalization of the productive apparatus. Gramsci refers to 'the experiments conducted by Ford and to the economies made by his firm through direct management of transport and distribution of the product' (SPN 285; Q22, §2, 2145). However, the more interesting questions which Gramsci raises concern whether these productive techniques signify a new type of society, and the ways in which workers are being made to conform to such new productive methods. Gramsci writes of the attempt in the USA to control alcohol consumption (the short-lived phenomenon of Prohibition) and the ways in which industrialists tried to interfere in the private lives of their workers by seeking to impose a puritanical code of regular living and monogamy. The question is whether this was an attempt to fashion or mould the workers into a new type of producer. As Gramsci writes of such attempts to extend factory discipline into the private lives of the workers, 'People who laugh at these initiatives (failures though they were) and see in them only a hypocritical manifestation of "puritanism" thereby deny themselves any possibility of understanding the importance, significance and objective import of the American phenomenon, which is *also* the biggest collective effort to date to create, with unprecedented speed, and with a consciousness of purpose unmatched in history, a new type of worker and of man' (SPN 302; Q22, §11, 2165). So the problem which Gramsci investigates in this particular notebook is of the wider implications of the type of industrial modernity represented by Fordist mass production and of the supposedly scientific methods of work represented by Frederick Winslow Taylor and Taylorism. This latter represented an attempt at the rationalization of labour, with the purpose of increasing efficiency and output of the workforce. If this signified a new stage of capitalist society, Gramsci's question is whether this would be a further contemporary example of a passive revolution. In other words, were these forms of capitalist modernity a means of extracting greater surplus value from the workers, and in that way of combating what Gramsci in orthodox Marxist fashion refers to as the declining rate of profit? This topic is included by Gramsci in his list of problems to be resolved or examined under the heading of 'Americanism and Fordism'. The seventh problem in his list refers to 'Fordism as the ultimate stage in the process of progressive attempts by industry to overcome the law of the tendency of the rate of profit to fall' (SPN 280; Q22, §1, 2140).

Gramsci's analysis of these phenomena is based on a comparison between New World (America) and Old World (Europe, especially Italy). Not that Gramsci refers to de Tocqueville, who in his classic *Democracy in America* suggested that the force of the democratic revolution of modernity could be seen with far greater clarity in America than Europe, since in the United States there was no *ancien régime* or hierarchy of traditional social strata to impede the workings of democracy. Gramsci's comparison of the USA and Italy focuses on two issues. In the first place, in America there were no unproductive, parasitic classes. In Italy, and Europe generally, on the other hand, there were societies where there did exist 'numerous classes with no essential function in the world of production, in other words classes which are purely parasitic'. Gramsci wrote that 'European "tradition", European "civilisation", is, in contrast, characterised precisely by the existence of such classes, created by the "richness" and "complexity" of past history' (SPN 281; Q22, §2, 2141). The second issue derived from this one was how hegemony was imposed in the respective societies of America and Europe. In the former, as Gramsci wrote, 'hegemony here is born in the factory and requires for its exercise only a minute quantity of professional political and ideological intermediaries' (SPN 285; Q22, §2, 2146). The contrast was with Europe where (at least this is implied) there would be greater difficulty in securing the assent of the subaltern classes to the existing society. Gramsci seems to be suggesting that in the American situation it was through the higher wages paid to workers in Fordist-type factories that consent or at least acceptance of the new order of society by the workforce was secured. In the American situation hegemony was achieved through a combination of force (smashing or intimidating the trade unions) and consent, with the latter dependent on what Gramsci calls 'high wages, various social benefits, extremely subtle ideological and political propaganda' (SPN 285; Q22, §2, 2145). The implication was that viewed from one aspect Americanism was an example of a passive revolution, in that it introduced modern methods of production and thus was in a certain sense progressive, yet it achieved this push towards greater modernity not through any revolutionary upheaval or forms of socialist politics, but by buying the workers off through higher wages and forms of intellectual discipline inculcated by such associations as Rotary Clubs and the YMCA, which fulfilled the functions carried out in Europe by Freemasons and the Jesuits (SPN 286; Q22, §2, 2146).

When Gramsci writes that in America 'hegemony is born in the factory', this recalls some of his early pre-prison writings on the factory councils and the attempt of the workers to emancipate themselves through taking over the productive apparatus and controlling production through institutions (the councils) set up at the point of production. In June 1920 Gramsci wrote that 'the revolutionary process takes place on the terrain of production, in the factory, where the relations are those between the oppressor and the oppressed, the exploiter and the exploited, where there is no such thing as liberty for the worker and no such thing as democracy' (PPW 164). In the notes on Americanism and Fordism Gramsci returns to 'the terrain of production, in the factory', and this time probes the question of whether the new methods of production were providing new means of dominance over the workforce rather than, through the factory councils, developing means of worker emancipation. Gramsci sees the American system of production as the rationalization of the productive process which involves an attempt at both physical and psychological control over the worker, seeking to mould human nature to the tasks of mass production. This combines both advanced and also anachronistic methods. Gramsci notes that 'rationalisation has determined the need to elaborate a new type of man suited to the new type of work and productive process' (SPN 286; Q22, §2, 2146). Through the rewards of high wages, on the one hand, and a kind of moral discipline exercised through institutions like Rotary Club and

YMCA, the capitalist system sought to mould the producers, the workers, into a productive being adapted to the new means of mass production. Yet in Gramsci's view this process in America had what he called an 'anachronistic' aspect, in that the American unions viewed the struggle as one of ownership of their jobs, of the defence of particular crafts. Gramsci states that the American version of the class struggle was 'similar to the struggle that took place in Europe in the eighteenth century' (SPN 286; Q22, §2, 2146), namely the idea of workers having a particular ownership of their craft. The implication is that this idea was in any case archaic in terms of the present structure of capitalist production, so that the American unions were in that respect rather backward, seeking to preserve a job or craft structure that had no future. Hence the attack on such a traditional concept of labour was a progressive one. Gramsci wrote that 'American workers unions are, more than anything else, the corporate expression of the rights of qualified crafts and therefore the industrialists' attempts to curb them have a certain "progressive" aspect' (SPN 286; Q22, §2, 2146). The word 'progressive' is placed by Gramsci in inverted commas, to suggest perhaps another aspect in which Fordism was one example of a passive revolution. It was in one way progressive in its development of the forces of production, yet it carried out this development by averting any social upheaval on the part of the subaltern classes. In that sense then while Gramsci in these notes was going back to some of his earlier focus on the factory and on the point of production, the examination of Fordism indicated the potential for these modern means of production to maintain the hegemony of the capitalist class more firmly, through the bait of higher wages and through the moulding of human beings and their disciplining to form them almost into productive machines.

SOCIALISM AND MODERNITY

That, however, is not Gramsci's final conclusion on the question of whether these modern methods of production are the means for extracting more surplus value from the worker and developing the dynamism of the productive process while impeding a revolutionary means of doing this. If this project were successful, then Fordism would represent a passive revolution in that respect. Gramsci's analysis is a highly insightful one of the whole dynamics of capitalist development and indeed of modernity as a whole. He makes it clear that the whole purpose of Taylorism was to tame the workers or to forcibly adapt them to the new productive system. As he writes, 'Taylor is in fact expressing with brutal cynicism the purpose of American society – developing in the worker to the highest degree automatic and mechanical attitudes, breaking up the old psycho-physical nexus of qualified professional work, which demands a certain active participation of intelligence, fantasy and initiative on the part of the worker, and reducing productive operations exclusively to the mechanical, physical aspect' (SPN 302; Q22, §11, 2165). The idea of Taylor was to make the worker into the equivalent of the trained gorilla, a human equivalent of a machine whose enhanced productivity was to the benefit of the capitalists. So in one respect modernity (this type of capitalist modernity) perfected what could be called the alienation of labour, though Gramsci does not use this term, the analysis of the alienated labourer offered in Marx's *Economic and Philosophical Manuscripts* of 1844 not being available to him.

This attempt to create a new type of labourer, what Gramsci calls 'a new type of worker and of man', extended to the private sphere and into the emotional and sexual life of the worker. A worker exhausted by debauchery and by excessive consumption of alcohol, not to mention a combination of both (and indeed the two might go together), would not be much use to the employer. Gramsci saw here the source of prohibition of alcohol and the monogamous marriage patterns of the American workers. Gramsci seems to be suggesting that whereas 'until recently the American people was a working people', with the vocation of work shared by working class and ruling classes alike, this was now changing with the emergence of a 'moral gap in the United States between the working masses and the ever more numerous elements of the ruling classes' (SPN 305; Q22, §11, 2168). To put it crudely, Gramsci seems to be suggesting that the workers were exemplars of sobriety and marital fidelity, because such were the traits required of modern workers and the 'most perfected automatism' required of them at work: 'The employee who goes to work after a night of "excess" is no good for his work.' It is not clear if Gramsci was endorsing the result of what could be called the socialization process of Fordist industry which would result in sober workers within a stable family structure, or whether he was just stating this as a fact, a result of the requirements of modern industrial production. He writes that 'this complex of direct and indirect repression and coercion exercised on the masses will undoubtedly produce results and a new form of sexual union will emerge whose fundamental characteristic would apparently have to be monogamy and relative stability'. In contrast, he suggests that this sober and stern morality is being honoured in the breach rather than the observance by the industrialists, and notably their wives and daughters who have nothing to do but travel and 'are continually crossing the ocean to come to Europe'. These members of the higher social classes succeeded in escaping Prohibition in their own country and were used to 'contracting "marriages" for a season', even getting married on the ship home and divorcing when the ship arrived back in the USA, according to the picture Gramsci presents. The wayward life of the upper classes has one result, which is to 'make more difficult any coercion on the working masses to make them conform to the needs of the new industry' (SPN 306; Q22, §2, 2168–69). Thus Fordist production required a new type of worker, and imposed the discipline and social sanctions which helped create the character of the new worker. Yet this process was hampered by the class divisions inherent in this new form of capitalist production, and by the split between the morality of the subaltern class and that of the upper classes, in Gramsci's presentation of the issue.

In some respects these views of Gramsci seem rather dated. The important point however is his insistence that modernity involves a protracted process which shapes human beings as producers, and imposes on them the discipline of industrial production. Equally important is the idea that it is the working class which could take over the process of modernity, and use the modern means of production for emancipatory purposes. Gramsci seems to be saying that the emergence of modernity came at a massive cost, but a necessary one, in a process in which natural or animal impulses had to be repressed and disciplined. Such development had been carried out through brute coercion and had been imposed by a ruling class, 'through the dominion of one social group over all the productive forces of society' (SPN 298; Q22, §10, 2161). In the course of history, 'the selection or "education" of men adapted to the new forms of civilisation and to the new forms of production and work has taken place by means of incredible acts of brutality which have cast the weak and the non-conforming into the limbo of the lumpen-classes or have eliminated them entirely' (SPN 298; Q22, §10, 2161). But how could this process (a necessary one) of adapting people to the new modern methods of production be carried out in a different way? And how had it been carried out in the non-capitalist environment of the Soviet Union, to which Gramsci refers in an elliptical way through his mention of the Bolshevik leader Trotsky and his project of the militarization of labour? Gramsci is here concerned with some fundamental problems of modernity. He is proposing that Fordism and Americanism are in some senses progressive since they are methods required by modern production, but they could be adopted and developed differently, so as to show a way out of the crisis of contemporary society. Yet Gramsci's analysis needs to be scrutinized in the light of our own contemporary post-Fordist society, where some of the presuppositions of his own analysis no longer hold. The key ideas here are those of the changed world of production (from Fordist to post-Fordist), and the recurrent problem of agency.

What Gramsci appears to be arguing is that what he calls 'Taylorism and rationalisation in general' are themselves 'the necessities of the new methods of work' (SPN 300; Q22, §10, 2162), in other words inescapable conditions of modernity. Gramsci also states that 'the new methods of production and work have to be acquired by means of reciprocal persuasion and by convictions proposed and accepted by each individual' (SPN 300; Q22, §10, 2163), by what we might call a reciprocal or dialogical process rather than imposition from above. In a paragraph which is not entirely clear, he suggests that in the society of his own day, there is a kind of crisis, since the practice of discipline and sobriety is not observed by 'those classes which are not tightly bound to productive work'. Those classes express an 'enlightened and libertarian conception', and it seems clear that in this context Gramsci is not using 'enlightened' in a positive sense. The argument implies that there is a sort of moral crisis throughout society, with the result that 'the psycho-physical attitudes necessary for the new methods of work are not acquired'. This moral crisis 'can be resolved only by coercion', but this would be 'self-coercion and therefore self-discipline', and the necessary coercion would be 'a new type, in that it is exercised by the *elite* of a class over the rest of that same class' (SPN 300; Q22, §10, 2163). He ends the paragraph by stating that 'the struggle against the libertarian conception means therefore precisely creating the *elites* necessary for the historical task, or at least developing them so that their function is extended to cover all spheres of human activity' (SPN 301; Q22, §10, 2163–64). But which class and which elites is Gramsci talking about here? One reading of this passage would be that he is referring to the organic intellectuals of the working class, who alone would be capable of the historical task of developing in the working class as a whole the habits and the morality appropriate to the productive tasks of modern industrial society. This then would be done through reciprocal persuasion rather than coercive imposition from above, and this function of the elites would be 'extended to cover all spheres of human activity'. Only in that way could the crisis of modern industrial society be resolved.

While the interpretation of this particular passage is only one possible one among others, Gramsci's overall argument throughout the notebook on 'Americanism and Fordism' is clear − it is that the working class is the agent of modernity and of the forms of productive activity needed for modern society. This is evident from one of the relatively few passages in the *Prison Notebooks* as a whole in which Gramsci refers to the factory council movement of the *biennio rosso* of 1919–20 and of the period of the periodical *L'Ordine Nuovo* which he edited (see Chapter 1 above). In this passage he contrasts Italy with America. Reflecting on the period of history before fascism took over in Italy, Gramsci emphasizes the role of the Italian skilled workers in leading the adoption of modern methods of work: 'In reality, skilled workers in Italy have never, as individuals or through union organisations, actively or passively opposed innovations leading towards lowering of costs, rationalisation of work or the introduction of more perfect forms of automation and more perfect technical organisation of the complex of the enterprise. On the contrary.' This is followed by an explicit reference to the events of the period of *L'Ordine Nuovo*, when Gramsci writes that 'a careful analysis of Italian history before 1922 ... must objectively come to the conclusion that it was precisely the workers who brought into being newer and more modern industrial requirements and in their own way upheld these strenuously' (SPN 292; Q22, §6, 2156). The words 'in their own way' are significant. They imply that the self-administration of the factory through the factory councils was the workers' own way of introducing the new methods of work appropriate for modern industrial production. Some of the industrialists, Gramsci notes, including the Fiat boss Agnelli, recognized this and tried to co-opt these modernizing practices of the workers by incorporating them into the work of the enterprise. Agnelli tried 'to absorb the *Ordine Nuovo* and its school into the Fiat complex and thus to institute a school of workers and technicians qualified for industrial change and for work with "rationalised" systems', yet these attempts were not successful (SPN 292; Q22, §6, 2156). Gramsci's argument is that it is through the activity and educative efforts of the working class that new methods of work and production could be applied and developed, so that in a broader sense the working class is the agent of modernity and industrial development. He is thus endorsing ideas of rationalized production and the need for the working class to adopt the new methods of work, which would be introduced not by coercion from above but by some kind of self-activity and, perhaps, by what could be called workers' control, as attempted for a brief period by the factory council movement. This form of modernity is contrasted by Gramsci with two other attempts to foster modern methods of industrial production, the Trotskyite militarization of labour on the one hand and the fascist corporative state on the other, so that the notebook on 'Americanism and Fordism' contains reflections, condensed and cryptic though they might be, on both Soviet communism and Italian fascism and their relationship to modernity and rationalized industrial production.

FORDISM IN COMMUNISM AND FASCISM

It was not only Trotsky among the Bolshevik leaders who expressed an interest in Fordist methods of production. Lenin himself wrote and spoke favourably of applying Fordism in the conditions of the Soviet Union. However, it is Trotsky to whom Gramsci refers in this context in the notebook on 'Americanism and Fordism', with specific mention of Trotsky's policy of the militarization of labour. This was an attempt, carried out in the period of war communism of 1918–21, to create labour armies, to organize the workforce as an army to carry out the necessary productive tasks of the new society. Not surprisingly this policy met with the opposition of the Soviet trade unions. Trotsky defended the militarization of labour at the Ninth Congress of the Russian Communist Party in March 1920, arguing that compulsion of labour 'would reach the highest degree of intensity during the transition from capitalism to socialism' (quoted in Deutscher 1959, 499). Trotsky argued that 'the militarization of labour, in this fundamental sense of which I have spoken, is the indispensable basic method for the organization of our labour force', and posing the question 'Is it true that compulsory labour is always unproductive?' retorted that 'this is the most wretched and miserable liberal prejudice: chattel slavery, too, was productive'. In the words of his biographer, Isaac Deutscher, who quotes these extracts from the debates at the Ninth Party Congress, Trotsky, 'the rebel *par excellence*, the expounder of permanent revolution, came very near to talking like an apologist for past systems of coercion and exploitation' (Deutscher 1959, 501). Deutscher explains that Trotsky's proposal was 'that the machinery for military mobilization should be employed for the mobilization of civilian labour', and that 'civilian labour was to be subjected to military discipline; and the military administration was to supply manpower to industrial units' (Deutscher 1959, 491–92).

Gramsci had come into contact with Trotsky during his period in the Soviet Union. The quite frequent references to Trotsky in the *Prison Notebooks* are mainly in connection with Trotsky's theory of permanent revolution, and are generally critical of this as an example of what Gramsci thought of as the war of manoeuvre, or a frontal assault on state power. Gramsci saw this as a mistaken reprise of the 1848 strategy of an uprising directly against the state, which he thought was bound to lead to failure in the complex world of civil society characteristic of Western as opposed to Eastern societies. These ideas are more fully discussed in the next chapter. In the section under discussion here, Gramsci is also critical of Trotsky, while noting the 'interest of Lev Davidovitch in Americanism' (SPN 302; Q22, §11, 2164) – Trotsky being always referred to in the *Prison Notebooks* either by his Russian first names, as here, or by his original surname of Bronstein. In this note Gramsci suggests that while the goal of imposing new methods of production (Fordist ones) on the workforce was correct, the means proposed of the militarization of labour were not the right ones to achieve that end: 'The principle of coercion, direct or indirect, in the ordering of production and work, is correct; but the form which it assumed was mistaken. The military model had become a pernicious prejudice and the militarisation of labour was a failure' (SPN 301; Q22, §11, 2164). It is not clear whether this statement endorsing coercion in the ordering of production and work was meant to apply to the new society of the post-revolutionary Soviet Union, or was intended to be valid more generally. In the light of what Gramsci wrote about the reciprocal persuasion and the references to *L'Ordine Nuovo* it seems more probable that it was with regard to the Soviet Union that he endorsed coercion (though not in the form of the militarization of labour), or at least accepted it as necessary in the conditions in which the Soviet Union found itself during and after the period of war communism (1918–21). In Gramsci's view, Trotsky's proposals for the militarization of labour, for making workers into members of a productive army commanded by military discipline, with severe sanctions for those who shirked their productive duty, 'was destined necessarily to end up in a form of Bonapartism', implying that Trotsky would have ended up as a dictator, just as the pursuit of collectivization and industrialization after 1929 led to the dominance of Stalin and his dictatorship. Hence Gramsci endorsed 'the inexorable necessity of crushing what threatened to become a form of Bonapartism' (SPN 301; Q22, §11, 2164).

Gramsci recognized the importance of imposing new methods of work, if need be (as in the case of the new society of the Soviet

Union) by coercive methods, while rejecting the methods used, for a brief period of time, in Soviet Russia in the extreme form of the militarization of labour. This was the mistaken way of introducing Fordism. By contrast, there are a number of remarks on fascism in this section of the *Notebooks*. This is presented by Gramsci as an alternative method of developing the productive infrastructure of society, but is seen as a passive revolution which proved to be a false or inadequate path to modernity. What could be called the deep structure or underlying argument of this notebook is the examination of Americanism and Fordism as typifying economic modernity. The notes in this notebook argue for a rejection of both the Soviet way and the fascist way of forcing the new production methods needed in a modern society onto the workforce. The implied conclusion was that the working class was the agent of modernity and the bearer of modern methods of production. However the modern production system could only be introduced and developed fully along a different path from the two routes taken by Soviet Russia and fascist Italy.

The analysis of fascism in this regard comes in some remarks about the corporative movement: 'The corporative movement exists' (SPN 293; Q22, §6, 2156), Gramsci notes. The corporative state was of course one of the ideological mainstays of Italian fascism. The idea, at least in theory, was to suppress class struggle by creating corporative institutions, presided over by the state, in which labour and capital would work harmoniously together, in the framework of the corporative state. The fascist state was meant to integrate the workers in an organized totality. As Mussolini proclaimed in a speech in 1929, 'The employed are integrated within the institutions of the regime: syndicalism and corporatism enable the whole nation to be organised. ... Labour and capital have ceased to consider their antagonism an inexorable fact of history; the conflicts which inevitably arise are solved peacefully thanks to an increasing degree of conscious class collaboration' (Griffin 1995, 63). The corporations were supposed not only to be institutions for the collaboration which put an end to class conflict, but were meant to channel investment and take decisions on production with a view to modernizing and developing the economy. In that sense the fascist regime, through the institutions of the corporations, claimed to be a modernizing state which would achieve the progressive development of the economy. These claims were more impressive in the theory than in the reality of the fascist regime.

Gramsci's analysis in the *Prison Notebooks* is allusive and indirect, but the question he poses was whether the fascist state, through the institutions of corporativism, really was economically progressive and whether it could be the instrument through which Italy's modernization could be furthered. Hence in this sense it fits in with his general analysis of modernity and the way in which Italy (and, it seems implicit, Europe in general) could move forward to gain the full fruits of modernity. If Americanism represented the necessary methods of modern production for which workers had to be educated and trained, was fascism and its corporative state moving towards this goal? The contrast which Gramsci makes between America and Europe involves the fact that European societies were rich in what Gramsci called parasitic classes who played no role in production, and hence were responsible for Italy's backward economy. Gramsci noted the contrast between 'the old, anachronistic, demographic social structure of Europe, and on the other hand an ultra-modern form of production and of working methods – such as is offered by the most advanced American variety, the industry of Henry Ford' (SPN 281; Q22, §2, 2140). The economic problems of Italy in particular and of Europe in general stemmed from the large number of those whom Gramsci in a memorable phrase called 'the pensioners of economic history', those who were 'economically passive elements' created in the course of the long history of Italy. 'This past history has left behind', Gramsci stated, 'a heap of passive sedimentations produced by the phenomenon of the saturation and fossilisation of civil-service personnel and intellectuals, of clergy and landowners, piratical commerce and the professional (and later conscript, but for the officers always professional) army' (SPN 281; Q22, §2, 2141). To these non-productive strata had to be added 'another source of absolute parasitism', namely the personnel of the state administration, and the existence of cities like Naples where large sections of the inhabitants gained their livelihood not in productive industry but in servicing the needs of the landowning groups who came to spend their money in the city. The economic structure of Italy was not a modern one, or rather its productivity was severely constrained by the mass of non-productive and parasitic groups. The contrast was with America, whose lack of past history meant that there were fewer, if any, of these groups left over from history. Gramsci is again wrestling with the problem of modernity, this time in its economic aspects, and the ways in which Italy (and Europe more generally) could be transformed into a modern society. America did not have 'this leaden burden' of the parasitic classes to support. So, Gramsci implies, the question is whether fascism and the fascist state could be the vehicle for economic and social modernization, for getting rid of the legacy of history, in the shape of the non-productive elements of Italian society. Gramsci noted the contradictions of fascism in this regard: 'In Italy there have been the beginnings of a Fordist fanfare: exaltation of big cities, overall planning for the Milan conurbation, etc.; the affirmation that capitalism is only at its beginnings and that it is necessary to prepare for it grandiose patterns of development' (SPN 287; Q22, §2, 2147). Yet at the same time fascism exalted rural ways of life and criticized Enlightenment views of modernity, a contrast, one may note, even more acute in German Nazism with its emphasis on industrial productivity opposed by its *völkisch* exaltation of the peasantry and the soil. In the case of Italian fascism Gramsci noted a whole package of antimodernist ideas. He listed these as 'a conversion to ruralism, the disparagement of the cities typical of the Enlightenment, exaltation of the artisanal and of idyllic patriarchalism, reference to craft rights and a struggle against industrial liberty' (SPN 287; Q22, §2, 2147).

In assessing whether fascism with its corporative state was a genuinely modernizing force, Gramsci notes that a number of conditions needed to be satisfied for this to be the case. Americanization (modernization of the economic structure) required a certain type of social structure (or at least, Gramsci noted, 'a determined intention to create it'), and a certain type of state. The former condition involved the absence or reduction of parasitic non-productive classes, while the latter was a state which was liberal in the sense of allowing the free self-development of civil society. Gramsci's words here should be quoted. He described the state needed for Americanization in the following terms: 'This State is the liberal State, not in the sense of free-trade liberalism or of effective political liberty, but in the more fundamental sense of free initiative and of economic individualism which, with its own means, on the level of "civil society", through historical development, itself arrives at a regime of industrial concentration and monopoly' (SPN 293; Q22, §6, 2157). This sentence is rather significant. It indicates not that Gramsci is a liberal, but that he saw the process of economic modernization as being achieved through the historical development of civil society and the development of modern industry which would through its own dynamic arrive at a system 'of industrial concentration and monopoly', perhaps following the path of capitalist development described by Marx in volume I of *Capital*. Marx analysed the process of capitalist development culminating in 'the constant decrease in the number of capitalist magnates' and in the emergence of 'the monopoly of capital' which 'becomes a fetter upon the mode of production which has flourished alongside and under it' (Marx 1976, 929). Whether or not Gramsci had this classic passage from Marx's *Capital* in mind when writing the sentence quoted above, it is clear that he saw fascism as incapable of satisfying either of the two conditions needed for effective Americanization, or modernization of production. In the first place, fascism did not get rid of the parasitic classes, in fact rather the opposite was the case. Gramsci wrote, referring to fascism, that 'the State is creating new *rentiers*, that is to say it is promoting the old forms of parasitic accumulation of savings and tending to create closed social formations' (SPN 293; Q22, §6, 2157). So the corporative trend was 'more a machinery to preserve the existing order just as it is rather than a propulsive force', since it created more unemployment. While some jobs were created through the corporations, they were 'organisational and not productive', posts for the unemployed of the middle classes, who would not survive in a situation of free competition.

Furthermore, not only did the fascist corporative state fail to diminish the parasitic strata of Italian society, but it obstructed the free development of civil society which Gramsci considered a necessary condition for economic modernization. Gramsci noted that 'the corporative movement exists' and he observed that it had involved juridical changes. Those changes had 'created the formal conditions within which major technical-economic change can happen on a large scale, because the workers are not in a position either to oppose it or to struggle to become themselves the standard-bearers of the movement' (SPN 293; Q22, §6, 2156). Gramsci posed the question of whether the corporative state could open up the possibility of genuine economic and social modernization. He asked whether 'corporative organisation could become the form of the new change', and whether this could be an example of Vico's 'ruses of providence', a phrase which itself echoes Hegel's idea of 'the cunning of reason' in which historical development brings about certain results irrespective of the actual intentions of the people involved. However, his answer to the question he posed remained sceptical of the capacity of fascism to be a genuinely modernizing force, precisely because of its dominance or policing control over the sphere of civil society. This is made clear in this sentence, referring to the corporative or fascist state: 'The negative element of "economic policing" has so far had the upper hand over the positive element represented by the requirements of a new economic policy which can renovate, by modernising it, the socio-economic structure of the nation while remaining within the framework of the old industrialism' (SPN 293; Q22, §6, 2157).

It is true that there are in the *Prison Notebooks* some passages which consider the possibility of fascism in its corporative form managing to contain its contradictions and develop the economy in the form of a passive revolution, without revolutionary upheaval. One such passage comes shortly after the lines previously quoted, where Gramsci points to what he calls a possible 'way out' of the contradictions of corporatism. Gramsci asks whether 'the corporative trend ... could yet manage to proceed by very slow and almost imperceptible stages to modify the social structure without violent shocks: even the most tightly swathed baby manages nevertheless to develop and grow'. Yet Gramsci dismissed this as an unlikely scenario, since 'the process would be so long and encounter so many difficulties that new interests could grow up in the meanwhile and once again oppose its development so tenaciously as to crush it entirely' (SPN 294; Q22, §6, 2158). It is not clear what these 'new interests' might be – perhaps this is an allusion to a post-fascist resurrection of the labour movement which would 'crush' the structures of the fascist state. In his study of Gramsci's life and thought, Giuseppe Vacca draws attention to the way in which Gramsci envisaged as a possibility that the fascist state would manage to rationalize production so that savings were not the preserve of the parasitic classes but were directly used for productive purposes (Vacca 2012, 137–45). This would lead to economic progress and genuine rationalization of the economy. In Gramsci's words, 'If the State were proposing to impose an economic direction by which the production of savings ceased to be a "function" of a parasitic class and became a function of the productive organism itself, such a hypothetical development would be progressive, and could have its part in a vast design of integral rationalisation' (SPN 315; Q22, §14, 2176). So here Gramsci explores the possibility that the fascist state could be the agent for a progressive (at least in the economic sense) development of capitalism, channelling savings directly to industry for productive purposes. Gramsci's words show how carefully he analysed the ideology of fascism, which exalted the totalitarian state as the supreme authority in which all conflicting interests were harmonized for a common good, and which claimed to be over and above particular interests, even those of the capitalist class. Fascist ideologists like Giovanni Gentile used a bastardized form of Hegelianism to justify this role of the fascist state. Gramsci writes of 'the historical justification of the so-called corporate trends, which manifest themselves for the most part in the form of an exaltation of the State in general, conceived as something absolute, and in the form of diffidence and aversion to the traditional forms of capitalism' (SPN 315; Q22, §14, 2177).

That was indeed the ideology of fascism, namely its exaltation of the state in general. In his examination of the possibility of a progressive economic function of the fascist state, Gramsci points out that if the corporative state were really to be the agent of a vast design of integral rationalisation then the state would have to promote genuine agrarian reform as well as industrial reform. This would involve a sort of technocratic recasting of property rights in which income would depend on fulfilling a productive role. At least this seems to be the meaning of Gramsci's statement that if there were agrarian and industrial reform then 'one could thus reduce all income to the status of technico-industrial functional necessities and no longer keep them as the juridical consequences of pure property rights' (SPN 315; Q22, §14, 2177). However, Gramsci seems to be deeply sceptical of the possibility that the fascist corporative state could act in this economically rational way, and he analyses the contradictions in the social base of the fascist regime. Fascism claimed to be a movement of ordinary people, but in reality it was tied to the interests of capital: 'in theory the State appears to have its socio-political base among the ordinary folk and the intellectuals, while in reality its structure remains plutocratic and it is impossible for it to break its links with big finance capital'. Gramsci further observed that 'it is the State itself which becomes the biggest plutocratic organism, the *holding* of the masses of savings of the small capitalists' (SPN 315; Q22, §14, 2177). His conclusion seems to be that the fascist state would just function as a guarantor and protector of parasitic savings, so that parasitic landed property would be strengthened and the interests of rentiers furthered. Instead of the fascist state acting as a promoter of economic rationalization and progress, it just existed to protect such non-productive savings and the interests of those classes of landed proprietors and petty-bourgeois rentiers, boosting the weight of those parasitic classes that American-style rationalization was meant to dispose of. Hence the fascist state could in no way be the progressive dynamic modernizing force its ideology proclaimed it to be. Gramsci's analysis of the possibility that the fascist state might play such a role involved an examination of the contradictions of fascism, the contradiction between its populist sometimes anti-capitalist rhetoric and appeal to ordinary folk and the intellectuals on the one hand and its links to finance capital and its role as the guarantor of non-productive savings on the other.

The conclusion is that this section of the *Prison Notebooks* contains an analysis of the modernizing role of both Soviet communism and Italian fascism, as possible agents of economic development. Because of its militarization of labour, Gramsci rejects the Soviet model, and presumably his criticism extends to the forced industrialization and collectivization from above that was the characteristic of Stalinism at the time of the Third Period, predicting imminent capitalist collapse. More clearly, Gramsci considered the possibility of a fascist road to economic modernity. He concluded that despite the rhetoric of fascism its modernizing role was rendered impossible by its failure to give civil society any autonomy under the dominance of the police (what he calls 'the negative elements of "economic policing"'), and by the real social base of fascism and its ties to finance capital and rentier interests. His admittedly brief allusions to the factory councils and to the willingness of the working class to accept and indeed foster economic modernization suggest that it was only the working-class movement which could be the agent of Americanism and Fordism, seen as crucial aspects of a productive industrial society. It is significant that Gramsci denies that Fordist mechanical methods of work result in the intellectual deadening of the worker. Indeed Gramsci argues that the reduction of work to a series of repetitive and mechanical movements is in a way liberating rather than restricting intellectual freedom and capacity: 'Once the process of adaptation has been completed, what really happens is that the brain of the worker, far from being mummified, reaches a state of complete freedom' (SPN 309; Q22, §12, 2170). The fate of the worker under conditions of mass production was far from being the trained gorilla that the industrialists perhaps wished to produce. On the contrary, 'not only does the worker think, but the fact that he gets no immediate satisfaction from his work and realises that they are trying to reduce him to a trained gorilla, can lead him into a train of thought that is far from conformist' (SPN 310; Q22, §12, 2171), in Gramsci's quite optimistic perspective. The mechanization of work in conditions of mass production thus liberates the worker to think non-conformist, perhaps revolutionary, thoughts. One could say that Gramsci's analysis leads to the conclusion that conditions of Fordist production might result in a lack of job satisfaction but also in the realization that true fulfilment comes not from work but from political engagement and revolutionary praxis. This of course is not stated explicitly, but Gramsci's analysis remains positive in its hope that the mechanization of labour does not necessarily lead to intellectual passivity but on the contrary that the liberation from absorption in the work at hand, which has been reduced to mindless mechanical operations, creates the conditions for intellectual activity. Such intellectual activity, as we saw in the analysis of intellectuals in the previous chapter, is characteristic of all human activity, of human beings as *homo faber*, as creative and active beings. That Fordist production does not dull the brain but liberates it for political activity seems to be Gramsci's argument here.

GRAMSCI AS A THEORIST OF MODERNITY

Gramsci does not explicitly use the term modernity. However, bringing together the two sections of the *Prison Notebooks* (in the SPN edition) which have been considered in this chapter (the 'Notes on Italian History' followed by 'Americanism and Fordism') one could argue that modernity was one of the central themes of the *Prison Notebooks*. The historical analysis showed how the form taken by the Risorgimento (and indeed earlier historical developments in Italy) had blocked Italy's path to modernity, or perhaps more accurately had produced an incomplete form of modernity. While Italy had created its own nation-state, this was one in which a historic bloc of northern industrialists allied to southern landowners remained dominant at the expense of workers and peasants, the 'bastard' form of nation-state, to use Gramsci's own label. The notes on Americanism and Fordism are equally reflections on modernity, this time focused more on the world of production rather than history and politics. American methods of mass production, as exemplified in what he calls 'an ultra-modern form of production and of working methods – such as is offered by the most advanced American variety, the industry of Henry Ford' (SPN 281; Q22, §2, 2140), were the necessary features of modern industrial production. Such forms of production were part of what Gramsci called 'links of the chain marking the passage from the old economic individualism to the planned economy' (SPN 279; Q22, §1, 2139). Gramsci examined the ways in which both the Soviet Union and the fascist economy attempted to develop new forms of, or control over, economic life, the former through a planned economy, the latter through the corporative state. Both were somehow distorted forms of modernity, the former at least in the shape of the militarization of labour, whereas fascism's supposed rationalization of the economy was thwarted by its failure to allow civil society to develop freely, as well as by its protection of parasitic classes and their non-productive economic function.

Gramsci's notes pose the question of 'whether we are undergoing a transformation of the material bases of European civilisation, which in the long run (though not all that long, since in the contemporary period everything happens much faster than in the past ages) will bring about the overthrow of the existing forms of civilisation and the forced birth of a new' (SPN 317; Q22, §15, 2179). His analysis suggests that such a transformation is indeed in train, the transformation to a new order of production. Condemnation and criticism of Americanism comes, in Gramsci's view, precisely from those non-productive sections of European society who have no place in this new order of production. Gramsci refers to them as 'the social groups "condemned" by the new order', or 'the remains of old, disintegrating strata' (SPN 317; Q22, §15, 2179). It is the working class alone which could use the modern methods of production as the basis for a modern society. This is suggested by Gramsci's statement that 'reconstruction' cannot be expected from those old parasitic social groups, 'but from those on whom is imposed the burden of creating with their own suffering the material bases of the new order. It is they who "must" find for themselves an "original", and not Americanised, system of living, to turn into "freedom" what today is "necessity"' (SPN 317; Q22, §15, 2179). Critics of Americanism, according to Gramsci, emerge or 'are due to the remains of old, disintegrating strata, and not to groups whose destiny is linked to the further development of the new method' (SPN 317; Q22, §15, 2179). It is clearly the working class which is referred to in these phrases as those whose fate depends on the new method of production, and those through whose own suffering or exploitation the new order is created. It is slightly confusing that in the last paragraph of the SPN chapter on 'Americanism and Fordism' Gramsci says that in the case of Americanism 'we are not dealing with a new type of civilisation', though this refers to Americanism 'understood not only as a form of café life but as an ideology of the kind represented by Rotary Clubs' (SPN 318; Q22, §15, 2180). The implication is that this is a very superficial understanding of Americanism, which in a broader sense does indeed represent a new type of civilization, or at least a new form of production and organization of the material base of society. Social reconstruction on such a new productive basis would sweep away the old, disintegrating strata, but it is the working class (those who create with their own suffering the material bases of the new order) which would be the agent of the new society based on their own control of the new productive methods. At least this seems one plausible interpretation of the idea of finding an original and not Americanized system of living, with the working class as the agent of the task of construction of a modern society.

Gramsci's notes on history and on the developments of capitalist production in his time (Fordism) are immensely stimulating, and so too is his quite condensed analysis of the corporative state and the contradictions of fascism between its modernizing rhetoric and reactionary reality. What emerges from these notes is his sense of fundamental changes in capitalism on a global scale, and their implications for the social structure of European society, with its survival of non-productive social strata impeding the progress of modernity. His analysis of passive revolution has also, as we have seen, given rise to a whole strand of controversy in international political economy using this term to open up a debate about the global economy and the nature of capitalist development (Morton 2010). What are the implications of his analysis for our contemporary conditions? Can we use Gramsci's approach to better understand the workings of the contemporary world of global capitalism and the possible development of a new order? The key problem here seems to be that while in one sense Americanism does seem to be a feature of contemporary globalization, if we mean the term to refer to the spread of American culture and lifestyles throughout the world, related to ideas of cosmopolitanism and a global more homogeneous culture (McDonald's and Coca-Cola), modern or postmodern production methods are post-Fordist rather than Fordist. This has implications both for the politics of Gramsci and for a Gramscian-style analysis of the contemporary world. There are some suggestive thoughts on this in the recent study by the political scientist Giuseppe Di Palma, in his book *The Modern State Subverted*. While his theme is not the analysis of Gramsci or his thought, rather like Gramsci he points to 'the context of the new world of work and production' (Di Palma 2014, 41), which was what Gramsci was trying to analyse in his own notes on Americanism and Fordism, seen as an examination precisely of the new world of production of his own time. Di Palma points out that 'the Fordist model *in toto* was more than an industrial model affecting ways of production and ways of working. It was a much broader *tout se tient*, sufficiently protected from obsolescence over time. A whole series of systemic disciplines, threads of a warp now unravelling, have been part of a model within which the citizen-worker conducted himself in predictable fashion' (Di Palma 2014, 41). He provides a long list of such disciplines, starting with 'stable occupations professionally specified and covering the span of a work life; full-time full employment; predictable occupational hierarchies and careers' and including 'standardised mass production in large productive units' (Di Palma 2014, 41). The thrust of Di Palma's argument is to point out that 'neoliberal intervention on the ongoing trans-formations in the world of work and production' has been responsible for the complete 'subversion' of the Fordist model (Di Palma 2014, 40). This subversion has undone the disciplines of the Fordist system, including guarantees of job security and the socialization of risk (guarantees and temporary cover during periods of unemployment) which were characteristic of the Fordist epoch. Developing arguments based on Ulrich Beck and his notion of 'risk society' (*Risikogesellschaft*), Di Palma paints a picture of a society which 'means to announce that class hierarchies mediated by solidarity no longer describe us and no longer have reasons to exist' (Di Palma 2014, 45). This supposed dissolution of class structure may reflect ideology more than reality, but this author paints a convincing picture of a world in which Fordist mass production has given way to post-Fordist small units of production, and to a world of work in which stable employment and a state which provided a certain degree of solidarity have been overcome by what he calls 'the flattening of both state and civil society on market-driven criteria' (Di Palma 2014, 9). This kind of analysis ties in with ideas of Zygmunt Bauman on the society of liquid modernity in which modern structures of family, workplace and certainty (*Sicherheit*) and predictability have been eroded (Bauman 2000). Fordism then has had its day, to be replaced by post-Fordist methods of work in a society of liquid modernity and growing insecurity.

There seem to be two possible responses to this analysis of society in its liquid or postmodern form of 'risk society', to amalgamate the perspectives offered by Bauman, Beck and Di Palma (the latter laying much more emphasis on the destructive impact of neo-liberal market relationships). The first is to suggest that this takes away from Gramsci's analysis much of its topicality as a picture of present-day (our day) capitalist production, and also from his picture (allusive and veiled though it is) of the working class as the agent of a true modernity in the world of production. If capitalist production is no longer Fordist, then it is doubtful if such production methods could create the agency (the working-class movement in the broadest sense) to master such production methods and provide the basis of a new society. It also seems to undermine Gramsci's perhaps rather puritanical picture of the morality of the working class, based on the family, as the necessary correlative of disciplined productive work in the factory. Di Palma writes of 'the popular attraction that the neoliberal narrative intends to elicit, as it emphasises the freedom and equality of a consumer society and a consuming citizen' (Di Palma 2014, 45). If such a narrative is hegemonic, it shifts attention away from the world of work to the sphere of consumption, presented as a world in which everyone can be free through their sovereignty as consumers, however illusory such ideas may be in practice. This would give a different sense to Gramsci's concept of Americanism: rather than standing for a new way of industrial production, 'Americanism' then seems to suggest a world of supposedly free consumers, interacting in a global market whose dictates must be followed by increasingly enfeebled nation-states. In the words of Manfred Steger, this would be a new 'global imaginary' which functions as a hegemonic ideology of 'market globalism' (Steger 2008, ch. 5). As for Fordism, that would belong to an epoch that has passed, and would not have the characteristic of being the basis for the reconstruction of society which Gramsci envisages. The analyses of history and of modern society presented in the 'Notes on History' and in 'Americanism and Fordism' would be interesting historical documents but ones which do not help us to make sense of our contemporary world.

However, there is another way of reading Gramsci's analysis, extending his method of analysis to contemporary transformations. His notes on Americanism and Fordism can be read as an attempt to analyse transformations in the world of work and production, explaining them as shaking up the traditional social structure of the Old World (Italy, and Europe in general) following the rationalization of the economy practised in the New World (America). Analyses of the present state of the global economy do in a sense follow in Gramsci's footsteps by exploring the political and economic and social implications of the transformed structure of the economy. If the world of Fordism has given way to post-Fordist production methods, then Gramsci's explorations are very relevant and so is his general perspective, namely that a new form of production gives rise to changed political agents and to a different world of politics. Indeed, his ideas might be employed to ask whether the development of production has also involved a passive revolution, in which the neo-liberal state has been a willing accomplice in the dismantling of the Fordist model, and has thus helped erode the solidaristic practices and relatively cohesive agencies of class politics on which previous attempts at revolutionary change rested. The third of what Gramsci calls 'the essentially most important or interesting problems' which he deals with in his examination of Americanism and Fordism could be quoted here. He asks the question 'whether Americanism can constitute an historical "epoch", that is, whether it can determine a gradual evolution of the same type as the "passive revolution" examined elsewhere' (SPN 279; Q22, §1, 2140). One could ask whether Americanism in its present form (which would be a form of what Steger calls 'market globalism', in a neo-liberal mode) does mean that we are in a new historical epoch. This could be one of passive revolution in which the exaltation of people as consumers in a privatized market has put paid definitively to any thoughts of complete or active revolution. Gramsci follows up this possibility by asking whether the new epoch (in his time) of Americanism might alternatively give rise not to passive revolution 'or whether on the other hand it does not simply represent the molecular accumulation of elements destined to produce an "explosion", that is, an upheaval on the French pattern' (SPN 280;

Q22, §1, 2140). In our time, any such explosion would not be on the French pattern alluded to by Gramsci (i.e. the Revolution of 1789), but might be achieved through a range of resistances carried out by movements like alternative globalization, or other 'molecular' movements focusing on particular issues or acts of opposition (for example environmentalist movements). This obviously goes off into speculation about future developments. It should however suggest that Gramsci's questions and methods of exploration of these issues are highly fruitful, even if in the conditions of our own time they might give rise to answers somewhat different from his – if indeed answers can be found to these problems.

SUGGESTIONS FOR FURTHER READING

For the historical background to Gramsci's thought on the Risorgimento, the survey by Lucy Riall, *Risorgimento: The History of Italy from Napoleon to Nation-State* (Basingstoke: Palgrave Macmillan, 2009), is useful and so too are the essays in John A. Davis (ed.), *Italy in the Nineteenth Century* (Oxford: Oxford University Press, 2000).

On 'passive revolution', the historical essays in John A. Davis, *Gramsci and Italy's Passive Revolution* (London: Croom Helm, 2009) are helpful. For wider discussions of the concept of 'passive revolution', see the special issue of *Capital and Class* 34, no. 3 (2010), on 'The Continuum of Passive Revolution', edited by Adam Morton, and also the book by Adam Morton, *Unravelling Gramsci: Hegemony and Passive Revolution in the Global Political Economy* (London: Pluto Press, 2007). The topic is also discussed in Neil Davidson, *How Revolutionary Were the Bourgeois Revolutions?* (Chicago: Haymarket, 2012), especially chapter 14.

On Americanism and Fordism there are some valuable pages (chapter 8) in Giuseppe Vacca's 2012 study *Vita e pensieri di Antonio Gramsci 1926–1937* (Turin: Einaudi, 2012), but this is not available in English, nor is a very useful article on Gramsci's thoughts on the fascist corporative state, and corporativism in general: Alessio Gagliardi, 'Il problema del corporativismo nel dibattito europeo e nei Quaderni', in F. Giasi (ed.), *Gramsci nel suo tempo* (Rome: Carocci, 2008).

5

POLITICS, STATE
AND CIVIL SOCIETY

This chapter deals with perhaps the most original of the reflections contained in Gramsci's *Prison Notebooks*: his thoughts on the nature of politics, his development of a theory of the state and its relation to civil society, and his attempt to sketch out the form of revolutionary politics appropriate to complex modern societies, a strategy to which he gave the name of war of position. This section takes up some 150 pages in the SPN, and is incredibly rich in concentrated reflection and analysis, while being (as with the *Prison Notebooks* in general) allusive and cryptic in places, often quite difficult to decipher and analyse. Yet it is these pages which contain the reflections central to the *Notebooks* as a whole, and which have to be understood in the context of the political situation with which Gramsci was confronted. These are not abstract reflections on the nature of the political conceived from a perspective of Olympian detachment (which was part of the charge which Gramsci levelled against the philosopher Benedetto Croce). These pages were written in an attempt to analyse the victory of fascism in Italy and the reasons for the defeat of the revolutionary surge in Italy and beyond, which had taken place in the aftermath of the First World War and of the Bolshevik Revolution of October 1917. The movement of the factory councils in Turin and other cities in the course of the *biennio rosso* or red two years of 1919–20 had been defeated. Two years later Mussolini had come to power, and fascism had established its hegemony. Whether that hegemony was temporary or longer-lasting remained to be seen, but what was clear was the defeat of the newly founded (in 1921) Italian Communist Party (PCd'I) and of the revolutionary hopes invested in it. The victory of fascism had, obviously, led to the incarceration of Gramsci. *The Prison Notebooks* provide a clear exemplification of the argument of Sheldon Wolin that 'most of the great statements of political philosophy have been put forward in times of crisis; that is, when political phenomena are less effectively integrated by institutional forms'. Wolin goes on to argue that 'Western political philosophers have been troubled by the wasteland that comes when the web of political relationships has dissolved and the ties of loyalty have snapped' (Wolin 2004, 9). This certainly applies to Gramsci's political philosophy. The *Notebooks* can be seen as partly a reflection on what went wrong, why the crisis of post-First World War Italy had led not to socialism or to the moral and intellectual reform (the phrase of Renan employed by Gramsci) envisaged in Marxism, but to fascism. But beyond that Gramsci was seeking to analyse the crisis of post-war politics, nationally and globally. This section of the *Notebooks* contains his analysis of organic crisis and of Caesarism (of which fascism was one form) as the response to that crisis. In analysing the dissolution of traditional politics which gave birth to fascism, Gramsci discusses, in the passages contained in this part of SPN, the role of political parties in general. More specifically, his analysis focuses on what he thinks should be the nature and role of a revolutionary party. He gives this the label of the modern Prince, echoing Machiavelli's presentation in 1513 of the Prince as the secular leader who could unify and liberate Italy.

The 'Notes on Politics', which form Part II of SPN, are divided into three chapters, including the first, given the heading of 'The Modern Prince', and the second, headed 'State and Civil Society', with the third called 'Americanism and Fordism', which was discussed in the previous chapter. The first of these three chapters deals primarily with the nature and the autonomy of politics – in other words, the idea that political activity is not determined simplistically by economic factors, but is a sphere in which creative leadership can shape developments. This leads Gramsci to reflect on the role and nature of the political party and the organization of the party, the concept of the modern Prince as a collective organism which in the conditions of modern politics is required to develop political leadership and inspire the masses. Politics is thus seen as separate from economics, while not entirely independent of it, and this involves Gramsci's critique of economism in its different forms, in other words of perspectives which reduce the sphere of the political and see it as determined by extrapolitical forces. In these pages, then, one can see why theorists like Ralph Miliband called Gramsci one of the most important political theorists of the twentieth century (in his inaugural lecture at Leeds), because Gramsci, while working in the Marxist tradition, is seeking to establish the creative role of the politician and of political leadership, rejecting the reduction of politics to a mere derivative of economic forces (Miliband 1975, 137).

The second chapter in Part II of the SPN, 'State and Civil Society', shows Gramsci confirming what he wrote in a letter to his sister-in-law Tania on 3 August 1931, in which he wrote that 'one of the subjects that has interested me most during recent years has been that of delineating several characteristic moments in the history of Italian intellectuals'. He explained that 'this interest was born on one hand from the desire to delve more deeply into the concept of the State' (LP2, 52). Such delving into the concept of the state is the subject matter of this section of SPN, which is also clarified by another of Gramsci's letters to Tania, this one written on 7 September 1931. In that letter he wrote that 'my study also leads to certain definitions of the concept of the State that is usually understood as a political Society (or dictatorship, or coercive apparatus, meant to mould the popular mass in accordance with the type of production and economy at a given moment) and not as a balance between the political Society and the civil Society (or the hegemony of a social group over the entire national society, exercised through the so-called private organisations, such as the Church, the unions, the schools, etc.)' (LP2, 67). Evidently then Gramsci was seeking to extend the traditional definition of the state by seeing it in broader terms than those envisaged by classical Marxism, at least as in the succinct definition of Engels, 'bodies of armed men'. The state had for Gramsci to be conceptualized in a different way, one which did justice to the growing complexity of civil society and the way in which so-called private organizations maintained the hegemony of ruling groups in society. Hegemony, the concept for which Gramsci has become most famous, was thus not purely, or perhaps even primarily, a matter of coercive force but depended on gaining consent through non-coercive means. All these crucially important ideas are articulated in these pages of the SPN, but often in a condensed and cryptic form which has to be explained and clarified.

The majority of the passages which appear in the SPN chapter on 'The Modern Prince' come from Notebook 13, one of the special notebooks given the title by Gramsci of 'Noterelle sul Machiavelli', or 'Little Notes on Machiavelli', and this notebook was written in the years 1932–34. It is significant that of the forty notes which constitute this notebook, all but one (§25) are C texts (i.e. reworking of notes appearing in earlier notebooks), and this suggests the importance which Gramsci gave to his notes on politics and the state. Those were among the ones which he most wanted to rewrite and reassemble in a special notebook. Of the thirty-four extracts which appear in the SPN chapter 'The Modern Prince', twenty come from Notebook 13. By contrast, the chapter on 'State and Civil Society' in SPN is much more heterogeneous. It contains extracts from no less than eleven of the twenty-nine notebooks, with eight from Notebook 6, written in 1930–32 (i.e. an earlier notebook), which Francioni calls 'the notebook of the State' (Francioni 1984). This suggests both that Gramsci's reflections on central concepts of the state, civil society and hegemony are scattered in a more fragmentary way throughout all of the *Quaderni*, and also that these were ideas on which he was working during the whole period of his imprisonment. In these notes, both on the modern Prince and on state and civil society, Gramsci was employing concepts well-established in political thought, but giving them a new meaning. He was seeking to work out a new theory of politics and political strategy appropriate to the conditions of modernity, and this led him to differentiate in fundamental ways the politics of complex societies from the tactics and strategy which had led to the victory of the Bolsheviks in Russia. These notes contain therefore a strikingly original redefinition of the bases of political thought, a revolutionary updating and rethinking of key concepts of political science, one could say.

It is in these pages that Gramsci develops his concept of hegemony, though this is nowhere presented as a separate section – there is no note in the whole of the *Prison Notebooks* devoted explicitly to an analysis of hegemony. Its meaning has to be gleaned from various passages, whether through analysis of particular historical episodes or, as in the notes in this section, reflecting on the limitations of economism – meaning by that views of politics which interpret political struggle narrowly as struggles to secure economic interests. Gramsci is arguing against such a view of political life, and in so doing develops an original and entirely new set of concepts for interpreting the sphere of the political.

INTERPRETING MACHIAVELLI

The chapter in SPN headed 'The Modern Prince' starts with two substantial extracts dealing with 'Machiavelli's Politics' and 'Machiavelli and Marx'. Gramsci was concerned to interpret Machiavelli and explain his conception of politics, and at the same time to update his analysis of political leadership to make it relevant to the world of modernity. Gramsci's analysis of Machiavelli uses the idea of the myth in the sense developed by the French thinker Georges Sorel, in his book of 1907, *Reflections on Violence*. It is in a way curious to see Gramsci invoking Sorel, the thinker from whom Mussolini said that he had learned the most. Sorel's concept of the myth was that of a body of images which would inspire people to action. The value of a myth was not that it was an accurate representation of reality, but its capacity to evoke emotions and to stimulate social movement. Sorel spoke of the myth of the general strike, an idea which (irrespective of its practicability) would deepen the sense of antagonism to the existing bourgeois order felt by the working-class movement, at

least in its syndicalist or trade-union component. Sorel, unlike
Gramsci, had no time for political parties. Indeed, he despised the
French socialist party and its leaders like Jean Jaurès, since he saw
parliamentary politics as a means of integrating the workers into
bourgeois society. For Sorel the value of the myth of the general
strike was that it kept alive the line of cleavage dividing the
workers' movement from existing society. It was to be compared
with other myths in history, such as the myth of the Second
Coming for the early Christians, or the sentiments animating the
soldiers of the French Revolution in battles like Valmy, embol-
dening them in their dynamism and holding out a vision of a
different social order (Sorel 1950, ch. 4).

Gramsci takes something from Sorel's concept of the myth,
while at the same time criticizing his conception of socialist politics.
He sees Machiavelli's book *The Prince* as an example of a Sorelian
myth, in that the vision it presents of a unified and independent
Italy was an imaginative picture which, in Gramsci's words, 'acts on
a dispersed and shattered people to arouse and organise its collective
will' (SPN 126; Q13, §1, 1556). Machiavelli was thus seeking
to develop forms of political consciousness and arouse people to
political activity through painting a picture of an outcome
attractive to the mass of the people, indeed in that way Machiavelli
(in Gramsci's presentation) 'merges with the people, becomes the
people' (SPN 126; Q13, §1, 1556). In Gramsci's presentation,
Machiavelli, whatever his reputation for deceit and cunning (as
conveyed by the popular usage of the term Machiavellian), was a
democrat, since he wished to reveal the secrets of the political
world for those 'not in the know' (i.e. the broad mass of the Italian
people). Machiavelli's text, *The Prince*, was a powerful means
of political education, and no dry academic treatise. In that way it
proclaimed a myth, a vision of an independent and united Italy, a
vision which could appeal to the mass of the people, irrespective of
its immediate practicality. Gramsci wrote that 'one may therefore
suppose that Machiavelli had in mind "those who are not in the
know", and that it was they whom he intended to educate politically' (SPN 135; Q13, §20, 1600). While 'anyone born into the
traditional governing stratum acquires almost automatically
the characteristics of the political realist', it was the 'Italian "people"

or "nation", the citizen democracy which gave birth to men like Savonarola and Pier Soderini' who were 'not in the know' but whom Machiavelli meant to educate through the publication of his treatise on politics. The same was true for Marxism, the 'philosophy of praxis'. It is somewhat puzzling that Gramsci writes that 'Machiavellianism has helped to improve the traditional political technique of the conservative ruling groups, just as the politics of the philosophy of praxis does' (SPN 136; Q13, §20, 1601). It is not clear why the politics of Marxism was of help to conservative ruling groups, unless it is implied that by educating the working class and forming political parties this made the ruling groups aware of the challenge that faced them, and in that way helped them improve their own political technique.

But Gramsci's main idea is clear enough. Machiavelli in his time wanted to enlighten the mass of the citizenry, to impart lessons in political practice, so to speak, so that they could become active citizens rather than subaltern subjects. This was, in the changed conditions of twentieth-century politics, exactly the task of the philosophy of praxis, or the politics of Marxism. The aim of Marxist politics was to enable the hitherto subordinate classes (workers and peasants) to emerge from their subalternity, and to impart to them the techniques of modern politics and the necessary organization to help them to do so. This required the formation of a collective will, or as Gramsci posed the question (SPN 130; Q13, §1, 1559), 'When can the conditions for awakening and developing a national-popular collective will be said to exist?' Machiavelli had shown the way, at least for his time, with his idea of popular militias, and through arousing the sentiments (the myth) of a unified Italy, which the Prince would lead. The task was the same for the philosophy of praxis, which had to develop, in the circumstances of modern (twentieth-century) politics, the collective will, this time based on the working masses who could be organized and educated through new forms of political activity. In particular, as we will show below, this led Gramsci to insist on the need for a political party of a new type, the modern Prince, and this followed on from his analysis of political parties in general.

While Gramsci uses Sorel's idea of the myth and applies it to Machiavelli's vision of a united Italy, he criticizes Sorel for his neglect of the need for a political party. Sorel's 'vision of things', Gramsci writes, 'leaves the collective will in the primitive and elementary phase of its mere formation, by differentiation ("cleavage")' (SPN 128; Q13, §1, 1557). It seems that Gramsci is saying that Sorel leaves out the necessary conditions for the development of a collective will of the hitherto subaltern groups, as though Sorel thinks a violent differentiation or feeling of hostility to the existing society would be sufficient. Gramsci accuses Sorel of seeing this sentiment of opposition as arising suddenly, without any political preparation or party organization. In the same way as Gramsci criticized his own contemporary Rosa Luxemburg and her view of the mass strike as suddenly arising and being sufficient as a revolutionary assault on the existing order (see 'War of Position', page 205 below), Gramsci thought Sorel was operating with a mechanistic and deterministic conception of revolution: 'In Sorel's case it is clear that behind the spontaneity there lies a purely mechanistic assumption, behind the liberty (will–life-force) a maximum of determinism, behind the idealism an absolute materialism' (SPN 129; Q13, §1, 1557). So we can sum up Gramsci's perspective as being one in which new forms of politics are needed, a modern Prince (the party) to carry out the task which Machiavelli writing in the early sixteenth century assigned to the Prince, as an individual leader. This idea of the political party as the modern Prince is absolutely central to Gramsci's politics, and one of the most original contributions of the *Prison Notebooks*. But before explaining the originality of Gramsci's analysis of parties in general and the modern Prince in particular, we can probe a bit more deeply into the question of why Machiavelli provides such an important set of themes for the *Quaderni*.

A further fundamental point in Gramsci's analysis concerns the creation of a new political order. In *The Prince* Machiavelli wrote that 'taking the initiative in introducing a new form of government is very difficult and dangerous, and unlikely to succeed'. He wrote that the reasons for this were that 'all those who profit from the old order will be opposed to the innovator, whereas all those who might benefit from the new order are, at best, tepid supporters of him' (Machiavelli 1988, 20–21). While not quoting this passage directly, Gramsci noted that 'the founding of new States or new national and social structures' was 'at issue in Machiavelli's *Prince*' (SPN 129; Q13, §1, 1558). Yet Gramsci's own concern was precisely with the creation of a new national and social structure, indeed of an international social structure, that of communism; and the *Prison Notebooks* are in some respects an examination of how this could be done, what kind of political strategy was needed to realize this, along with some observations on the attempts to do this in the Soviet Union. Gramsci insisted that it was through actions and political organizations which had 'a long-term and organic character' that the project of a new political order could be attempted. So for that reason the kind of leadership and political organization appropriate to such a project in the conditions of modern politics, in which the masses could participate, had to be an organism, not an individual leader. This marks the difference of the modern Prince from the Prince figure, the *condottiere*, of Machiavelli's time. Gramsci's words here could not be clearer: 'The modern Prince, the myth-prince, cannot be a real person, a concrete individual. It can only be an organism, a complex element of society in which a collective will, which has already been recognised and has to some extent asserted itself in action, begins to take concrete form.' And this organism, he wrote, had been already provided by history – 'it is the political party' (SPN 129; Q13, §1, 1558). The corollary of this belief in the necessity of a political party as the modern Prince was that the figure of the individual leader, so important for Machiavelli, was in some sense archaic in the modern world or suitable only where a feeling of imminent danger was present. Gramsci alluded to the figure of General Boulanger, whose movement was directed against the parliamentary regime of the Third French Republic. Boulangism fanned the nationalist passions of revenge against Germany and developed an embryonic form of National Socialism (see extracts in Girardet 1966, 129–40). Yet it is hard to avoid the thought that Gramsci was thinking about Italian fascism and Mussolini when he wrote of 'a great danger which precisely fans passion and fanaticism suddenly to a white heat, and annihilates the critical sense and the corrosive irony which are able to destroy the "charismatic" character of the condottiere (as happened in the Boulanger adventure)' (SPN 129; Q13, §1, 1558). The great danger alluded to here could be the danger (as perceived by dominant classes and petty-bourgeois groups) of socialist revolution in post-war Italy (and Europe generally), which fanned their passion and made them put their trust in a condottiere, namely Mussolini – of whom Boulanger was some kind of anticipation. This leads on to the discussion of Gramsci's ideas on organic crisis and the concept of Caesarism, dealt with below.

THE AUTONOMY OF THE POLITICAL: AGAINST ECONOMIC DETERMINISM

There is a further reason for Gramsci's focus on Machiavelli. If Benedetto Croce was the contemporary figure with whom the *Prison Notebooks* are a kind of dialogue, the Florentine thinker of the sixteenth century is someone from the past with whom Gramsci engages in a kind of conversation in the course of developing his own form of Marxist politics. As Maurice Finocchiaro points out, 'Machiavelli is unquestionably one of the most frequent topics of reflection in the Prison Notebooks', with two special notebooks devoted to him, the extensive set of notes in Notebook 13, plus a much shorter one, Notebook 18, though this is only four pages long (Finocchiaro 1988). Furthermore, Gramsci puts the name of Machiavelli as the rubric of many other paragraphs scattered throughout the *Quaderni*. The key idea of Gramsci's preoccupation with Machiavelli can be simply expressed as a perspective emphasizing the creative role of political leadership (though not in the form of the supposedly charismatic leader or *Duce*) and of politics in general that is not to be reduced to the mere expression of economic forces. In arguing in this way, Gramsci was developing an analysis of the political which was critical of certain tendencies in Marxism, those that can be given the label of economism. Machiavelli is seen as an analyst of politics but not merely as a political scientist, presenting abstract laws of politics in an academic sense. The important point for Gramsci was that Machiavelli was someone who advocated a new order, but not in the sense of a utopia or abstract fantasy of the perfect society. Here again Gramsci was making a comparison between Machiavelli and the philosophy of praxis, or Marxism, or perhaps using the analysis of

Machiavelli as a coded way of developing Marxist political analysis. In presenting what he saw as Machiavelli's view of politics he was developing in a coded or Aesopian way his own perspective on the autonomy of politics – on politics as a field of activity not determined by inflexible economic laws, as some versions of Marxism (economism) tended to portray it. Gramsci is very scornful of what he calls 'economistic superstition', and following Engels states that 'many people find it very convenient to think that they can have the whole of history and all political and philosophical wisdom in their pockets at little cost and no trouble, concentrated into a few short formulae' (SPN 164; Q13, §18, 1595).

What then does Gramsci's opposition to economism amount to? He sees Machiavelli as the jumping-off point, since it was Machiavelli who focused on politics as a separate dimension of human activity, with its own laws, distinct from ethics. Gramsci was concerned in the *Prison Notebooks* to establish, as he put it, 'the place that political science occupies or should occupy in a systematic (coherent and logical) conception of the world, in a philosophy of praxis' (SPN 136; Q13, §10, 1568). This passage in the SPN is taken from Notebook 13, §10, of which an earlier (A-text) version appears in Notebook 8, §61, which has the rubric (given by Gramsci) 'Machiavelli', whereas the revised C text has no rubric. The Gramsci scholar Maurice Finocchiaro notes that 'this note is *an exception* to the rule that later versions are improved elaborations of the earlier ones' (Finocchiaro 1988, 124). The earlier version starts off by asking 'what is politics; that is, what place should political activity occupy in a systematic (coherent and logical) conception of the world, in a philosophy of praxis?' (QE3, 271; Q8, §61, 977), so in this first version Gramsci poses the question as relating to political *activity* rather than political *science,* but both versions ask the same question: 'In what sense can one identify politics with history, and hence all of life with politics?' (SPN 137; Q13, §10, 1569). One could then say that Gramsci is operating with an expansive, or expanded, concept of politics, if we take the early version as the clearer one: politics is all of life, and must not be seen as totally conditioned by the economic structure of society. Indeed Gramsci firmly places politics in the superstructure, but states that 'political activity is precisely the first moment or first level; the moment in which the superstructure is still in the unmediated phase of mere wishful affirmation, confused and still at an elementary stage' (SPN 137; Q13, §10, 1569). It is quite hard to make sense of this sentence, because Gramsci's overall analysis seems to be that it is through political activity that hitherto subordinate groups can organize themselves, that political parties are formed and that the movement to a new society can take place.

Certainly Gramsci takes a very positive view of politics, in the broadest sense, and indeed of politicians, at least of the potentially creative role of politicians aiming at the creation of a new political order. This too is related to Machiavelli, presented by Gramsci as 'an active politician, who wishes to create a new balance of forces and therefore cannot help concerning himself with what "ought to be" (not of course in a moralistic sense)' (SPN 172; Q13, §16, 1577). Once again one can see the parallel between Machiavelli, in Gramsci's interpretation of him, and Marxism or the philosophy of praxis as Gramsci conceived it as an activist or voluntarist and non-economistic philosophy. If Machiavelli wanted to 'create a new balance of forces', this too was the project of Marxism, which was concerned with 'what ought to be'. The classical perspective of Marxism was to see a new form of society emerging in the womb of the existing order, in the terms of one of Marx's letters ('the capitalist order of economy emerged from the womb of the feudal order of economy', quoted in Avineri 1969, 151). In that way the preconditions for a future society were being prepared within the framework of the existing social order. Yet the essential point of Gramsci's analysis is that such a new society could not be seen as an arbitrary conception: as he writes, '"what ought to be" is therefore concrete; indeed it is the only realistic and historicist interpretation of reality, it alone is history in the making and philosophy in the making, it alone is politics' (SPN 172; Q13, §16, 1578). What is meant by the term 'historicist' is discussed in the following chapter of the present volume. What is of interest here is the importance Gramsci gives to politics ('history and philosophy in the making') and to the role of what he calls the active politician, described in this same passage as 'a creator, an initiator' though one who 'neither creates from nothing nor does he move in the turbid void of his own desires and dreams'.

It seems as though Gramsci is seeking to establish the creative role of the active politician and of politics in general. A new social order cannot be created automatically by the unfolding of economic forces. It requires will and political activity, and the leadership of a political party. On the other hand, such activity has to be based, so Gramsci says, on the particular force which one believes to be progressive. The active politician is engaged in 'strengthening it to help it to victory', so that 'one still moves on the terrain of effective reality, but does so in order to dominate and transcend it (or to contribute to this)' (SPN 172; Q13, §16, 1578).

These are crucial passages in Gramsci's political theory. One may ask some critical questions here. Is Gramsci overestimating the capacity of politicians to be active and creative? To what extent, at least in the present order of world politics, are politicians constrained by the very powerful economic forces of a globalized economy so that their capacity for creative leadership is limited? And who would be examples of 'the active politician' helping the 'particular force which one believes to be progressive'? Clearly for Gramsci this particular force was the working class, and the rural proletariat, organized and led, as we shall see, by the political party and its organic intellectuals linked to the working class, perhaps, like Gramsci himself, springing from the hitherto subaltern groups of society. Applying Gramsci's own analysis to the conditions of contemporary (twenty-first-century) society, one may ask what is the nature of the progressive force on which an active politician could base their creative political activity, and whether in the conditions of liquid modernity (Bauman 2000) there is such a coherent political force or agency as Gramsci envisaged. A cohesive working class led by a working-class party does not seem to be a feature of the present world of advanced capitalist states or indeed newly emergent capitalist societies (the so-called BRICS countries of Brazil, Russia, India, China and South Africa). Pursuing the same line of thought, one could ask whether Gramsci's own analysis of hegemony, to be explained further on in this chapter, leads to more pessimistic conclusions about the capacity of politicians and political parties to perform such a creative role, faced with global hegemonic pressures and with powerful agencies of legitimation of the existing order, for example newspapers controlled by individuals such as Rupert Murdoch and (at one stage, before he went off to work in an old people's home) Silvio Berlusconi with the power to diffuse a worldview hostile to radical change.

Nevertheless, the significance of Gramsci's overall analysis is clear. 'Politics is life' since only through political action could there be movement toward a different kind of society, and such movement will not come about in a mechanistic way through the automatic development of economic forces. That is the thrust of Gramsci's critique of the various forms of economism. His perspective clearly emphasizes the importance of political action: 'An appropriate political initiative is always necessary to liberate the economic thrust from the dead weight of traditional policies.' Such a political initiative is needed to form 'a new, homogeneous politico-economic historical bloc, without internal contradictions' (SPN 168; Q13, §23, 1612). This involved the attempt to establish a new set of ruling ideas, a new hegemony, which perspectives based on economism never envisaged. These ideas are clearly expressed in a long paragraph in Notebook 13, paragraph 18, with the rubric 'Some Theoretical and Practical Aspects of "Economism"', which appears as pages 158–67 of the SPN (Q13, §18, 1589–97). In this extended note Gramsci takes issue with economism, and argues that it is merely a crude parody of Marxism to portray it as holding that all political action can be explained as a result of economic interests. Gramsci discusses two forms of economism, the first being economic liberalism – what in Italian is called *libero scambio*, translated in SPN as 'free trade'. The second form of economism is syndicalism, or trade-union politics. What Gramsci says about free-trade liberalism could well apply to doctrines of neo-liberalism and global free trade today. He sees this as the politics of a 'dominant and directive social group'. It is interesting that the two adjectives used in Italian are *dominante e dirigente*, suggesting a difference between two forms of power. Such free-trade liberalism is justified by its adherents as freeing the economy from the state. But as Gramsci rightly points out, such economic liberalism is enforced and maintained by the state. It is not a question of the economy spontaneously carrying on, as someone like Hayek might maintain with his conception of catallaxy (the free self-ordering of the market). As Gramsci says: 'laissez-faire liberalism is a political programme, designed to change – in so far as it is victorious – a State's leading personnel'. Economic liberalism is a 'form of State "regulation", introduced and maintained by legislative and coercive means' (SPN 160; Q13, §18, 1590).

The other form of economism is syndicalism, or theoretical syndicalism, in other words the idea of trade-union activity as sufficient to challenge the existing order, with the consequent underestimation, or rather complete neglect, of political action. For Gramsci this is an example of ideas developed by a subaltern class which prevent it from rising above the economic-corporate phase to achieve 'ethical-political hegemony in civil society and domination in the state'. Gramsci does not restrict the term economism to trade-union activity narrowly defined. It is significant that he refers to Fabianism and to 'a notable part of labourism', as well as to the theorist Henri de Man. The SPN translates *parte notevole del laburismo* as 'an important part of the Labour Party'. It might be that Gramsci intended the term to have a wider significance beyond the British Labour Party, to refer to movements, whether of trade union or party, that had a restricted horizon, concerned with improving conditions in the framework of the existing society rather than moving to the stage of capturing hegemony in the sphere of civil society and dominance in the state. At any rate he saw economism, in its different forms, as a way in which the independence and autonomy of the subaltern group were sacrificed or subordinated to the intellectual hegemony of the dominant group. Syndicalism was for him just one aspect of free-trade liberalism, 'justified with a few mutilated (and therefore banalised) theses from the philosophy of praxis' (SPN 160; Q13, §18, 1590).

Gramsci therefore explains that it is a caricature to see Marxism as simply a crude view that politics is determined by economic interests. He quotes an article from a French journal, reproduced in an Italian review of the foreign press, in which it was argued that 'in pure Marxism, men taken as a mass obey economic necessity and not their own emotions', and that 'everything is governed by debits and credits'. For Gramsci this was a complete distortion of Marxism, though it was a form of vulgarized Marxism which had a certain appeal as 'economistic superstition' to the popular masses and to mediocre intellectuals. But in such a form 'the philosophy of praxis loses a great part of its capacity for cultural expansion among the top layer of intellectuals' (SPN 164; Q13, §18, 1595). However, the main point was that this presentation of Marxism as a crude materialism was a misrepresentation. Gramsci here alludes, as on many occasions, to the statement in Marx's preface to *A Contribution to the Critique of Political Economy* concerning the 'ideological forms in which men become conscious of this conflict and fight it out', 'this conflict' referring to the conflict between the 'material productive forces' of society and the 'existing relations of production'. It was this statement that Gramsci alludes to when he writes that 'the thesis which asserts that men become conscious of fundamental conflicts on the level of ideology is not psychological or moralistic in character, but structural and epistemological' (SPN 164; Q13, §18, 1595). So Marxism is not a simplistic philosophy which holds that it is only a narrow concept of economic self-interest which motivates people and which is at the basis of political struggles. One phrase which Gramsci uses is taken from the first of Marx's *Theses on Feuerbach*, which criticizes Feuerbach for seeing practice only 'in its dirty-judaical manifestation' (*schmutzig-jüdisch*). This may be an unfortunate phrase to use, but Gramsci uses it to suggest that Marxism does not see human activity or practice (*praxis*) in such a way, as motivated only by narrow economic concerns, but gives due place to the ideological forms and ideas through which human beings see political activity: 'The search for "dirty-Jewish" interests', Gramsci writes, 'has sometimes led to monstrous and comical errors of interpretation, which have consequently reacted negatively on the prestige of the original body of ideas' (SPN 165; Q13, §18, 1595). The reaction against such a distorted view of Marxism leads to the need for a different perspective, and this is one way in which Gramsci came to emphasize the concept of hegemony.

The example which he used was that of the Boulangist movement, which was alluded to above. This could have been a coded way of analysing reasons for the success of fascism in Italy. Gramsci argues that to analyse a movement like Boulangism, 'economism asks the question: "who profits directly from the initiative under consideration?"' (SPN 166; Q13, §18, 1596). But this was a completely inadequate approach to the question. Analysis of such a movement had to look at its social basis and the way in which such a movement changed the balance of forces in society as a whole. In other words, how had such a movement (if successful) established its hegemony: in Gramsci's words which conclude this extended note, 'an analysis of the balance of forces – at all levels – can only culminate in the sphere of hegemony and ethico-political relations' (SPN 167; Q13, §18, 1597). Economism not only provided a distorted view of Marxism, but economistic perspectives were inadequate to explain political conflict. Movements like Boulangism (and by implication fascism) had to be explained as attempting to establish hegemony, so that political struggle was not just a question of immediate material interests and personal or group profit and loss. Politics was a matter of getting beyond the economic-corporate level. In order to end their position of subordination, subaltern groups had to get beyond that narrow level of economic interest, and establish their capacity to lead in the sphere of ideas. The passages just quoted come from Notebook 13, but the early version of this paragraph appears in Notebook 4, with a different ending. The first version of the sentence just quoted states that the research into a movement like Boulangism 'must be carried out in the sphere of the concept of hegemony'. This is followed by a short paragraph which alludes to Lenin, referred to here, as throughout the *Prison Notebooks*, as Ilyich. The concept of hegemony, Gramsci wrote in this A text,

> should be regarded as Ilyich's greatest contribution to Marxist philosophy, to historical materialism: an original and creative contribution. In this respect, Ilyich advanced Marxism not only in political theory and economics but also in philosophy (that is, by advancing political theory, he also advanced philosophy).
>
> (QE2, 187; Q4, §38, 464–65)

Lenin is invoked here because he criticized economism, and in so doing advanced both political theory and philosophy. Politics therefore has to be understood not in a crude way as the struggle to defend economic interests. Such a perspective leaves everything on the plane of economic-corporate relations. Politics is a struggle to establish hegemony, a concept which requires further explanation. The task of the political party is, for Gramsci, to gain hegemony, and so we first need to explain his views on political parties in general, and in particular his concept of the modern Prince.

THE POLITICAL PARTY AS THE MODERN PRINCE

Gramsci's concept of the modern Prince is a brilliant conceptualization of the need for a political party to perform, in the conditions of modern politics, the function which Machiavelli saw the ideal figure of the individual Prince carrying out in sixteenth-century Italy. The political party is a necessary vehicle of political education, as well as being the institution through which leaders emerge who could develop consciousness of the working class from the economic-corporate level to the higher stage of achieving hegemony. The crucial pages of SPN relevant here are those of pages 175 to 185, which constitute the section on 'Analysis of Situations: Relations of Force' (all of which comes from Notebook 13: Q13, §2, 1561 and Q13, §17, 1579ff.), and the section headed 'The Political Party', which takes up pages 147 to 157 of SPN which brings together passages from Notebooks 12, 13, 14 and 15.

In the first of those sections, Gramsci analyses in fairly orthodox Marxist fashion different moments or levels in the 'relations of force'. The first level is that of the economic structure of society, which provides the data on which it is possible 'to discover whether in a particular society there exist the necessary and sufficient conditions for its transformation' (SPN 181; Q13, §17, 1583). But the next level is the most significant in the present context. Gramsci here points to three stages in the relation of political forces, starting with the economic-corporate level, in which members of particular trades or professions feel a sense of solidarity and cohesion, which however does not link them in a wider unity with members of the same social class. The second moment is that of class solidarity, 'but still in the purely economic field', as Gramsci notes. The third moment is the stage when the interests of a particular class are seen in much broader terms, 'posing all the questions around which the struggle rages not on a corporate but

on a "universal" plane, and thus creating the hegemony of a fundamental social group over a series of subordinate groups' (SPN 182;
Q13, §17, 1583–84). To this political moment, itself divided into
three stages, Gramsci adds the third level, that of military struggle,
and clearly in this stage he is thinking of the Italian Risorgimento,
to which in fact he alludes explicitly, echoing his previously
articulated criticism (see Chapter 4 above) of the Action Party
and 'the disastrous absence of politico-military leadership' in the
course of the Italian Risorgimento. Gramsci makes it clear that all
of these stages or moments are necessary for the subordinate class to
establish its hegemony, and here again there is the clear criticism
of mechanistic or economistic perspectives, according to which
economic developments on their own would trigger political
developments: 'It may be ruled out that immediate economic crises
of themselves produce fundamental historical events'. Gramsci
illustrates this with reference to the French Revolution: in that
case, as in others, 'the rupture of the equilibrium of forces did not
occur as the result of direct mechanical causes'. The Revolution of
1789 'occurred in the context of conflicts on a higher plane than
the immediate world of the economy' (SPN 184; Q13, §17,
1587). The crucial factor, Gramsci suggests, and with reference not
merely to the French Revolution, is the process of development
from economic factors to political ones and also military ones, 'a
process which has as its actors men and their will and capability',
in other words the factor of political leadership is decisive.

It seems clear that the following lines refer to the failure of the
Italian Left to prevent the rise of fascism. When Gramsci writes
that 'if this process of development from one moment to the next
is missing ... the situation is not taken advantage of, and contradictory outcomes are possible: either the old society resists and
ensures itself a breathing-space, by physically exterminating the
elite of the rival class and terrorising its mass reserves', this can be
taken to be a clear reference to the fascist suppression of rival
socialist and communist (and other) parties, and the use of the
squadristi to terrorize those masses opposing fascism. The alternative possibility was (and this echoes the phrase of *The Communist
Manifesto* concerning 'the common ruin of the contending classes')
that 'a reciprocal destruction of the conflicting forces occurs, and a

peace of the graveyard is established, perhaps even under the surveillance of a foreign guard' (SPN 185; Q13, §17, 1588). So political action and will and capability of political leaders are needed if politics is to be advanced above the economic-corporate level, and this is where the role of the political party is crucial.

Gramsci makes it clear that in the era of modern politics the people, the masses, have entered the political arena. This is the era where in the most advanced states '"civil society" has become a very complex structure and one which is resistant to the catastrophic "incursions" of the immediate economic element (crises, depressions, etc.)' (SPN 235; Q13, §24, 1615). This quotation comes from the chapter on 'State and Civil Society' and is analysed further in the next section. The crucial point for present purposes is that political struggle involves the masses, and therefore political parties are necessary structures for waging political conflict. But what exactly is Gramsci's understanding of a political party? He states in the most explicit way possible that 'the protagonist of the new Prince could not in the modern epoch be an individual hero, but only the political party' (SPN 147; Q13, §21, 1601). Yet there can be many different types of party. Gramsci notes that a party could be an intellectual group, 'constituted by an elite of men of culture' (SPN 149; Q17, §37, 1939), and it seems clear that here, not for the first time in the *Prison Notebooks*, he has in mind the figure of Benedetto Croce. Such an elite grouping has 'the function of providing leadership of a cultural and general ideological nature for a great movement of interrelated parties' (SPN 150; Q17, §37, 1940), almost as we might say a sort of think tank for conservative forces. Gramsci also refers in a veiled way to parties of the fascist type, which he describes in an allusive way as 'a type of party constituted this time not by an elite but by masses'. Such masses have no other function than to show loyalty, and they are 'kept happy by means of moralising sermons, emotional stimuli, and messianic myths of an awaited golden age, in which all present contradictions and miseries will be automatically resolved and made well' (SPN 150; Q17, §37, 1940). This seems a good description of fascist or Caesaristic parties, which mobilize the masses not in a democratic way but precisely through 'messianic myths of an awaited golden age', where the mass following is merely an instrument of a demagogic leader.

Clearly the party which Gramsci saw as playing the role of the modern Prince is neither the elite party nor the fascist-type mass party. The nub of his view comes in Gramsci's statement that for a party to exist, 'three fundamental elements (three groups of elements) have to converge' (SPN 152; Q14, §70, 1733): the three elements are firstly the mass element, which constitutes the bulk of the party membership. Yet Gramsci emphasizes that this mass element needs leadership: 'They are a force in so far as there is somebody to centralise, organise and discipline them.' This force is the second element, the leadership, 'endowed with great cohesive, centralising and disciplinary powers', and also 'with the power of innovation', which presumably means innovation of a political or policy-making kind, to innovate in deciding strategy and tactics of the party. The third element in a political party is described by Gramsci as 'an intermediate element, which articulates the first element with the second and maintains contact between them'. There have to be fixed proportions between these three elements, but it seems clear that for Gramsci it is the leadership element which is the most important. It seems equally clear that he is referring to his own party and to his own political experience when he writes that 'since defeat in the struggle must always be envisaged, the preparation of one's own successors is as important as what one does for victory', so that to make arrangements for 'the eventuality of its own destruction' is one of the chief tasks of the party leadership. Gramsci here seems to be making an implicit criticism of the failure of the PCd'I to anticipate the outlawing of the party by the fascist regime. But if these three elements together constitute a party, what are the functions of parties in general and of the party as a modern Prince in particular? Is Gramsci's concept of the party merely a restatement in different words (drawing inspiration from Machiavelli) of a Leninist conception of the vanguard party in which the party was constituted by a group of professional revolutionaries, whose task was to bring class consciousness to the workers who otherwise would only attain what Lenin called 'trade-union consciousness', or in Gramsci's language the stage of 'economic-corporate' awareness? Is Gramsci's concept of the modern Prince little different from the ideas of the party as expounded in Lenin's text *What Is to Be Done?*, in which he argued that without a vanguard party the working class would only attain the level of trade-union consciousness (Lih 2008)?

It is clear that for Gramsci the party as the modern Prince has a fundamentally educational role, in the sense that it is the agent, the necessary agent, for the process of moral and intellectual reform which is needed for subaltern groups to emerge from their subordinate condition. Indeed Gramsci compares the party, in this guise of the modern Prince, with God or with a Kantian categorical imperative, which places the political party in a high position indeed. It is not only that, as Gramsci puts it, 'the modern Prince, as it develops, revolutionises the whole system of intellectual and moral relations'. Further than that, Gramsci writes that 'in men's consciences, the Prince takes the place of the divinity or the categorical imperative, and becomes the basis for a modern laicism and for a complete laicisation of all aspects of life and of all customary relationships' (SPN 133; Q13, §1, 1561). This seems to suggest that it is through the political party that the citizens of a particular society develop their ideas. Indeed it may arouse suspicion that Gramsci envisages here a totalitarian and all-controlling party, if he is comparing it with the categorical imperative, the highest source (at least in Kantian thought) of moral obligation and duty. Gramsci certainly sees the political party as having a policing function, which in his argument can be either progressive or regressive. He emphasizes that a regressive party seeks to 'carry out its policing function in order to conserve an outward, extrinsic order which is a fetter on the vital forces of history'. Evidently this refers to the fascist party, contrasted with a party which exercises such a policing function 'in the sense of tending to raise the people to a new level of civilisation expressed programmatically in its political and legal order' (SPN 155; Q14, §34, 1691). This is the role of the modern Prince, which has the educational task of diffusing a new consciousness and, in Gramsci's words again, 'to raise the backward masses to the level of the new legality'. Gramsci does see the role of the party (the modern Prince) as totalitarian in the sense of diffusing and propagating a 'total' or all-embracing view of the world. He makes the same distinction between progressive and regressive totalitarianism, taking totalitarian to mean an all-embracing *Weltanschauung*, or view of the world. Gramsci writes that a totalitarian policy aims at 'ensuring that the members of a particular party find in that party all the satisfactions that they formerly found in a multiplicity of organisations' and that 'when the given party is the bearer of a new culture – then one has a progressive phrase'. This is contrasted with what is clearly a reference to the fascist party, seen as a party which 'wishes to prevent another force, bearer of a new culture, from becoming itself "totalitarian" – then one has an objectively regressive and reactionary phase, even if that reaction (as invariably happens) does not avow itself, and seeks itself to appear as the bearer of a new culture' (SPN 265; Q6, §136, 800).

Clearly this is not a pluralist perspective, but (so it is argued here) it is neither Leninist nor totalitarian in the sense of forcing beliefs onto a passive population, or manipulating them in the fascist way of, to use Gramsci's own words, 'messianic myths and emotional stimuli'. The party is seen as the instrument of political education. In our own time such a statement naturally arouses fears of indoctrination and brainwashing. Yet working-class parties in liberal-democratic systems were traditionally seen as agents of political education and of raising the cultural level of their members. A classical example of this could be seen in the pre-1914 German Social Democratic Party (Sozialdemokratische Partei Deutschlands, SPD), with its attempt to create a socialist counter-culture through a whole host of associational activities. Admittedly such activities included smoking clubs, which might not have been conducive to the health or educational level of their members, but on a more serious note the political party in the classical social-democratic perspective was seen as a channel for the political education of its members. Similarly in Britain organizations like the WEA (Workers' Educational Association) and the Plebs League, though not the preserve of any one political party, were seen as channels through which workers could share in the culture which orthodox bourgeois channels of education and culture denied them. So one can suggest that Gramsci's concept of the party was totalitarian only in the sense that the political party of the working class was in his view the agent for the formation of a new collective will, and would be the means through which the mass of workers would develop the new culture which Marxism could provide.

As we shall see in the following chapter, Gramsci saw Marxism as the culmination and transcendence of all previous culture, and in that way the political party would be the channel for the process of moral and intellectual reform needed as a precondition for a successful war of position in complex societies, ideas which are explained further in the next section. The political party as the modern Prince also had the function of training and selecting new leaders: as Gramsci writes, 'parties may be said to have the task of forming capable leaders; they are the mass function which selects, develops, and multiplies the leaders which are necessary if a particular social group ... is to become articulated, and be transformed from turbulent chaos into an organically prepared political army' (SPN 191; Q13, §31, 1628).

In assessing the significance of these ideas, perhaps the critical point to be made is not that this is a recipe for totalitarianism in the meaning of a rigid system of party *apparatchiki* or a bureaucratized system of one-party domination such as emerged in the Soviet Union. The problem rather seems to be one of whether in contemporary politics in liberal-democratic systems, political parties have become hollowed out into mechanisms for getting out the vote and little else. The contemporary literature on political parties focuses on the ways in which they have become increasingly controlled from the top, and in which their educational role is very limited (Mair 2013). Gramsci makes large claims for the political party in general, and for his idea of the party as the modern Prince in particular. He stresses the role of the party in spreading the new culture and view of the world which Marxism represents, and also as a channel through which the new leaders, perhaps the new organic intellectuals (as discussed in Chapter 3 above) could emerge. But if in the world of today political parties in general have become little more than electoral machines, often controlled by the party bureaucracy or leadership, then there seems little hope that any political party could carry out the functions which Gramsci envisages the modern Prince performing. Similar remarks could apply to the 'creative' function of politicians which he describes in this section of the SPN. If politicians are not trusted or have little credibility, then it seems improbable that they could be the agents for creating a new social and political order, or be the effective initiators of what Gramsci called 'a new equilibrium among the forces which really exist and are operative'. For Gramsci the two axes or agents of political action are *class* and *party,* with the two of course closely linked. Gramsci notes that 'every party is only the nomenclature for a class', with the corollary that when classes and class division are no longer features of society, then political parties would cease to exist. With evident reference to the communist party (any such party, not the Italian one in particular), the sentence just quoted continues by saying 'it is obvious that the party which proposes to put an end to class divisions will only achieve complete self-fulfilment when it ceases to exist because classes, and therefore their expressions, no longer exist' (SPN 152; Q14, §70, 1732). Does that mean that in a classless or communist society there would be no need for political parties because parties are nothing other than the political expression of class interests? This seems to be implied by the sentence just quoted. However, Gramsci does not dwell on this point, because he is interested in the role of political parties in the here and now, as organizations which are necessary in political struggle. Again, this raises the question of the applicability of these ideas to our own times: if parties have been undermined and are now little more than structures to mobilize electors at election time and to prepare for elections, has the sphere of political involvement moved from political parties to social movements, to the sphere of 'civil society'? This is a topic on which, as we shall see below, Gramsci had a good deal to say.

RULERS AND RULED: LEADERSHIP AND THE MASSES

The pages of the *Prison Notebooks* dealing with the concept and role of political parties are among the most insightful in the whole work. As we have seen, Gramsci sees the political party as the modern Prince, as a vitally important organization through which political action can take place. Such political action cannot be the spontaneous sudden upheaval, as anticipated by Sorel and his idea of the general strike, or by Rosa Luxemburg with her invocation of the mass strike. Gramsci suggests that political action to create 'new national and social structures' must have 'a long-term and organic character' (SPN 129; Q13, §1, 1558). It is the party which is a necessary institution for developing a whole new view of the world and instructing its members in that set of ideas. But can the political party, as a mass organization, achieve that end? One of the most significant studies of political parties, and it is one to which Gramsci refers, was that of Robert Michels in his book of 1911, *Political Parties*. Michels derived from his study of the German SPD his famous 'iron law of oligarchy', with its pithy summary: 'Who says organisation, says oligarchy' (Michels 1959). Michels's argument, simply put, rested on his study of the SPD, whose avowed aim was to organize the working class into a coherent and democratic political force which could capture political power. Yet, in his argument, the organization of the party needed to achieve this end created a party bureaucracy, or oligarchy, to which the mass of the party remained subordinate. The party then became an organization ruled by an elite, and that elite became ever more reluctant to challenge the wider society, since, as Michels wrote, 'what is the point of a social revolution for them? Their own social revolution has been achieved'; in other words the party elite had established its own power over the wider membership, and had little interest in jeopardizing the party organization by radical politics (see Beetham 1977 and Schwarzmantel 1994, ch. 4, for discussions of Michels).

Gramsci refers explicitly to Michels's work in the *Prison Notebooks*, again in a rather condensed way, but his remarks are suggestive and important. If Michels is right, then the role of the party is not that of a modern Prince but merely of a structure which gives rise to a new elite, and a non-revolutionary one at that. Gramsci's reference to Michels states that 'to write a history of a political party, it is necessary to confront a whole series of problems of a much less simple kind than Robert Michels, for example, believes – though he is considered an expert on the subject' (SPN 150; Q13, §33, 1629). The criticism of Michels seems to be that Michels isolates the study of the party from wider factors in society at large, since Gramsci writes that 'it will be necessary to take some account of the social group of which the party in question is the expression and the most advanced element' (SPN 151; Q13,

§33, 1629–30), with the implication that this was not something that Michels dealt with. Indeed Gramsci goes further in suggesting that any history or analysis of a particular political party 'can only emerge from the complex portrayal of the totality of society and State', so that 'to write the history of a party means nothing less than to write the general history of a country from a monographic viewpoint'. It is hard to avoid the impression that Gramsci is talking about his own experience and the history of the PCd'I in the following sentence, concerning 'the real effectiveness of the party, its determining force, positive and negative, in having contributed to bringing certain events about and in having prevented other events from taking place' (SPN 151; Q13, §33, 1630). One could read this sentence as an interrogation of the role of the communist party (and other non-fascist parties too) in *not* having prevented certain events, namely the coming to power of fascism. But there are two questions one can ask about Gramsci's analysis of political parties. First, does he respond to Michels's challenge that political parties, even – or especially – those of a socialist or communist kind, end up as bureaucratized organizations with an elite cut off from the mass membership, rather than the organic intellectuals that Gramsci saw as the new leaders? And second, does Gramsci's emphasis on the party contrast with his earlier pre-*Prison Notebooks* views which saw the factory councils as the nucleus of a new social order, and seemed to suggest that factory councils were more significant in the class struggle than the political party? Has Gramsci moved from a more workerist bottom–up perspective to a Leninist, Jacobin type of democratic centralism which sees leadership coming from above – with consequent elitist implications, whatever his stance on Michels might be?

While Gramsci does not respond directly to Michels's iron law of oligarchy, some of the pages in the *Quaderni* do seem to show Gramsci wrestling with the question of elitism and the possibility of democracy in party organizations, and in large organizations generally. Pages 185–90 of SPN, given the heading 'Bureaucracy', are a kind of response to Michels and the problem of elites in conditions of modern mass politics. 'As political and economic forms develop historically', Gramsci wrote, 'a new type of functionary is increasingly being produced – what could be described as "career" functionaries' (SPN 186; Q13, §36, 1632). This shows Gramsci's recognition of the realities of modern politics, in which mass organizations were needed and which consequently created what he called this 'new type of functionary' (SPN 186; Q13, §36, 1632), 'a fact of prime significance for political science, and for any history of the forms taken by the State'. Gramsci's answer to the challenge posed by Michels's analysis seems to lie in his (Gramsci's) distinction between bureaucratic centralism and genuinely organic centralism, which according to Gramsci is realized in democratic centralism. He described the latter as 'a centralism in movement – i.e. a continual adaptation of the organisation to the real movement, a matching of thrusts from below with orders from above' (SPN 188; Q13, §36, 1634). So how is Gramsci suggesting that such organic or democratic centralism could be prevented from turning into bureaucratic centralism, and where are examples of each form of centralism to be found? As in several places in the *Prison Notebooks*, the answers are not very clear, given the cryptic form of expression. It would seem that the following description of bureaucratic centralism could refer to the evolution of the Bolshevik Party and the danger of bureaucratic degeneration in the Soviet Union with the Stalinization of the party organization, even if the words in brackets suggest that Gramsci also has other examples in mind:

> The prevalence of bureaucratic centralism in the State indicates that the leading group is saturated, that it is turning into a narrow clique which tends to perpetuate its selfish privileges by controlling or even by stifling the birth of oppositional forces – even if these forces are homogeneous with the fundamental dominant interests (e.g. in the ultra-protectionist systems struggling against economic liberalism).
>
> (SPN 189; Q13, §36, 1634)

Gramsci lays the blame for 'the unhealthy manifestations of bureaucratic centralism' on 'a lack of initiative and responsibility at the bottom, in other words because of the political immaturity of the peripheral forces' (SPN 189; Q13, §36, 1634). But it is not clear how such political immaturity could be overcome. At any rate, it is clear what a healthy form of centralism would involve, since Gramsci says that 'this continuous effort to separate out the "international" and "unitary" element in national and local reality is true concrete political action, the sole activity productive of historical progress. It requires an organic unity between theory and practice, between intellectual strata and popular masses, between rulers and ruled' (SPN 189; Q13, §36, 1635). Much of his historical analysis, as we saw in the previous chapter, sought to explain those factors which prevented the organic links between intellectuals and the people in a national-popular unit. In Italy the attachment of intellectuals to the Papacy and their failure to link themselves to the people were examples of such a lack of organic unity. So does Gramsci really provide an answer to Michels's elitist hypothesis? It is clear that Gramsci is aware of the danger of bureaucratic centralism, both within particular political parties, and more generally in terms of a failure of intellectuals to be responsive to the mass of the people. He denies that such a divorce between party elite and mass membership is an *inevitable* result of the logic of mass organization, which is what Michels asserts. In opposition to the iron law of oligarchy Gramsci offers the idea of democratic centralism as an antidote to such bureaucratic deformations. Democratic centralism as Gramsci conceives it 'offers an elastic formula, which can be embodied in many diverse forms; it comes alive in so far as it is interpreted and continually adapted to necessity' (SPN 189; Q13, §36, 1634).

The Gramsci scholar Maurice Finocchiaro makes much of Gramsci's lines that democratic centralism 'consists in the critical pursuit of what is identical in seeming diversity of form and on the other hand of what is distinct and even opposed in apparent uniformity, in order to organise and interconnect closely that which is similar' (SPN 189; Q13, §36, 1634). Finocchiaro (1988, 162–63) relates these two types of centralized administration (bureaucratic versus democratic types of centralism) to two types of revolution, passive revolution (analysed in previous chapters) and democratic revolution. So we could conclude that Gramsci is aware of Michels's elitist challenge. He does not deny that there will always be a division between rulers and ruled, indeed for Gramsci that is one of the fundamental elements of politics: 'there really do exist rulers and ruled, leaders and led. The entire science and art of politics are based on this primordial, and (given certain general conditions) irreducible fact' (SPN 144; Q15, §4, 1752). But where Gramsci parts company with elitist theorists like Michels is in his historicizing this question – asking 'is it the intention that there should always be rulers and ruled, or is the objective to create the conditions in which this division is no longer necessary? In other words, is the initial premise the perpetual division of the human race, or the belief that this division is only an historical fact, corresponding to certain conditions?' (SPN 144; Q15, §4, 1752). Clearly Gramsci tends towards the latter belief, though this does not imply that the division between rulers and ruled will ever disappear completely. He implies that this division can take more or less democratic forms, depending on the type of leadership, and on the initiative of the ruled. Again we are back to the question of political parties as the channel for developing leaders: 'The principle once posed that there are leaders and led, rulers and ruled, it is true that parties have up till now been the most effective way of developing leaders and leadership' (SPN 146; Q15, §4, 1753). As for the ruled, we can refer to a passage from an earlier section of the *Prison Notebooks*, in the chapter 'On Education', where Gramsci states that '[democracy] must mean that every "citizen" can "govern" and that society places him, even if only abstractly, in a general condition to achieve this. Political democracy tends towards a coincidence of the rulers and the ruled (in the sense of government with the consent of the governed), ensuring for each non-ruler a free training in the skills and general technical preparation necessary to that end' (SPN 40; Q12, §2, 1547).

Gramsci thus grapples with the challenge of elitist thought. The political party is seen as a crucial institution in forming new types of leaders, but only on condition that democratic centralism does not degenerate into bureaucratic centralism, a danger of which Gramsci was very much aware. But how does the educative role of the political party, the modern Prince, relate to other forms of organization, more spontaneous and oriented towards the base? What is the relationship between organization and conscious leadership (provided by the party) and spontaneity (the mass movement, in the workplace, for example)? In the paragraphs given the heading of 'spontaneity and conscious leadership' Gramsci does refer to the factory council movement as it developed in Italy in the *biennio rosso* of 1919–20, and in which Gramsci was an active participant (see Chapter 1 above). This section, pages 196 to 200, comes from Notebook 3, an earlier notebook written in 1930, and is a B text (i.e. one not picked up and rewritten later in a special notebook). In this reference to the Turin movement, Gramsci does not negate or deny the value of the factory councils, or denigrate spontaneity. Talking of the leadership of the Turin movement and accusations levelled against it that it was spontaneist, he states that 'this element of "spontaneity" was not neglected and even less despised. It was *educated*, directed, purged of extraneous contaminations; the aim was to bring it into line with modern theory – but in a living and historically effective manner' (SPN 198; Q3, §48, 330). Indeed this extract ends with a critique by Gramsci of 'a scholastic and academic historico-political outlook which sees as real and worthwhile only such movements of revolt as are one hundred per cent conscious, i.e. movements that are governed by plans worked out in advance to the last detail or in line with abstract theory (which comes to the same thing)' (SPN 200; Q3, §48, 332). This is something which Gramsci rejects, asking the question 'can modern theory be in opposition to the "spontaneous" feelings of the masses?' By 'modern theory' he means Marxism, and his answer to the question is clear. He notes that such spontaneous feelings are those which 'have been formed through everyday experience illuminated by "common sense", i.e. by the traditional popular conception of the world', and in answer to the question whether 'modern theory' can be in opposition to such a spontaneous conception, his answer is definite: 'It cannot be in opposition to them' (SPN 199; Q3, §48, 330–31). The aim must be to raise such spontaneous movements 'to a higher plane by inserting them into politics', and the failure to do so 'may often have extremely serious consequences' (SPN 199; Q3, §48, 330). How then could such a link be achieved between spontaneous movements and conscious leadership? This raises fundamental questions of hegemony and of organization, of how subaltern classes could achieve hegemony, and whether the terrain for this is to be found in the institutions of civil society, and how civil society relates to the state.

More fundamentally, all of these questions lead Gramsci to seek to develop a strategy for radical politics appropriate to the complex societies of modern times, and to differentiate such a strategy (which he calls war of position) from the one (war of movement) which led the Bolsheviks to power in Russia in 1917. This is the most original and exciting part of the *Prison Notebooks*, contained in the second chapter of the 'Notes on Politics' which form Part II of SPN. The fundamental topics of hegemony, the analysis of the state and civil society, and the concepts of war of position contrasted with permanent revolution and war of movement are all contained in that part, under the heading 'State and Civil Society', and these have to be examined and analysed, along with the concepts of Caesarism and the crisis of the state, as exemplified in fascism.

CAESARISM AND THE CRISIS OF THE STATE

That chapter of Part II of SPN, headed 'State and Civil Society', begins with two sets of extracts dealing with 'observations on certain aspects of the structure of political parties in periods of organic crisis' and with the concept of Caesarism. Here, as in other parts of the *Prison Notebooks*, Gramsci starts with an analysis of particular historical and political phenomena, from which he develops his more general theory concerning state and civil society and political strategy, and indeed hegemony. So it is always with reference to specific historical or contemporary events and processes that Gramsci's theoretical framework is elaborated. Hence a key concept like hegemony is never explicated in an abstract way or given a separate extended exposition, but (as we saw with reference to Gramsci's analysis of the Moderates and the Action Party in the Italian Risorgimento) is expounded more allusively, as it emerges from the concrete political and historical analysis.

The 'period of organic crisis' which forms the topic of the first extract in the 'State and Civil Society' chapter is clearly the period of crisis in European politics opened up by the First World War and the Russian Revolution, with fascism in Italy (and later in

Germany) as responses to this crisis. In Gramsci's reflections, this is presented as 'the crisis of the ruling class's hegemony', when the traditional ruling groups could no longer rely on the acquiescence of those who previously accepted their rule. In such a situation, Gramsci writes, 'social classes become detached from their traditional parties', and, obviously referring to Italian fascism and the leadership cult of Mussolini, 'the field is open for violent solutions, for the activities of unknown forces, represented by charismatic "men of destiny"' (SPN 210; Q13, §23, 1602–3), with Mussolini clearly fitting the bill here. While the discussion here is presented by Gramsci in quite general terms, the analysis is guided by the underlying thought that this crisis of hegemony did not result in the victory of the working class, but in the seizure of power by fascism. So Gramsci is here probing the question of why this was so. Why was the revolutionary upsurge defeated, and why was fascism victorious? Reflecting on this question led Gramsci to formulate a new strategy for the subaltern classes to come to power, a strategy which took account of the complexity of civil society and the mass organizations which characterized modern politics.

Before explaining Gramsci's conception of such a new strategy, we need to explain further his general conception of organic crisis and what makes such a crisis an organic one, as compared with much less significant political conflicts which do not threaten or challenge the whole structure of the political order. The post-war crisis which led in Italy to the victory of fascism was certainly an organic one, since what was at stake was the structure and existence of the liberal-democratic state as such, not particular policies of any one government. In Gramsci's words, it was a 'crisis of authority' which was precisely 'the crisis of hegemony, or general crisis of the State' (SPN 210; Q13, §23, 1603). In Notebook 13, from which the extract on organic crisis is taken, Gramsci distinguishes between organic phenomena and conjunctural ones. In an earlier notebook, number 7, written between 1930 and 1933, he also makes the distinction between 'big politics' and 'little politics', *grande politica* and *piccola politica*. It would be a political error of considerable significance, in Gramsci's view, to confuse what is merely conjunctural with what is organic: the former type of politics is what could be called day-to-day politics, which operates within the framework of the existing order. To see conjunctural politics as challenging the whole political structure is a serious mistake. Gramsci seems to mean that thinking that particular events or struggles, perhaps at the economic level, signify an attack or challenge to the whole political system is an illusion. It stems from the kind of economism he was concerned to criticize, since those prone to such an illusion present 'every political and ideological fluctuation as a direct expression of the structure', an error which Gramsci thought 'must be combated on the theoretical level as a primitive infantilism, or it should be combated in practice with the authentic testimony of Marx, the author of concrete political and historical works' (QE3, 173; Q7, §24, 871). It seems that Gramsci is suggesting that to mistake particular struggles, even if they appear to be victories, as having organic implications in the sense of portending a real crisis of the state, is a serious underestimation of the resilience of the established order. An organic crisis could only lead to a revolutionary outcome if the hegemony of the ruling groups had been seriously undermined and a conception of an alternative political order had captured the minds of the hitherto subaltern groups. The appeal in the last quotation from Gramsci to Marx, writer of concrete works of politics and history, makes a reference to Marx's study of the *coup d'état* of Napoleon III in 1851, *The Eighteenth Brumaire of Louis Bonaparte* (Marx 1973c). In the context in which Gramsci refers to it in this quotation (Marx as the author of studies of particular political and historical situations) its significance is that no particular political situation can be analysed in purely abstract or general terms – the particular features of the conjuncture have to be scrutinized in detail, without jumping to the conclusion that any particular fluctuation in the political and ideological sphere or in the economy necessarily or simultaneously implies transformation of a deeper more structural kind. The existing order has a greater capacity for self-defence, and these are ideas Gramsci develops further in his discussion of war of position when he writes that economic crisis does not necessarily lead to the crumbling of the existing order. Gramsci wrote that in war 'it would sometimes happen that a fierce artillery attack seemed to have destroyed the enemy's entire defence system, whereas in fact it had only destroyed the outer perimeter' (SPN 235). Similarly in politics: 'a crisis cannot give the attacking forces the ability to organise with lightning speed in time and in space; still less can it endow them with fighting spirit' (SPN 235; Q13, §24, 1615–16).

The implications of Gramsci's analysis are very important, and much broader than the specific case of fascism in post-First World War Italy. Economic crisis might be a necessary, but certainly not a sufficient, condition for (progressive) political change, since for such change to be possible the attacking forces must have established the greater attraction of their own ideas and have convinced other groups of the attraction of such oppositional ideas. To mistake particular conjunctural events for organic ones is to mistake the nature of political struggle and the necessary maturation of political forces which could mount a challenge to the existing order. These reflections in the *Prison Notebooks* come from the bitter experience of having witnessed the defeat of revolutionary hopes in post-war Italy and the success of fascism in the political struggle. These ideas might find an echo in our own time of the early twenty-first century, where economic crisis, albeit not on the scale of 1920s Europe, does not seem to have opened the way to any progressive restructuring of the existing order. The crisis, or rather the response to the present crisis, seems to be conjunctural rather than organic, in the absence of ideas for an alternative society which could convince the broad masses of society.

What then is Gramsci's analysis of the genuinely organic crisis of the state or crisis of hegemony in 1920s Italy from which fascism emerged triumphant? The crisis of the liberal-democratic state in Italy arose from the erosion of the ruling group's hegemony because of the war and because of the newly found activism of the masses. Why had fascism emerged triumphant from this organic crisis? Gramsci sees fascism, at least in its Italian version, as a form of Caesarism, and this is the term he uses to analyse the phenomenon in the *Prison Notebooks*, though it should be remembered that for him Caesarism is a broader term than fascism, since there are different varieties of Caesarism, with fascism being a subspecies of the family of Caesaristic regimes. Caesarism involves a series of events culminating 'in a great "heroic" personality', as Gramsci puts it

(SPN 219; Q13, §27, 1619), citing Julius Caesar, Napoleon I, Napoleon III and Cromwell as examples of Caesaristic leaders, and Bismarck is added later as another example of a Caesaristic leader. Caesaristic leaders come to power, in the Gramscian analysis, in 'a situation in which the forces in conflict balance each other in a catastrophic manner; that is to say, they balance each other in such a way that a continuation of the conflict can only terminate in their reciprocal destruction' (SPN 219; Q13, §27, 1619). There are clear echoes here of two important Marxist texts. In the first place this alludes to the *Communist Manifesto* with its evocation of the historical series of class struggles, 'a fight that each time ended, either in a revolutionary reconstitution of society at large, or in the common ruin of the contending classes' (Marx 1973b, 68). But the more important reference is to Marx's *The Eighteenth Brumaire of Louis Bonaparte*, in which the *coup d'état* of Napoleon III in 1851 is analysed in terms which Gramsci echoes himself. In that text Marx presents Napoleon's coming to power as stemming from the fear of the possessing classes that parliamentary democracy might open up a road to power for the working class. The economically dominant class thus abandoned parliamentary democracy and switched support to Napoleon, who also practised a form of demagogic populist politics appealing to the dislocated strata of society (the lumpenproletariat, 'the whole indeterminate fragmented mass, tossed backward and forwards, which the French call *la bohème*') and to the army as well ('Vive Napoléon! Vive les saucissons!') (Marx 1973c, 197–200).

Caesarism therefore, in Gramsci's analysis, is similar to Marx's conception of Bonapartism (as expounded in *The Eighteenth Brumaire*) – it arises in a situation of a balance of class forces, or a sort of stalemate of the class struggle, a kind of power vacuum which enables a seemingly heroic or charismatic leader to seize control of the state, from Julius Caesar through the first Napoleon down to twentieth-century examples such as Mussolini and Hitler. Unlike Marx and his conception of Bonapartism, Gramsci distinguishes between progressive and reactionary forms of Caesarism, where the former progressive kind would be exemplified by Julius Caesar and Napoleon I (and presumably Oliver Cromwell, though Gramsci does not explicitly cite him in the camp of progressive

Caesarism), and Napoleon III and Bismarck would be examples of reactionary Caesarism. Mussolini would be another example of the latter. Gramsci describes the difference between the two forms of Caesarism as follows: 'Caesarism is progressive when its intervention helps the progressive force to triumph, albeit with its victory tempered by certain compromises and limitations. It is reactionary when its intervention helps the reactionary force to triumph – in this case too with certain compromises and limitations … ' (SPN 219; Q13, §27, 1619). But there are two significant aspects to Gramsci's analysis of Caesarism, and to fascism as a form of Caesarism. The first is that (unlike the fascist variety) Caesarism could exist without the figure of a heroic leader. Gramsci cites the (British) MacDonald National Government of 1931 as an example of this. Presumably the idea here is that the National Government represented a kind of balance of class forces, which maintained the existing class structure. Gramsci could be suggesting that a government of this kind (even without a charismatic or demagogic leader) increased the autonomy of the state and gave more weight to the executive, free from any control from below. This was certainly an important theme in Marx's analysis of Bonapartism, which emphasized how the Bonapartist state reinforced executive power and towered over society.

The second aspect of Gramsci's analysis is that the conditions of modern Caesarism, are quite different from earlier examples of the phenomenon. Gramsci distinguishes modern Caesarism (i.e. fascism) from previous forms of the phenomenon. The distinction rests on the difference between the bases of modern and earlier types of Caesaristic dictatorial rule. The latter (premodern) forms of such rule by a single figure rested on the army, whereas in the modern world the bases of Caesaristic rule are more complex, in line with the nature of civil society and the mass organizations of modern politics. These lines are significant for Gramsci's analysis of modern politics and indeed of the conditions under which political struggle is carried out. He notes that 'in the modern world, with its great economic-trade-union and party-political coalitions, the mechanism of the Caesarist phenomenon is very different from what it was up to the time of Napoleon III'. Unlike earlier forms of Caesaristic dictatorship which relied on straightforward military force, the means of domination of fascism (modern Caesarism) are more complicated, just because of the complexity of civil society and its associational life: 'The functionaries of the parties and economic unions can be corrupted or terrorised, without any need for military action in the grand style – of the Caesar or 18 Brumaire type' (SPN 220; Q13, §27, 1620). The whole nature of politics had changed, and so not only the means through which fascism maintained itself were different, so too was any political strategy which could confront and oppose fascism. In this sense Gramsci was broadening out his analysis of fascism or Caesarism, using the lessons painfully learned from the victory of fascism to develop a new and original analysis of state and civil society. On the basis of that expanded notion of the state (see below) came a new conception of the political strategy appropriate to the complexity of state and civil society in the age of modernity. The crucial distinction Gramsci draws is between such a new conception and what he calls in this section 'the Jacobin/Forty-eightist formula of the so-called "Permanent Revolution"' (SPN 220; Q13, §27, 1620). This slogan of 'Permanent Revolution' was employed by Marx in 1850, in the 'Address to the Central Committee of the Communist League', proposing that the bourgeois revolution of 1848 should be carried further, 'until all the more or less propertied classes have been driven from their ruling positions, until the proletariat has conquered state power' (Marx 1973b, 323). In Gramsci's own time it was Trotsky who took up the slogan of permanent revolution. In the context of revolutionary politics in Russia at the beginning of the twentieth century this meant that the working class would be the agent of the (bourgeois) revolution to overthrow Czarism and then proceed immediately to socialist revolution. The crucial point for Gramsci's political analysis was that slogans and analyses based on such perspectives of direct and rapid attack on the state were outdated. They no longer had any applicability in an age of mass organizations and complex civil society, in which it was necessary to develop new ideas of political struggle which grasped the need for different techniques of political action. In this respect Gramsci expresses his ideas with exemplary clarity: 'Modern political technique became totally transformed after Forty-eight; after the expansion of parliamentarism and of the associative systems of union and party, and the growth in the formation of vast State and "private" bureaucracies (i.e. politico-private, belonging to parties and trade unions)' (SPN 221; Q13, §27, 1620). This transformation of the nature of political life in the conditions of modernity (mass participation in politics, complex and diversified associational life) explains the nature of modern Caesarism and the more complex ways in which it maintained its power. Power in fascism (and in the modern state more generally) is not simply a question of coercive might but of more subtle forms of domination wielded by a whole range of associations and organizations. Gramsci notes 'the transformations which took place in the organisation of the forces of order in the wide sense'. Those forces of order included not only 'the public service designed for the repression of crime' – what we could call the repressive organs of state power (see Miliband 2009, 38, what he calls that branch of the state apparatus concerned with 'the management of violence') – but, in Gramsci's words, 'the totality of forces organised by the State and by private individuals to safeguard the political and economic domination of the ruling classes' (SPN 221; Q13, §27, 1620).

To sum up, the *Prison Notebooks* can be seen as reflecting on the organic crisis opened up by the impact of the Great War and the Bolshevik Revolution. Gramsci sees fascism as a form of Caesarism, in which a dangerous charismatic man of destiny (Mussolini, in the Italian case) comes to power in a situation of an equilibrium of class power, as analysed in Marx's study of Bonapartism. The dominant classes abandoned their traditional parties (which operated in the framework of the liberal-democratic state) and switched to fascism. Yet fascism was distinct from earlier forms of Caesaristic dictatorship, because it achieved power through parties and mass organizations rather than purely through military force. In that sense it had achieved hegemony, and also exploited the weaknesses and inadequacy of the socialist and communist parties. This seems to be what Gramsci alludes to when he writes that 'in the modern world Caesarism also has a certain margin ... and in particular can count on the relative weakness of the rival progressive force as a result of its specific character and way of life' (SPN 222; Q13, §27, 1622). The lessons to be learnt, suggests Gramsci, involve abandoning direct attacks on the state, whether in the manner of the 1848 tactics of permanent revolution, or of a modern reworking of that strategy in the same vein, whether by Trotsky or by Rosa Luxemburg. A new form of political action has to be developed. In a later passage, also taken from the special Notebook 13, 'Notes on Machiavelli', Gramsci dates the temporal dividing line not from 1848 but from 1870, but with the same emphasis on the complexity of politics in the modern age. He writes that in the period after 1870 'the internal and international organisational relations of the State become more complex and massive, and the Forty-Eightist formula of the "Permanent Revolution" is expanded and transcended in political science by the formula of "civil hegemony"' (SPN 243; Q13, §7, 1566).

These are crucial ideas for the politics of our own time. Political struggle is conceptualized in entirely new ways, and the terrain of politics is seen by Gramsci in a much broader way. It is as though reflecting on the phenomenon of fascism and the reasons why it has succeeded in seizing power Gramsci came to a much more subtle theory of politics and the political strategy required in the modern age. He developed a new theory of state and civil society, and these terms in their Gramscian usage need fuller explanation.

CONCEPTS OF THE STATE

The *Prison Notebooks* are rightly taken to be a classic of political theory (and of social theory in general) because they offer new ways of conceiving politics, and the conditions of political action in the age of modernity. One could say that Gramsci was offering a new paradigm (in Thomas Kuhn's sense) through which politics could be viewed. However, he uses traditional concepts of politics, namely state and civil society, but redefines these concepts, presenting a new language of political analysis, which adds new or redefined concepts such as hegemony and war of position to the traditional vocabulary of political theory. Clearly, state and civil society are basic and hallowed terms of political theory, but they appear in a new guise in Gramsci's attempt at conceptual redefinition and exploration – though this is always carried out with specific reference, as noted above, to particular historical or contemporary events and processes.

It is through analysing the couplet state/civil society that this redefinition on Gramsci's part takes place. Gramsci changes the definition of the state, expanding it from the relatively narrow sense of an apparatus of coercion ('bodies of armed men') to make the term 'the state' a much broader one. It is now seen as the whole set of institutions which work to elicit the consent of people to a particular political order. In that way the state includes a broad range of associations which are usually not thought of as political, or part of the state, but which in this expanded conception of the state form part of its apparatus. One of the clearest statements of such an extended conception of the state appears in Notebook 15, one of the miscellaneous notebooks, written in 1933, which contains one of the few autobiographical reflections in the whole of the *Quaderni*, paragraph 9. This is entitled 'Autobiographical Notes' and it bears out what was said above analysing the *Quaderni* as a reflection on the victory of fascism and the implications of socialist defeat. Gramsci starts the note with the sentence, 'How I have begun to judge disasters of character with greater indulgence' (Q15, §9, 1762). These paragraphs give some clue to the conditions under which the *Prison Notebooks* were written, since Gramsci is analysing the ways in which a person would change under conditions of extreme pressure. He envisages someone who in normal conditions would sincerely say that if the choice were between survival and cannibalism, he would kill himself rather than resort to cannibalism. However, when actually faced with that choice, 'he would become a cannibal and would not consider in any way killing himself'. The person who, in full possession of his physical and moral faculties, would be horrified at the thought of eating a fellow human being, by the time it came to make the choice was a different person who would proceed to cannibalism without any qualms. In the same way, Gramsci considered, those who condemned someone for not holding out in harsh conditions for another year when that person had managed to resist for several years already forgot that that person had been changed by suffering, and so was not the same person as he was initially when he had been more able to resist.

The following note, paragraph 10 in Notebook 15, is headed 'Machiavelli: Sociology and Political Science', and appears in

SPN on pages 243–44 in the context of a critique of Bukharin's *Historical Materialism* (Gramsci's critique is more fully discussed in the next chapter). Gramsci here gives us the basis of his expanded notion of the state, as the subject matter of political science: 'If political science means science of the State, and the State is the entire complex of practical and theoretical activities with which the ruling class not only justifies and maintains its dominance, but manages to win the active consent of those over whom it rules, then it is obvious that all the essential questions of sociology are nothing other than the questions of political science' (SPN 244; Q15, §10, 1765). The crucial idea here is obviously that the state includes all those institutions and organizations which succeed in gaining people's acceptance of the political order. The implications are clear: the state is much broader than those governmental institutions which exercise coercion, so that the state would include all institutions which elicit consent. Furthermore, it is not just through coercion, or even primarily through coercion, that the existing order is maintained, but through the active consent of those over whom power is wielded. This would suggest that institutions like the educational system or the mass media are part of the state in this broader sense, since they certainly seek to win the active consent of the members of that particular political order.

However, this seems to imply that institutions and processes that one would normally consider part of civil society are in fact part of the state. Gramsci seems to be arguing this at least in some of his observations. For example, in an earlier notebook, number 6, Gramsci discusses a review of a book by the French writer Daniel Halévy. Gramsci notes that according to Halévy 'the most important events of French history from 1870 until the present day have not been due to initiatives by political organisms deriving from universal suffrage, but to those either of private organisms (capitalist firms, General Staffs, etc.) or of great civil servants unknown to the country at large, etc.' – Gramsci's summary of the review (SPN 261; Q6, §137, 801). Gramsci draws out the implications as follows: 'But what does that signify if not that by "State" should be understood not only the apparatus of government, but also the "private" apparatus of "hegemony" or civil society?'

(SPN 261; Q6, §137, 801). A similar extension of the term 'state' to cover and include civil society comes when Gramsci discusses the idea of the nightwatchman state, in which the functions of the state 'are limited to the safeguarding of public order and of respect for the laws', in Gramsci's summary. The term 'nightwatchman state' comes from the German socialist Lassalle's ironic description of the classical liberal conception of the state, whose remit was supposed to be strictly confined to the maintenance of law and order. This conception has been taken up in our own time by theorists like Hayek, who argued that the functions of the state as a coercive body should be limited to enforcing general rules of just conduct. Hayek wrote of 'the basic liberal principle of limiting coercion to the enforcement of general rules of just conduct'. For Hayek that principle found expression in the ideas of the natural rights of the individual and of the separation of powers (Hayek 1978, 137). Commenting on the concept of the nightwatchman state, Gramsci argues that 'in this form of regime (which anyway has never existed except on paper, as a limiting hypothesis) hegemony over its historical development belongs to private forces, to civil society – which is "State" too, indeed is the State itself' (SPN 261; Q26, §6, 2302).

There are problems with such an expanded conception of the state, since it seems to swallow up the idea of civil society as a sphere independent of the state. For several theorists, the significance of civil society with its plethora of freely constituted organizations lies precisely in the fact that it is, and should be, a sphere separate from the state. Certainly Gramsci seems to be wrestling with this complicated question of the nature of the state and its relationship to civil society. In a passage taken from Notebook 6 (a miscellaneous notebook, but with many passages dealing with the problem of the state), Gramsci offers another formulation, still in the context of the liberal conception of the state as 'nightwatchman', or as he puts it in this formulation 'the *gendarme*–nightwatchman State'. This formulation states that 'the general notion of State includes elements which need to be referred back to the notion of civil society (in the sense that one might say that State = political society + civil society, in other words hegemony protected by the armour of coercion)' (SPN 263; Q6, §88, 763–64). This (often quoted) passage envisages the ultimate goal of the coercive elements of the state (presumably political society) as, Gramsci's words again, 'withering away by degrees, as ever-more conspicuous elements of regulated society (or ethical State or civil society) make their appearance' (SPN 263; Q6, §88, 764).

This last passage introduces another concept which needs explanation, that of the ethical state. Such an ethical state is here linked or made synonymous with both regulated society and civil society. It seems clear that Gramsci is talking about a possible future society, 'a State without a State', as he puts it in a rather confusing way, claiming both that this 'was present to the greatest political and legal thinkers', and also that such thinkers 'placed themselves on the terrain of pure science', though he then follows this by saying this concept is 'pure utopia' (SPN 263; Q6, §88, 764). What seems to be envisaged here is the idea of a future society, a regulated society, in which the coercive aspects of the state would be reduced and eventually outweighed by civil society in which human beings would govern themselves through free association rather than forcible state direction. Yet this is seen as a gradual process, not a sudden leap from coercion to association. Gramsci writes of 'a coercive organisation which will safeguard the development of the continually proliferating elements of regulated society, and which will therefore progressively reduce its own authoritarian and forcible interventions' (SPN 263; Q6, §88, 764). But, according to Gramsci, this process would not 'conjure up the idea of a new "liberalism", even though the beginning of an era of organic liberty be imminent'. The idea of an era of organic liberty is clearly synonymous with regulated society, and the basic thought seems to be of a gradual progression to such a (self-)regulated society. In more classically Marxist language this seems to invoke the idea of a transition to socialism, in which the state gradually begins the process of withering away, eventually approaching the idea of a classless and hence stateless society.

In SPN, the passages just quoted from Notebook 6 are followed by a passage from Notebook 8, another miscellaneous one, to which in the original Gramsci gives the rubric 'Economic-Corporate Phase of the State'. This paragraph evidently refers to the Soviet Union and to the building of a new state. Gramsci argues that 'no type of State can avoid passing through a phase of economic-corporate primitivism', and draws the conclusion that 'the content of the political hegemony of the new social group which has founded the new type of State must be predominantly of an economic order ... the superstructural elements will inevitably be few in number ... cultural policy will above all be negative, a critique of the past' (SPN 263; Q8, §185, 1053). One can surmise that these are references to the process of building socialism in the Soviet Union, to debates about constructing the economic base for socialism in the period of the New Economic Policy (1921–28) and also in the years of breakneck industrialization which followed that. Gramsci seems to be saying that the culture or superstructural elements of this new society would initially be few, but that a new culture was being created, at least in broad outline, and that this culture was trying 'to be consistent with the new structure as it is formed'. On the basis of the new economy there might arise a new culture which would give 'hegemony to the new class'. Gramsci thus suggests that a culture or superstructure appropriate to the new economic system was in the process of being formed, or at least he holds out the hope that this might be the case. He makes a contrast between this process and 'the period of the mediaeval communes' where culture remained under the control of the Church, and hence remained 'anti-economic in character (i.e. against the nascent capitalist economy)'. From this he derives the conclusion that 'Humanism and the Renaissance were reactionary, because they signalled the defeat of the new class, the negation of the economic world which was proper to it, etc.' (SPN 264; Q8, §185, 1053–54). This can be interpreted as above all an analysis of what happened in Italy. Gramsci seems to be saying that Italy had historically failed to develop a modern culture in tune with the conditions of modern (i.e. capitalist) economic production. In line with his analyses of intellectuals (see Chapter 3 above), his argument implies that in Italy the intellectuals had been captured by the traditional structures of Papacy and Holy Roman Empire, rather than linked in a national-popular movement with the bourgeoisie (and later with the working class). The new society of the Soviet Union, he is implying, or hoping, would by contrast eventually develop a culture in line with the new productive forces and cement the hegemony of the new class.

If these lines of Gramsci's seem to offer the perspective of transition to a situation of regulated society, in which the state 'will be identified with civil society' (i.e. a non-coercive form of state), Gramsci's idea of ethical state deserves more analysis. This concept seems to derive from Hegel, who in his *Philosophy of Right* placed the state as the highest form of political and human association, through which people could achieve their full freedom. Such freedom could not be realized in civil society (*bürgerliche Gesellschaft* – which could equally be translated as bourgeois society), because such society was one of conflicting needs and interests, which could not attain the universality or full flowering of ethical life which Hegel thought was only possible in and through the state. A distorted form of this Hegelianism was to be found in fascist ideology, which elevated the idea of the state in a totalitarian way, as witnessed by the statement in *The Doctrine of Fascism* (written by Gentile and Mussolini in 1932) proclaiming that 'for the Fascist, everything is in the State, and nothing human or spiritual exists, much less has value, outside the State. In this sense Fascism is totalitarian, and the Fascist State, the synthesis and unity of all values, interprets, develops and gives strength to the whole life of the people' (Lyttelton 1973, 42). In a paragraph in Notebook 8 with the rubric 'Ethical or Cultural State' ('Stato etico o di cultura'), Gramsci presented his idea on the ethical state, or the cultural state (using the two phrases as synonyms), as follows: 'Every state is ethical in as much as one of its most important functions is to raise the great mass of the population to a particular cultural and moral level, a level (or type) which corresponds to the needs of the productive forces for development, and hence to the interests of the ruling classes' (SPN 258; Q8, §179, 1049). The state is thus linked to a particular form of economy. It is noteworthy that when Gramsci discusses how the state fulfils this function, he refers to 'the school as a positive educative function, and the courts as a repressive and negative educative function', calling them 'the most important State activities in this sense'. But according to Gramsci this aim of raising the cultural and moral level of the mass of the population in line with the prevailing economic system was also carried out by institutions in civil society: 'a multitude of other so-called private initiatives and activities tend to the same end-initiatives and activities which form the apparatus of the political and cultural hegemony of the ruling classes' (SPN 258; Q8, §179, 1049), so that hegemony is achieved both through the state in the broader sense and also by 'so-called private initiatives'. All states then were ethical in seeking to adapt the culture of the population to the prevailing economic system. This seems a highly valid point. In contemporary times the emphasis of states on expanding higher education as a means of equipping more and more young people for jobs in a globalized economic system (if they can find any jobs), and insisting that higher-education institutions foster entrepreneurial values and a positive attitude to business values, seems to illustrate what Gramsci meant in these lines. The liberal-democratic state is ethical, though not really in a moral sense, but in the way in which its function consists in spreading the values and educational perspectives appropriate to the dominant economic system.

Gramsci however maintained that the only genuinely ethical state was one created by 'the social group that poses an end of the State and its own end as the target to be achieved' (SPN 259; Q8, §179, 1050). This was a coded way of referring to the communist or socialist movement, with its proclaimed goal of a stateless and classless society. Its aim was 'to put an end to the internal divisions of the ruled, etc. and to create a technically and morally unitary social organism' (SPN 259; Q8, §179, 1050). The implication of this seems to be that the only really ethical state is the non-coercive state which has been absorbed by civil society, in other words the only ethical state is a kind of non-state, a regulated society where state functions have been taken over by civil society. In the periods before this end is achieved, the state uses both coercive and non-coercive methods to (so to speak) 'fit' the population to the needs of the economy. The failure to do this, as with the Italian mediaeval communes, meant a situation of historical backwardness. In Italy, Gramsci seems to suggest, there had been a failure to create a modern state adequate for its historical tasks. There had been what he called a 'rift between "spiritual" and "temporal" in the Middle Ages', and this rift was being re-enacted in modern times. Gramsci speaks of 'the crisis of the State', and of a 'process of disintegration of the modern State' which he said was a process 'far more catastrophic than the mediaeval historical process' (SPN 270–71; Q6, §10, 691). In this connection Gramsci uses another term to be added to his lexicon of types of state, beyond 'night-watchman state' and 'ethical state'. This is the term 'integral state', which helps explain what he means by his remarks about the catastrophic process of the disintegration of the modern state. For some commentators on Gramsci, the idea of the integral state constitutes the specifically Gramscian contribution to state theory. Liguori interprets the idea of the integral state as meaning that Gramsci combines in such a definition the idea of the state as organized force with the idea of civil society as the range of private or so-called private organizations through which hegemony is exercised and consent elicited. Both are part of the state in this 'integral' or extended sense (Liguori and Voza 2009, 802).

As with all of Gramsci's ideas, they have to be interpreted in the context of a broad historical perspective. Gramsci argues that the crisis of the Middle Ages involved the separation between spiritual and temporal, meaning that intellectuals were captured, metaphorically, by the Church, and detached from the temporal, the rising bourgeoisie. Gramsci's analysis is highly condensed and allusive, so it is not easy to make sense of it, but his argument appears to be that the crisis of the Middle Ages was ended by the epoch of the French Revolution. In this period the bourgeoisie was able to create an integral state, appropriate to the new productive forces. In his words, 'the social grouping that had been economically the motor force in Europe throughout the millennium was able to present itself as an integral "State", possessing all the intellectual and moral forces it needed to organise a complete and perfect society'. Yet in the contemporary (for Gramsci) world, this integral state was again in crisis, in a process of disintegration, since the intellectuals were deserting it, but this time '"without a Pope"' in 'an unstable diaspora of great cultural personalities', which again might be a reference to Croce and other contemporary intellectuals (SPN 270–71; Q6, §10, 691).

Without forcing the analysis or reading too much into these condensed remarks, one could suggest that Gramsci is calling for the formation of a new integral state, to end the catastrophic crisis of the modern state. Such an integral state would in its turn be a powerful instrument, a genuinely ethical state, which would raise the level of the population to equip it for the productive and other tasks needed for the modern world, and would incorporate the intellectuals (the new organic intellectuals) into the process, thus ending the separation of spiritual and temporal, intellectual and producer, which the modern world had recreated. But just as the integral state of the French Revolutionary epoch had been based on the bourgeoisie, 'the social grouping that had been economically the motor force in Europe', so the new integral state would have to be based on a definite 'motor force', the working class, in alliance with the rural proletariat. The integral state would thus be a powerful agent of modernity in its own right, bringing together intellectuals and workers in a new organism. Gramsci's remarks about the only truly ethical state being one created by the grouping which wished for the end of the state suggest that this integral state might be one which anticipated its own demise, once it had achieved the tasks it set out to accomplish, raising the level of the population in line with the new collectivist economy which was emerging in the womb of capitalism. Is Gramsci therefore a statist? It is true that this attempt at interpretation of his idea of the integral state is somewhat speculative, given the allusive nature of his remarks on the subject. It is clear that he had as an ultimate goal the disappearance of the state, but that this was premised as the end of a long period of historical evolution. His view of the modern crisis of the state stemmed from the idea that the integral state created by the bourgeoisie was no longer able to organize a complete and perfect society. A new integral state was needed, based on a different economic system and animated by different social forces. At the same time as his discussion of these different forms or types of state, liberal, ethical, integral (and also, by implication, fascist), Gramsci was grappling with the relationship between state and civil society. Hegel had seen civil society as subordinate to the state, with the state as the higher form of ethical life. Marx had reversed the relationship, seeing the state as in some sense determined by the structure of civil society, and had famously insisted in the 1859 Preface to *A Contribution to the Critique of Political Economy* that 'the anatomy of this civil society, however, has to be sought in political economy' (Marx 1973a,

425). What then is Gramsci's perspective on these matters, and how do his views on civil society relate to his perspective on the war of position?

THE SPHERE OF CIVIL SOCIETY

As with his theory of the state, Gramsci's analysis of the concept of civil society can be seen as a case of 'new wine in old bottles', in other words using a well-established concept but giving it a new definition and transforming its significance. As noted above, the concept of civil society is a venerable idea in social and political theory. For theorists of the Scottish Enlightenment like Adam Ferguson in his 1767 *Essay on the History of Civil Society*, the term referred to the modern commercial society in which its members engaged in trade and as a result gentler manners of civility became the norm, replacing (in Scotland) the rude and primitive clan society where war was the normal means of social interaction (Ferguson 1995). This idea of the modernity of civil society was enormously influential, and was taken up by Hegel in his *Philosophy of Right*. Hegel saw civil society as one stage or moment, through which human beings would develop their sociability and community. Civil society was such a stage, higher than the family (a unit based on feelings of love for the immediate family members), but lower than the state. In civil society, precisely because of its commercial nature, human beings saw each other in instrumental terms, as means to the satisfaction of their own interests. Civil society was thus one in which individuals came into contact with each other as traders or consumers, an essentially modern society, but it could not (for Hegel) realize the full solidarity or ethical life which was possible only through the state. The state alone could develop the universal interests of its citizens. Indeed for that reason he viewed civil servants as the universal class, since they served the state and in that way were agents of the common interest that the state represented. The state was in a metaphorical sense 'higher' than the conflicting interests of civil society (Hegel 1952).

For his part Marx in this respect as in others turned Hegel on his head. While respecting the distinction between state and civil society Marx saw the state as in a sense derivative from civil society. If, following the quote previously given, the anatomy of civil society was to be found in political economy, the class structure of modern society was the foundation of the state, and the role of the state was to preserve the dominance of the ruling class. Civil society was thus fundamental, and the state was part of the superstructure, with civil society as the class-divided society whose economic foundations formed the base. For Marx, therefore, it could be said, simplifying the issue, that civil society was the sphere of the economy, and the state constituted the political superstructure which helped maintain the class divisions of society. Far from being universal, the state was rather particular, it was not an ethical state but a powerful coercive body which propped up the class structure of civil society.

Gramsci gives considerable importance to the sphere of civil society, but the *Prison Notebooks* show him developing a different perspective on this hallowed term, one which has been enormously influential on more recent discussions of the concept. Indeed there has been much discussion on the way in which Gramsci seems to use the term 'civil society' in different ways. There is a careful examination of this problem in the book by Cospito (2011a, 85–100 and 266–75). Cospito's diachronic reading of Gramsci suggests that there is a heightened or more intense use of the term civil society by Gramsci in the year 1932, and that this is a sign that Gramsci was using the term as a means of developing his thought away from a rigid or schematic way of looking at political phenomena. While the first reference to civil society in the *Quaderni* comes already in Notebook 1, §130, there is clear reference to Hegel's use of the term in Notebook 6, §24, where Gramsci writes:

> One must distinguish civil society as Hegel understands it and in the sense it is often used in these notes (that is, in the sense of the political and cultural hegemony of a social group over the whole of society; as the ethical content of the state) from the sense given to it by Catholics, for whom civil society is, instead, political society or the state, as opposed to the society of the family and of the church.
>
> (QE3, 20; Q6, §24, 703)

This indicates that Gramsci's use of the concept is (often – but not always) one which indicates that civil society constitutes the sphere through which hegemony is developed and maintained. Cospito notes (2011a, 89) that in Notebook 6, §81, which was written between March and August 1931, the link between civil society and hegemony is made explicit in the rubric of this paragraph, the first time that 'hegemony' appears in the title of a paragraph: 'Hegemony (Civil Society) and Division of Powers' (SPN 245; Q6, §81, 751). Civil society is thus distinguished from the sphere of the economy, and in this sense Gramsci departs from Marx who sees 'the anatomy of civil society in political economy'. This view of civil society as distinct both from the economic structure and also from the state in the narrow coercive sense is clearly expressed by Gramsci in a paragraph of Notebook 10, which appears in the *Further Selections*: 'Between the economic structure and the state with its legislation and its coercion stands civil society, and it is this latter which has to be radically transformed, in concrete terms and not just in the written word as it appears in statutes and learned books' (FSPN 167; Q10 II, §15, 1253). The problem then is to understand the often different ways in which Gramsci defines the term, the ways in which his usage differs from that of other theorists, and the political implications of his interpretation of the concept. In understanding his meaning, it has to be seen in terms of his idea of the integral state. The state for Gramsci was not purely a coercive body but included those institutions which sought to establish the hegemony of the ruling group and elicit consent from subaltern classes. While the quotation just given suggests that civil society is distinct from both economy and the state, it is often the case that for Gramsci state in the broader or 'integral' sense includes civil society: 'by "State" should be understood not only the apparatus of government, but also the "private" apparatus of "hegemony" or civil society', in Gramsci's words (SPN 261; Q6, §137, 801). An important definition of civil society comes in the notes on intellectuals (discussed in our Chapter 3 above) where Gramsci establishes what he calls 'two major superstructural "levels"', and he distinguishes these levels as follows: 'the one that can be called "civil society", that is the ensemble of organisms commonly called "private", and that of "political society" or "the State"'. The former level, according to Gramsci, corresponds to 'the function of "hegemony"' while the latter level corresponds 'to that of "direct domination" or command exercised through the State and "juridical" government'. Civil society is thus part of the state, in the integral or expanded sense, and it is that part of the state through which the ruling group establishes its hegemony. Civil society is the sphere of hegemony, contrasted with the '"direct domination" or command exercised through the State and "juridical" government' (SPN 12; Q12, §1, 1518). There thus appears to be a sharp contrast between the institutions of civil society which secure the consent of subordinate classes to the established order, and the coercive apparatus of political society, or 'the State' in the narrow sense, which exercises direct domination through what could be called the management of violence (the repressive arms of the state apparatus). Hegemony and domination are thus the two ways in which the state in the broader integral sense maintains the power of the ruling group, through civil society and juridical apparatus respectively. Yet in an earlier notebook, number 4 (the first of the 'Appunti di filosofia', 'Notes on Philosophy'), Gramsci presents this distinction as merely one of method rather than one which is significant in real life. He criticizes the economistic theory of free trade which maintains that 'economic activity belongs to civil society and that political society must not intervene in its regulation'. For Gramsci, at least in this paragraph, the distinction between political and civil society 'is purely methodological and not organic; in concrete historical life, political society and civil society are a single entity' (QE2, 182; Q4, §38, 460). If political society and civil society are the same, this must be because they both together act to secure the dominance of a ruling group, and the distinction between the two becomes blurred in real life, in concrete historical life.

Civil society for Gramsci thus forms part of the state in the broader integral sense, and it is precisely the greater complexity of civil society and its associational life that marks off modern politics from the politics of the era of 1848. In his conception of civil society Gramsci includes the educational system, the Church, the press and more generally what we would now call the mass media, and the complex of voluntary associations which form the network of the sphere between individuals and the state. While it is hard to find in Gramsci an extended or explicit definition of the term civil society, he clearly sees it in terms of a range of associations which act as important institutions through which the existing structure of society is defended. Gramsci states that 'in the case of the most advanced States, where "civil society" has become a very complex structure and one which is resistant to the catastrophic "incursions" of the immediate economic element (crises, depressions, etc.)', a different conception of politics and political strategy is needed (SPN 235; Q13, §24, 1615). It is thus clear what Gramsci means by the term civil society: it is that network of associations, including the educational system, the Church, the mass media, which is separate from the state in the narrow coercive sense, but (according to Gramsci) which forms an integral part of the state in the broader meaning, because both sets of institutions (coercive state and civil society) act to maintain the hegemony of the dominant class. So much is indicated by Gramsci's statement 'of what the State (in its integral meaning: dictatorship + hegemony) really is' (SPN 239; Q6, §155, 810). The significance of these words is that there is a kind of division of labour between the two parts of the integral state: its coercive or repressive organs exercise dictatorship, whereas it is through civil society that hegemony is maintained and the legitimation of the existing order achieved. But a number of problems are raised by Gramsci's interpretation of civil society, and there has been much debate about this aspect of the *Prison Notebooks*.

In the first place, where does civil society fit into the classical Marxist distinction between base and superstructure? As we have seen, Marx wrote that 'the anatomy of civil society is to be found in political economy', which suggests that the true face of civil society is the economic structure of society. Civil society is therefore part of the base, since its determining features are located in the economic base, which is the foundation of society. But Gramsci gives civil society a different interpretation. It is not a fundamentally economic concept, for him, but seems to represent the terrain on which people become aware of the deep-seated cleavages in society and achieve consciousness of social structure. If civil society is for

Marx part of the base, arising on the economic foundation, the Italian political theorist Norberto Bobbio argues that Gramsci gives a more significant role to civil society, since it is through the institutions of civil society that hegemony is secured, so that those institutions play a more important role than that accorded to them by classical Marxism. Bobbio (1988) suggests that in a sense Gramsci moves away from the classical Marxist presentation, by adding to the classic base/superstructure distinction another dichotomy within the superstructure, between civil society (the sphere of hegemony) and the state (as a coercive instrument). The classical Marxist conceptualization sees the economy as foundational and determining, whereas Gramsci seems to present civil society as an equally important locus through which the existing order is maintained – and also challenged. Cospito's analysis draws our attention to the fact that even in Marx the discussion of civil society and its place in the base/superstructure distinction is not so clear-cut (Cospito 2011a, 267). He refers us to a letter of 1846 by Marx to a Russian correspondent, Annenkov, where civil society seems to be distinguished from the economic base: 'Assume particular stages of development in production, commerce and consumption and you will have a corresponding social system, a corresponding organisation of the family, of social estates or of classes, in a word, a corresponding civil society' (Marx and Engels 1975, 30). For his part Gramsci sees the complexity of civil society as the fundamental feature which marks out modern democracies and represents so many bulwarks of the existing order: 'The massive structures of the modern democracies, both as State organisations, and as complexes of associations in civil society, constitute for the art of politics as it were the "trenches" and the permanent fortifications of the front in the war of position' (SPN 243; Q13, §7, 1567). Gramsci therefore sees civil society as a decisive arena in the class struggle. Civil society is seen, differently from Marx, not as the sphere of the economy, but as part of the integral state, a part which is crucial for disseminating the ideas and habits of common sense through which the existing order is maintained. If civil society is so important, then this raises the question of how it could be challenged, or how the hitherto subaltern classes could use the arena of civil society to oppose the hegemony of existing ideas. How could these trenches or bulwarks be captured by the working-class movement and its political party?

In one of the most famous and often-quoted passages from the *Prison Notebooks*, Gramsci contrasts East and West, East being represented by Russia, where the Bolsheviks had carried out their revolution, West by the modern democracies with their complex civil society: 'In the East the State was everything, civil society was primordial and gelatinous; in the West, there was a proper relation between State and civil society, and when the State trembled a sturdy structure of civil society was at once revealed. The State was only an outer ditch, behind which there stood a powerful system of fortresses and earthworks: more or less numerous from one State to the next, it goes without saying – but this precisely necessitated an accurate reconnaissance of each individual country' (SPN 238; Q7, §16, 866). This paints a picture of the structure of modern mass democracies with their network of civil-society associations as being much more resilient and resistant to radical or revolutionary challenge than was the case in Russia in 1917. If civil society formed such a 'powerful system of fortresses and earthworks', then what were the implications for political strategy? This led Gramsci to sketch out his concept of war of position.

WAR OF POSITION

The significance of the *Prison Notebooks* lies partly in the fact that in his reflections on the defeat of the revolutionary movement in post-war Europe, and the triumph of fascism in Italy, Gramsci developed the idea of a political strategy different from that which had led the Bolsheviks to victory in Russia. Precisely because of the difference between East and West, between societies marked by a weak ('primordial and gelatinous') civil society and those of the West with their 'sturdy structure of civil society', a new form of politics was needed which took account of the complex structure of modern democracies. Gramsci's concept of war of position is developed through a critique of what he calls war of manoeuvre, or frontal attack on the state. It is such a war of manoeuvre that he saw represented in the views of the Polish revolutionary Rosa

Luxemburg, with her conception of the mass strike, and by the Bolshevik leader Trotsky with his idea of permanent revolution. Both theorists are seen by Gramsci as presenting ideas of political action which are not relevant to the situation of advanced or complex modern democracies, and hence doomed to defeat. Luxemburg was inspired by the Russian Revolution of 1905 to write her pamphlet of 1906 on *The Mass Strike, the Political Party and the Trade Unions* (Luxemburg 1906). Luxemburg became known for her emphasis on the mass movement as the source of revolutionary consciousness, while not denying the significance of either socialist party or trade-union organization. In an earlier article, 'Organisational Questions of the Russian Social Democracy', Luxemburg had criticized Lenin's vanguard-party idea, ending her article with the statement that 'historically, the errors committed by a truly revolutionary movement are infinitely more fruitful than the infallibility of the cleverest Central Committee' (Luxemburg 1961, 108).

In the *Prison Notebooks* Gramsci criticizes Luxemburg (referred to simply as 'Rosa') for the 1906 pamphlet. He sees this work as 'one of the most significant documents theorising the war of manoeuvre in relation to political science' (SPN 233; Q13, §24, 1613). The gist of his criticism was that Luxemburg's view was 'a form of iron economic determinism', or what Gramsci called 'out and out historical mysticism, the awaiting of a sort of miraculous illumination' (SPN 233; Q13, §24, 1613–14), in which economic crisis opened the way for insurrection and the overthrow of the existing order. In Gramsci's view this was too simplistic and grossly overestimated the fragility of that existing society, just as in modern warfare a sudden attack on enemy trenches could not be successful unless it took into account 'the whole organisational and industrial system of the territory which lies to the rear of the army in the field' (SPN 234; Q13, §24, 1615). Gramsci suggested that the existence of a complex civil society meant that an insurrectionary attack on the state neglected the fact that 'the superstructures of civil society are like the trench-systems of modern warfare' – they made the existing order much less susceptible to a frontal attack. In a telling parallel, Gramsci states that 'in wars among the more industrially and socially advanced States', the war of manoeuvre 'must be considered as occupying the same position as siege warfare used to occupy previously in relation to it', and the same was true 'in the art and science of politics'. The suggestion is that just as no one in modern times would consider waging war by siege warfare, so too the idea of a direct assault on the state was equally archaic in arenas where there was a developed civil society, 'in the case of the most advanced States, where civil society has become a very complex structure' (SPN 235; Q13, §24, 1615).

If Gramsci saw Rosa Luxemburg as one representative of the outmoded war of manoeuvre, he presents Trotsky (referred to in the *Prison Notebooks* by his real name of Bronstein) as also advocating a mistaken revolutionary strategy, one which was derived from the Russian situation, 'a reflection of the general-economic-cultural-social conditions in a country in which the structures of national life are embryonic and loose, and incapable of becoming "trench or fortress"' (SPN 236; Q7, §16, 865). Gramsci sees Trotsky's formula of permanent revolution (derived from Marx's slogan of 1848) as limited to a historical period in which mass political organizations of the working class and the range of associations in civil society were all absent. The idea of permanent revolution or what Gramsci called war of manoeuvre had been effective in Russia in 1917 because of the relative backwardness of that society, in particular the 'primordial and gelatinous' nature of civil society. But in developed modern societies, a different strategy was needed, to which Gramsci gave the label of war of position. He calls the 'transition from the war of manoeuvre (frontal attack) to the war of position in the political field as well' the most important question of the post-war period. Trotsky/Bronstein, says Gramsci, 'can be considered the political theorist of frontal attack in a period in which it only leads to defeats' (SPN 238; Q6, §138, 801). It thus has to be replaced by a war of position.

But what exactly is such a war of position, and what are the political implications of such a strategy? The concept raises a number of problems, theoretical and empirical. Gramsci writes that where 'the internal and international organisational relations of the State become more complex and massive' then 'the Forty-Eightist formula of the "Permanent Revolution" is expanded and transcended in political science by the formula of "civil hegemony"'

(SPN 243; Q13, §7, 1566), a quote we have already cited above. It would seem then that war of position means a protracted struggle in and through the institutions of civil society, perhaps as preparation for a final direct assault. It is not entirely clear what a war of position would involve, as a practical political strategy. Gramsci seems to envisage such a war of position as a protracted and difficult process, as when he writes that 'the war of position demands enormous sacrifices by infinite masses of people' (SPN 238; Q6, §138, 802). Rather confusingly, in the light of the passage previously quoted in which siege warfare is contrasted with more modern means of warfare, the war of position is also equated with 'siege warfare' which 'is concentrated, difficult, and requires exceptional qualities of patience and inventiveness' (SPN 239; Q6, §138, 802). The picture which emerges from these rather cryptic remarks is of what could be called slow burn revolution, if not exactly a long march through the institutions (one of the slogans used in radical movements of the 1960s) then something like an extended struggle to establish a presence in the (meta-phorical) trenches of civil society. Perhaps the post-Second World War strategy of the PCI (Partito Comunista Italiano, after 1944) could be taken as an example of such a war of position: building up a presence in local government by control of municipalities like Bologna, establishing cultural events like the annual Festa dell'Unità, seeking to create a range of cultural associations and institutions, and generally create what one study of the French Communist Party (Kriegel 1972) called a counter-society as a kind of base from which to mount a challenge to the broader structure of social power.

Gramsci, it is fair to say, does not explain in any detail what is meant by his term war of position. If the slogan or formula of permanent revolution gives way to that of civil hegemony this suggests that before any attempt to take over or challenge the state could be made, the radical or oppositional forces have first to establish their hegemony in the sphere of civil society. This was one of the lessons drawn by Gramsci from his study of Italian history and, as he saw it, the failure of the Italian Risorgimento, at least of its radical strand. In the 'Notes on Italian History', discussed in our previous Chapter 4, we find the clear statement of this perspective: 'A social group can, and indeed must, already exercise "leadership" before winning governmental power (this indeed is one of the principal conditions for the winning of such power)' (SPN 57; Q19, §24, 2010). The war of position, then, must consist of oppositional groups exercising intellectual leadership, or 'establishing the apparatus (mechanism) of their intellectual, moral and political hegemony', as Gramsci wrote that the Moderates had done in the Italian Risorgimento, whereas the more radical Action Party had failed to do this (SPN 59; Q19, §24, 2011).

If this is what is entailed by the war of position as a strategy appropriate to the conditions of modern mass politics, there seem to be a number of problems with it, which apply both in Gramsci's time and in contemporary politics. One problem is *how* the trenches of civil society could be taken over by oppositional forces. If civil society forms part of the integral state and its components (like the educational system and mass media) are means through which ideas of the dominant groups in society are diffused, is there a space for an alternative civil society, or the possibility of capturing part of civil society for radical politics? Take the example of the mass media: in an age when large sections of the popular press and TV media are owned by media moguls like Rupert Murdoch and Silvio Berlusconi, to take some obvious examples, how could a war of position challenge the grip of such powerful media and the massive financial resources they command? Perhaps contemporary events such as (in the UK) the attempts to regulate the media and constrain their intrusive phone hacking and unscrupulous prying into private lives might be an example of one aspect of such a war of position. Others might point to the use of the Internet and social media as new channels through which a war of position might be waged and some of the trenches of civil society conquered, or at least inroads made into them. In a more pessimistic vein, an analysis such as that offered by Jürgen Habermas in his *Structural Transformation of the Public Sphere* suggests the greater manipulation of public opinion by mass media and powerful economic interests, and their control of popular culture (Habermas 1989). Long gone are the days when salons and other forums of *bürgerliche Öffentlichkeit* or bourgeois public opinion were able to engage a wider public in rational debate and scrutinize actions of the state and of public officials. In an age of spin doctors and state surveillance of communication, let alone the phenomenon analysed by some social scientists of bowling alone – the decline of associative life in America highlighted by Robert Putnam (2000), among others – how could civil society be the sphere of a successful war of position challenging established ideas? Again, some theorists or political scientists might point to movements like alternative globalization as an engagement of civil society, waging a war of position by proposing alternative models of globalization and by arousing public opinion against the inequalities inherent in global capitalism. However, such movements are often rather episodic, lack enduring organization, and are prone to sudden upsurges and downturns, rather than the steady advance and taking over of positions and established institutions which is suggested by Gramsci's term war of position.

Some of the problems presented in this questioning of the idea of the war of position echo what was said in the chapter on intellectuals concerning the possibility of new organic intellectuals of the working class. If Karabel is right, contemporary society is marked by a diminishing space (institutional and organizational) for such intellectuals to be formed (Karabel 1976). If the power of neo-liberalism as a global ideology in the contemporary world is so great, diffused through institutions like the International Monetary Fund and World Bank, and if (to take one contemporary British example) the study of economics in universities is increasingly ideological in giving a monopoly to perspectives in line with that view of the world (even though there are presently (2013) student protests against the rather one-sided intellectual content of economics courses as currently taught), then it is not clear how or where or by what agencies a war of position might be effectively conducted. But this may all be too pessimistic. However, it is a possible development of Gramsci's own position. He shows, very convincingly, how the institutions of civil society constitute a line of defence of the existing order, so that even if the state were to be attacked or destabilized, then the organizations of civil society could still withstand such direct assault: 'the State was only an outer ditch, behind which there stood a powerful system of fortresses and earthworks' (SPN 238; Q7, §16, 866). Or perhaps the metaphor could be used the other way round – for any successful attack on the state to be made, first the institutions of civil society have to be penetrated, yet this might be more difficult in our contemporary age than at the time Gramsci was writing.

Another problem with the war of position has been identified by theorists like Perry Anderson. The charge here seems to be that if the war of position sketched out by Gramsci in his *Prison Notebooks* does consist in establishing a kind of bridgehead in civil society, or permeating its institutions by establishing a presence there, whether cultural or more narrowly political, then how does this differ from reformism? If the war of position entails getting integrated within the institutions of civil society, then this could lead to absorption into those institutions and to the waning of any transformative project. Even a politics of presence might have the same result, if that means achieving power at a local or municipal level. This could result in efficient running of a city or region, but without any impetus to take that further towards a hegemonic project of transforming the wider society. In other words, engagement in the trenches or earthworks of civil society might result in integration within those same structures, and thus the classic dilemma of reform/revolution is re-enacted, only with a different language. Anderson suggests that Gramsci's war of position might be little different from Kautsky's *Ermattungsstrategie*, a strategy of exhaustion or war of attrition, whereby the continued pressure of social democracy at all levels would lead to the exhaustion or surrender of the dominant groups (Anderson 1976–77). Yet the record of the German SPD was rather one of integration into the wider society, while achieving a better standard of life for the mass of its members. This was certainly no minor achievement, but it seems far removed from the process of total cultural renewal and political transformation which Gramsci aspired to, as will become clearer in the following chapter which looks at how he thought Marxism could become a new popular philosophy and provoke an intellectual, as well as political, revolution.

There emerge from these pages on 'The Modern Prince' and 'State and Civil Society' entirely new perspectives on central questions of politics (the state, civil society, the nature of politics) and of political action (the role of the party, the possibility of a political strategy very different from that of the Bolsheviks in 1917), which completely revise and reconstruct traditional concepts of politics. It is for that reason that the *Prison Notebooks* constitute a classic text of political theory: Gramsci is formulating a new language of politics, even if he is using the same words (party, state, civil society) that have been used by earlier theorists of the political. From the modern Prince to the war of position, he is adding to the lexicon of modern politics, in an attempt to sketch out a new way of doing politics, one which is suitable for the characteristics of advanced modern societies. The aim of such a new form of political action would be to transform the mentality of citizens of such societies in a process of moral and intellectual reform, to take the phrase which Gramsci borrowed from Renan. If this process was profoundly political, involving the creation of new agencies of politics, it was also a philosophical and intellectual process. That leads on to Gramsci's views on the study of philosophy and the problems of Marxism, the third part of SPN, and that forms the material of the following chapter.

SUGGESTIONS FOR FURTHER READING

The literature on Gramsci's ideas on state, party and civil society is enormous. There are useful analyses by Peter Thomas, *The Gramscian Moment* (Leiden: Brill, 2009) and James Martin, *Gramsci's Political Analysis: A Critical Introduction* (Houndmills: Macmillan, 1998). Equally vast is the literature on hegemony: a useful introduction is by Peter Ives, *Language and Hegemony in Gramsci* (London: Pluto Press, 2004), and see also Joseph Femia, *Gramsci's Political Thought: Hegemony, Consciousness, and the Revolutionary Process* (Oxford: Oxford University Press, 1981). Different perspectives on hegemony are offered in the articles by Gwyn Williams, Thomas Bates, Joseph Femia, Chantal Mouffe and Peter Ives, which are collected in volume 2 of the four-volume set of articles on Gramsci edited by James Martin, *Antonio Gramsci: Critical Assessments of Leading Political Philosophers* (London: Routledge, 2002). This volume also contains important articles on Gramsci's views on the state and civil society by Perry

Anderson, Anne Showstack Sassoon, Joseph Buttigieg, Geoffrey Hunt and Walter Adamson.

On civil society and Gramsci's analysis of the concept, the essay by Norberto Bobbio is an essential point of reference: 'Gramsci and the Concept of Civil Society', in J. Keane (ed.), *Civil Society and the State: New European Perspectives* (London: Verso, 1988).

6

PHILOSOPHY AND MARXISM

THE PHILOSOPHY OF PRAXIS

This chapter deals with Gramsci's ideas on philosophy and on the nature of Marxism, following the heading of Part III of SPN, 'The Philosophy of Praxis'. This was the term frequently employed by Gramsci in the *Notebooks* to refer to Marxism. While it seems clear that one reason for the use of this term was as a substitute for the politically more dangerous term of 'Marxism', which could have led to censorship of any writings referring explicitly to Marxist philosophy and politics, Gramsci's use of this term arose out of more than the concern to avoid censorship. The philosophy of praxis conveys and summarizes Gramsci's distinctive interpretation of Marxism. As we shall see, the second part of the writings contained in Part III of the SPN consists of a prolonged critique of what Gramsci considered to be a deterministic or mechanistic version of Marxism, as contained in the book written by the Russian Bolshevik Nikolai Bukharin, published in English translation under the title of *Historical Materialism*, with the subtitle *A System of Sociology* (Bukharin 1925). Gramsci refers to this book as the *saggio popolare*, popular essay. His extensive critique of this book uses it as the target against which to develop his own view of a much more activist Marxism, which takes its inspiration from Marx's *Theses on Feuerbach*, in particular the third thesis. This third thesis criticizes a one-sided materialist doctrine (such as put forward by the English 'utopian' socialist Robert Owen) which holds that human beings are determined by their environment. Owen, for example, believed that changing the environment in which workers laboured in his factories would change the nature of those workers and induce in them more altruistic attitudes of cooperation and association rather than selfish and ignorant motives. The third of Marx's *Theses on Feuerbach* takes issue with such one-sided materialism, asserting that 'the materialist doctrine concerning the changing of circumstances and upbringing forgets that circumstances are changed by men and that it is essential to educate the educator himself'. This could only be achieved through a process of human activity or self-changing, through 'revolutionary praxis'. *Umwaelzende Praxis* is the phrase used in the original German – translated by Gramsci as *rovesciamento della praxis* in his own translation of the *Theses on Feuerbach*. The third thesis on Feuerbach ends with this sentence: 'The coincidence of the changing of circumstances and of human activity or self-changing can be conceived and rationally understood only as *revolutionary practice* [*umwaelzende Praxis*]' (Marx 1973a, 422, emphasis in the original). The implication is clear: human beings are not determined in a mechanistic or passive way by their environment, but through their own activity (self-activity) they change that environment, and in so doing change themselves.

This perspective is in many ways the key to Gramsci's own understanding and development of Marxism, as expressed by his use of this term the philosophy of praxis. Marxism could not, or should not, be reduced to a sociology, by which Gramsci meant a positivistic search for laws which operated regardless of human will and consciousness, determining human activity. In his perspective, it was through coming to self-awareness and achieving a critical consciousness of the world and their place in it that human beings would be able to change society. This process, necessarily a very complex and protracted one, was what was meant by praxis. Thus his use of the term the philosophy of praxis to describe Marxism was not just, or even primarily, a coded term to fool the censor, but expressed ideas fundamental to his philosophy and political theory, and these ideas are expounded in the sections of the *Quaderni* (*Notebooks*) contained in this Part III of the SPN.

It is worth pointing out, in seeking to place these sections in the context of the *Notebooks* as a whole, that most of the extracts in Part III of the SPN come from two of the special notebooks in which Gramsci assembled and rewrote many of the notes contained in earlier notebooks, where they appeared as the A texts. The notes in the first chapter of Part III of the SPN ('The Study of Philosophy') come primarily from Notebook 10, written in the years 1932 to 1935, which contains two parts to which Gramsci gave the title 'The Philosophy of B. Croce'. The fact that he gave so much attention to criticizing the thought of Croce is highly significant for the ideas expounded in the *Prison Notebooks*. In Chapter 4 we have seen how Gramsci's views on history and politics were developed in opposition to Croce's presentation of the history of Europe since 1815 and of Italy since 1871, and more generally in critique of Croce's presentation of 'the religion of liberty' as the dominant theme of modern European history. Gramsci's *Prison Notebooks* are in many ways a kind of critical dialogue with the ideas of Croce, seen as the dominant figure of European liberal thought, a kind of 'lay Pope' as Gramsci himself described Croce in a letter to his sister-in-law Tatiana of 7 September 1931, referred to in our Chapter 2 above: 'Ben. Croce, for example, is a sort of lay pope and he is a very effective instrument of hegemony even if from time to time he comes into conflict with this or that government, etc.' (LP2, 67).

These extracts, taken primarily from Notebook 10 in which Gramsci had assembled his critique of Croce (and there are many notes scattered through the *Notebooks* quoting and criticizing Croce), suggest another crucial way in which Gramsci developed his ideas through criticizing opposing perspectives. If Bukharin's deterministic and mechanistic brand of Marxism was one target to be criticized, then equally Croce's idealism and his kind of historicism were also objects of Gramsci's criticism and provided a foil through which his own brand of Marxist historicism was to be expounded. At the risk of some simplification, we can therefore see this section of the *Prison Notebooks* (SPN Part III, 'The Philosophy of Praxis') as showing Gramsci developing his original version of Marxism in opposition to two very different philosophies. The first is that of Croce's speculative idealism and his view of history. Gramsci was also opposing what he thought was Croce's misrepresentation of Marxism (or the philosophy of praxis), which Croce presented as being nothing more than a crude materialism. The second was Bukharin and his, in Gramsci's view, reduction of Marxism to positivist sociology. Through combating these two antagonists, Croce and Bukharin – corresponding to idealism and materialism, if one can put it in those simple terms – Gramsci developed a distinctive view of philosophy in general and of Marxism in particular, albeit in sometimes cryptic terms and allusive language forced on him by the circumstances of imprisonment.

Of the thirty-two extracts from the *Notebooks* contained in the first chapter ('The Study of Philosophy') of Part III of the SPN, fifteen are from Notebook 10 entitled 'The Philosophy of Benedetto Croce', while eight are from Notebook 11, also one of the special notebooks written between 1932 and 1933, with the title (this time not given by Gramsci but by the editor of the 1975 complete edition, Valentino Gerratana) 'Introduction to the Study of Philosophy'. It is this Notebook 11 which contains the final and fullest version of Gramsci's critique of Bukharin's ideas as contained in *Historical Materialism* or the 'popular essay' (*saggio popolare*) as Gramsci usually refers to it. So it is not surprising that the editors of the SPN took the overwhelming majority of the extracts in the second chapter of Part III ('Problems of Marxism') from Notebook 11, which provides twenty-nine of the forty extracts contained in that chapter. But we can start our exposition with the first of the extracts in the first chapter ('The Study of Philosophy') of Part III of SPN. This is a long extract from Notebook 11, and these twenty pages in the SPN (323–43) contain a wealth of ideas in which Gramsci expounds his conception of philosophy and his interpretation of Marxism as a philosophy of praxis representing the culmination of modern thought.

WHAT IS PHILOSOPHY?

One of the central points in this section is the assertion which Gramsci makes that in an important sense philosophy is not the preserve of an intellectual elite, or limited to the speculations of professional philosophers. His argument is that 'everyone is a philosopher' (SPN 323; Q11, §12, 1375), since all people have a conception of the world and express this in their action, even if their conception of the world may be incoherent and implicit rather than systematic and explicit. This is what Gramsci calls the 'spontaneous philosophy' which is 'proper to everybody', in so far as all human beings are thinking beings who exercise intellectual activity and to that extent are themselves philosophers. This spontaneous philosophy, according to Gramsci, has three components. The first is language, seen by him as 'a totality of determined notions and concepts and not just of words grammatically devoid of content'. Yet everyday philosophy, if we can call it that, is also contained in what he calls common sense and good sense, the former representing ideas commonly held in the society at large, if in an unreflective and uncritical sense, whereas good sense seems to be for him a more refined and reflective or critical consciousness, almost a higher stage of common sense in which the assumptions and preconceptions of common sense have been assessed and perhaps rejected in the light of a critical self-consciousness. Good sense may thus be the result of a process of education in which the philosophy of the philosophers has infiltrated and refined the beliefs commonly accepted in society at large. As we shall see, the task of Marxism (philosophy of praxis) was in Gramsci's view to engage with common sense and connect with popular beliefs so that out of those popular beliefs would emerge a deeper critical consciousness. The third element of spontaneous philosophy is what Gramsci calls folklore, as exemplified in popular religion and the popular beliefs and superstitions, though this does not seem very different from what he called common sense, also referring to relatively incoherent or unreflective beliefs held by people at large.

If, according to Gramsci, everyone is a philosopher and carries with them a body of notions expressed through language, common sense and popular religion and other unreflective beliefs, this body of thought is often incoherent and contradictory. As human beings, members of society, we uncritically absorb the values and beliefs of the particular social group to which we belong, and in that sense carry with us a mass of often contradictory ideas, some of them, as Gramsci said, 'prejudices from all past phases of history' which coexist with more modern ideas and 'intuitions of a future philosophy which will be that of a human race united the world over'. Popular philosophy is thus unsystematic and unreflective, contradictory and based on the prejudices of particular social groups, and in many cases on the values of dominant or superior social groups. This of course engages with the master theme of hegemony. Gramsci writes of a group (and it is clear he is here referring to subordinate groups, primarily that of the working class) having two competing conceptions of the world, one expressed in action, if only in an episodic and spasmodic way ('occasionally and in flashes'), the other expressed in words, but this is a set of beliefs taken over from a dominant group. In 'normal times' a subordinate group takes over the beliefs 'borrowed from another group', and this is a sign of 'submission and intellectual subordination', since the working class (to make this explicit) is accepting a worldview which is not essentially its own (SPN 327; Q11, §12, 1379). This is one aspect of hegemony, to which the philosophy of praxis can provide a challenge.

Gramsci's conception of the task of philosophy is that it educates and transforms common sense and is the means through which a new culture and *Weltanschauung* (view of the world) is transmitted to the mass of the people, and this is an essential part of the revolutionary transformation of society. There are a number of assumptions here which need careful probing. Gramsci argued that philosophy could not be divorced from politics, and that the philosophy of the philosophers (of the leading intellectuals) should not be divorced from the philosophy of the broad masses of society. It is interesting that Gramsci makes several points of comparison between Marxism, the philosophy of praxis on the one hand, and religion, in particular the practice of the Catholic Church, on the other. The Catholic Church, he argues, was always concerned to avoid a divorce or separation between the intellectuals and the 'simple', the broad masses (SPN 328; Q11, §12, 1381). In his view, Marxism was the movement of thought and practice which could achieve this link between refined philosophy and the common sense of the masses in ways which idealist philosophy, such as that of Croce, could not do. Gramsci writes that 'one of the greatest weaknesses of immanentist philosophies in general consists precisely in the fact that they have not been able to create an ideological unity between the bottom and the top, between the "simple" and the intellectuals' (SPN 329; Q11, §12, 1381). The term 'immanentism' is one which needs explaining in its own right (see further on in this chapter), but here it is clear that Gramsci is talking about Croce and philosophers in the idealist tradition who, at least in Gramsci's view, did not aim to develop their philosophy in contact with the broad masses of society. It was only Marxism that could function as the educator of society in the widest sense, to refine common sense and raise the unreflective ideas of the hitherto subaltern groups to a higher level, in other words to achieve and diffuse a new culture. This would be a task, he wrote, 'far more important and "original" than the discovery by some philosophical "genius" of a truth which remains the property of small groups of intellectuals' (SPN 325; Q11, §12, 1378). Only in that way could philosophy 'purify itself of intellectualistic elements of an individual character and become "life"' (SPN 330; Q11, §12, 1382). So philosophy, on this view, could not but be 'political', since 'the relation between common sense and the upper level of philosophy is assured by "politics"' (SPN331; Q11, §12, 1383).

One obvious comment on this is that Gramsci has a very expansive conception of philosophy, seen as a process of imparting intellectual order, refinement and coherence to the mass of beliefs held in a particular society (common sense). Philosophy is not seen by him as a specialized activity carried on by professional philosophers (the intellectuals), or at least if it is, then that activity has to engage with the beliefs and practices of the broad masses of the population (the simple, as Gramsci calls them, in reference to the attempts by the Catholic Church to avoid any divorce between these two groups). Philosophy cannot be divorced from everyday life, and has to be understood as a constant project to develop and raise the level of coherence of common sense: 'philosophy is criticism and the superseding of religion and "common sense"'. This raises a number of problems, when applied to the conditions of contemporary (i.e. twenty-first-century) society. One could say that the development of philosophy (and of academic work in general) has been in the opposite direction from that envisaged by Gramsci, in other words in ever more specialized fields which have little contact with the broad masses, or little concern with refining or developing the concerns of common sense.

Gramsci takes a quite different view of what philosophy is, or should be. Every person is a philosopher in giving expression to a distinctive view of the world, however incoherently or crudely that might be done. Specialized or professional philosophers are no different from the rest of humanity, in that they carry on the activity of philosophizing which is what all people as thinking beings do. The specialized or professional philosopher does this with more coherence and logicality than the average person in the street, and has an awareness of the history of thought and of philosophy which enables such a professional philosopher to situate contemporary developments in the context of previous attempts by philosophers to address the same problem. Gramsci's view of philosophy was that it should not be seen as the practice of individuals in a closed intellectual circle seeking to attain some esoteric truths reserved for a restricted group of great thinkers. Philosophy as he conceived it was 'above all ... a cultural battle to transform the popular "mentality" and to diffuse the philosophical innovations which demonstrate themselves to be "historically true" to the extent that they become concretely – i.e. historically and socially – universal' (SPN 348; Q10 II, §44, 1330). Interestingly Gramsci invokes a new type of philosopher, whom he called the 'democratic philosopher'. Such a philosopher would be convinced that his personality was in 'an active social relationship of modification of the cultural environment' (SPN 350; Q10 II, §44, 1332). This 'democratic philosopher' could only thrive in conditions of freedom of thought and of expression, so that Gramsci thought that these liberal and democratic freedoms provided the necessary conditions for a new type of philosopher to emerge.

MARXISM AS POPULAR PHILOSOPHY

Gramsci's argument in the *Prison Notebooks* is really twofold. First, that it is only Marxism or the philosophy of praxis which is equipped theoretically and practically to carry out this task of linking the philosophy of the philosophers or intellectuals to the concerns and beliefs of the common man and woman. While the Catholic Church historically had tried to do that, its philosophy was unable to cope with modernity and the upsurge of popular forces. Catholicism might, historically, have tried to avoid having one doctrine for the intellectuals and a different one for the simple, but it did not see its task as one of raising the simple to the level of intellectuals. Marxism, on the other hand, was a philosophy and a movement which had such an aim at its heart. The second point is that Gramsci thought that since Marxism envisaged a unity of theory and practice, seeing the two intrinsically linked, the politics of Marxism (and indeed of modernity in general, of which Marxism was the most advanced expression, as we will see below) brought with it the creation of agencies and instruments through which this task of moral and intellectual reform or creation of a new and higher culture could be achieved. The political party was a crucial instrument of political education, in the sense of transmitting the philosophy of praxis to the mass of the population: 'One should stress the importance and significance which, in the modern world, political parties have in the elaboration and diffusion of conceptions of the world.' Gramsci writes of political parties as functioning as laboratories, as elaborating 'new integral and totalitarian intelligentsias', understanding 'totalitarian' in the sense of a total and integral view of the world, one which was appropriate to the conditions of modernity (SPN 335; Q11 §12, 1387). One may ask whether in conditions of contemporary politics, political parties in fact do carry out that educational role, and whether Gramsci's view of the political party as the institution for the unification of theory and practice is sustained in the conditions of contemporary politics. Political parties have long ceased to carry out such educational functions and are rather regarded with suspicion in many contemporary Western democracies as vehicles not so much for the incubation of new intellectual elites but rather as channels for ambitious power-seekers to climb to power. Parties live in a house of power, as Max Weber put it – they are therefore vehicles in the conditions of mass politics in a competitive electoral system for getting out the vote, but it is clear that Gramsci saw the political party as much more than this, as one of the key institutions for educating its members and in that way spreading a new culture. The party, as we have seen in Chapter 5 above, was the modern Prince which would provide the leadership in conditions of modern mass politics. So we can summarize Gramsci's ideas here as suggesting that unlike the theory and practice of Catholicism, Marxism was the only body of thought in contemporary times which could 'construct an intellectual–moral bloc which can make politically possible the intellectual progress of the mass and not only of small intellectual groups' (SPN 332; Q11 §12, 1385). It could achieve this through the (Marxist) political party which would not only 'recruit individuals out of the working mass', presumably to be the new leaders, but would 'raise the intellectual level of ever-growing strata of the populace' (SPN 340; Q11, §12, 1392).

Does this mean that Gramsci thought that Marxist philosophy would be or was the *only* system of thought that would be able to achieve this aim of educating the masses? If so, does this imply a system of thought that is unable to accept any pluralism of ideas, and so has dangerous monolithic tendencies? It certainly seems that Gramsci thought that the philosophy of praxis was a truly modern body of thought, representing the summation of all previous philosophy. Further on in Part III of the SPN comes an extract from a different notebook from the ones previously quoted, namely Notebook 16, also one of the special notebooks, this one written in 1933–34, given the title by Gramsci 'Argumenti di cultura 1', 'Arguments of Culture 1'. Paragraph 9 of this notebook has the rubric 'Some Problems in the Study of the Development of the Philosophy of Praxis', and in this long note Gramsci developed the idea that Marxism was the modern equivalent to the (Protestant) Reformation. He argued that 'the Lutheran Reformation and Calvinism created a vast national-popular movement through which their influence spread' (SPN 394; Q16, §9, 1859). Gramsci makes use of a comparison between Renaissance and Reformation, an antithesis used by Croce. Croce had suggested that the Renaissance was a movement of intellectual elites which did not penetrate into mass consciousness. Renaissance intellectuals like Erasmus were theoretically innovative but their ideas remained restricted to a narrow circle of humanists and cultivated individuals. The Reformation, by contrast, presumably because of such innovations as the translation of the Bible into the vernacular language, was a historical movement which *did* involve the mass of the people. Croce quotes Erasmus as saying that this popular implantation came at the expense of intellectual development: 'wherever Lutheranism reigns, there is the death of letters'. For his part Gramsci suggests that out of the Protestant Reformation was born the German nation, 'as one of the most vigorous in modern Europe' (SPN 394; Q16, §9, 1859).

However, the crucial point is that for Gramsci the philosophy of praxis was in a sense the combination of Renaissance and Reformation, and indeed the culmination of all modern thought. It combined intellectual innovation and new ideas (like the Renaissance) with popular appeal (like the Reformation), and was a philosophy which involved the creation of a new *Weltanschauung* that was distinctively modern and secular. It was thus superior to all its rivals, notably to modern liberalism of which Croce was the most sophisticated representative and innovator. Gramsci sees Marxism as a total philosophy or view of the world which has the advantage over its competitors not just of being a synthesis or transcendence of previous philosophies, but being the view of the world most in tune with modernity, as an analysis of modern society and also as the worldview which can raise the educational level of the masses. So we could say not just that Gramsci has an expansive view of philosophy, but also a similarly broad view of Marxism as the summation of previous philosophies and as the vehicle for spreading a new culture throughout society to educate the broad mass of the population. This was in contrast to philosophies such as that of Croce, whose liberalism was a restricted movement unconcerned with making itself life by contact with the broad masses. Notebook 4 contains the first of Gramsci's four 'Notes on Philosophy' ('Appunti di filosofia'), with this first set of notes on philosophy headed 'Materialism and Idealism', thus indicating the twin targets of Gramsci's critique, namely a deterministic one-sided materialism, on the one hand, and Crocean idealism on the other. In paragraph 3 of this Notebook 4, which has the rubric 'Two Aspects of Marxism', Gramsci wrote that 'modern philosophy is a continuation of the Renaissance and of the advanced phase of the Reformation, but its methods are those of the Renaissance; they are bereft of the popular incubation of the Reformation, which created the solid foundations of the modern state in the Protestant nations' (QE2, 142; Q4, §3, 423). By modern philosophy Gramsci means here the philosophy of liberalism, as exemplified by Croce, which had failed, or not even tried, to educate or transform the consciousness of the mass of the population. Historical materialism, on the other hand, at least in the form in which Gramsci envisaged it, 'corresponds to the Reformation + French Revolution, universalism + politics' (QE2, 142; Q4, §3, 424), so that it could achieve the popular implantation which modern philosophy in the form of contemporary liberalism never could.

None of this is meant to suggest that Gramsci thought, to put it crudely, that Marxism had all the answers, that it was a creed which could explain simplistically all aspects of modern life. Nevertheless, there is a sentence in Notebook 11, paragraph 12, which suggests, in a cryptic form, Gramsci's belief that the philosophy of praxis would be able to win mass adherence because it was a philosophy adequate to explain the problems of the age. He writes that 'mass adhesion or non-adhesion to an ideology is the real critical test of the rationality and historicity of modes of thinking', stating that 'constructions which respond to the demands of a complex organic period of history always impose themselves and prevail in the end', even if such constructions passed through intermediary phases and expressed themselves 'in more or less bizarre and heterogeneous combinations' (SPN 341; Q11, §12, 1393). Gramsci's totalistic view of Marxism is certainly at odds with contemporary scepticism towards 'grand narratives'. His view that it would be a philosophical event of great significance if a mass of people could 'be led to think coherently and in the same coherent fashion about the real present world' (SPN 325; Q11, §12, 1378) rests on certain assumptions that a common worldview is possible and that the evolution of modernity has led to a certain uniformity in conditions of life such that a shared worldview is possible and that such a worldview can make sense of a unified world. Before discussing the problems of such a perspective, it is necessary to explore further Gramsci's views about philosophy in general and Marxism in particular, by exploring notions of historicism and immanentism, since both terms are crucial to understanding the ideas put forward in Part III of the SPN.

HISTORICISM

Part III of the SPN contains several pages of notes, taken primarily from the special Notebooks 15 and 16, in which Gramsci develops his own conception of Marxism, or the philosophy of praxis. One term which he employs frequently is 'historicism', or in Italian *storicismo*, and therefore any understanding of Gramsci's ideas has to involve explanation of what he means by this term. On page 399 of the SPN Gramsci writes of the philosophy of praxis as 'the greatest form of "historicism", total liberation from any form of abstract "ideologism", the real conquest of the historical world, the beginnings of a new civilisation' (SPN 399; Q16, §9, 1864). It is clear that Gramsci thought of Marxism as summing up previous philosophies when he wrote that the philosophy of praxis 'presupposes all this cultural past: Renaissance and Reformation, German philosophy and the French Revolution, Calvinism and English classical economics, secular liberalism and this historicism which is at the root of the whole modern conception of life' (SPN 395; Q16, §9, 1860) and also going beyond them as the worldview which (alone) could make sense of the conditions of life in the modern world.

The concept of historicism originated in German thinkers like Herder, arguing against a particular unilateral or unilinear view of historical progress which they attributed, rightly or wrongly, to the Enlightenment and its theorists. Against a view of history as a straightforward process of liberation from error and the attainment of reason through the sloughing off of error and superstition, historicist thinkers proposed a view of history which suggested that each period of history had its distinctive character and ideas. History therefore could not be seen as uninterrupted progress to truth, but in terms of a succession of different societies each of which had its own value and way of looking at the world. The German philosopher Herder, for example, used a historicist method to suggest that each nation had its distinctive culture, expressed through folk traditions and folklore, each nation therefore through its particular culture having something of value to contribute to world history. In that sense he mocked Enlightenment philosophers like Voltaire who presented French culture of the Enlightenment as being of universal value and the model which all of humanity had to follow (for general discussions of historicism see Beiser 2011 and Morera 1990). For Gramsci, the supreme modern example of historicism was to be found in Hegel who in his *Phenomenology of Spirit* traced out the course of world history, analysing it as the story of 'Spirit', the force of the Idea which objectified itself in a whole series of different societies, each of them marked by internal contradictions, until the final stage of world history had been reached in which the mystical or idealistic force of 'Spirit' recognised itself in the society it had created, and saw that society as the final objectification of the Idea made rational and realized as the final outcome of the whole historical process. For Croce, whom Gramsci saw as the dominant figure of contemporary liberalism, history was a rational process in which the 'religion of liberty' would win out, despite attempts of reactionary regimes (including fascism) to oppose the idea of freedom (Roberts 1987). Historicism therefore, whether in the form of Hegel or Croce, or indeed Herder, was not incompatible with an idea of progress, though in some of its forms this historicist perspective ran the risk of relativism, in the sense that if each period or epoch of history gave rise to a distinctive ideology or worldview which was characteristic of that society, then how could any of those distinctive forms of life be held superior to another, since each of them reflected the customs and practices of that society as it was constituted at that particular moment of history?

Gramsci tells us in the course of his criticism of Bukharin's version of historical materialism, that 'the philosophy of praxis is absolute "historicism", the absolute secularisation and earthliness of thought, an absolute humanism of history. It is along this line that one must trace the thread of the new conception of the world' (SPN 465; Q11, §27, 1437). It is clear that he saw Marxism as a philosophy which 'opens up a completely new road, renewing from head to toe the whole way of conceiving philosophy itself' (SPN 464; Q11, §27, 143). By insisting on the historicity of Marxist thought, Gramsci meant that a Marxist perspective was critical of the very notion of eternal verities and rejected an ahistorical concept of human nature, seen as unvarying throughout all ages of human history. In Notebook 10, Gramsci has a paragraph with the rubric 'Introduction to the Study of Philosophy: What Is Man?', and his answer is to say that 'man is a process and more exactly the process of his actions' (SPN 351; Q10 II, §54, 1343). There is no general concept of human nature, but Gramsci sees human nature as a process, one through which human beings act on the natural world and change themselves and their fellow human beings through their activity. In the SPN, this note from Notebook 10 is (rather confusingly) followed without any break by a passage taken from an entirely different notebook, number 7, which contains the second of Gramsci's 'Notes on Philosophy'. Paragraph 35 of that notebook has the rubric 'Materialism and Historical Materialism', in which Gramsci engages with the assertion of the German philosopher Feuerbach that 'man is what he eats' (*der Mensch ist, was er ißt*). Gramsci rejects, here as elsewhere, the crude materialism which sees human beings as the simple product of their environment, or, in this case, of their food. As he says, one could just as well argue that 'man is his clothing', or 'man is his housing', since these are all important features of social life (SPN 354; Q7, §35, 884). His conclusion is that the most satisfactory answer to the question 'What is man?' is 'that "human nature" is the "complex of social relations"', 'because it includes the idea of becoming (man "becomes", he changes continuously with the changing of social relations) and because it denies "man in general"' (SPN 355; Q7, §35, 885, though in the original Italian there are no parentheses and no inverted commas round 'becomes').

Thus 'historicism' for Gramsci points to the fact that ideas and concepts are transitory, related to a particular social structure. Hence there can be no abstract concept of human nature as something unchanging and eternal. Indeed Gramsci goes so far as to say that 'the nature of man is "history"' (SPN 355; Q7, §35, 885), meaning by that expression that human beings in one sense create themselves and create the world in which they live, but that this is a continuous process dependent on the activity of the human agent. This leads Gramsci to pronounce that 'everything is political, even philosophy or philosophies ... and the only "philosophy" is history in action, that is, life itself' (SPN 357; Q7, §35, 887). Everything is politics because it is through history, and the human activity of politics that constitutes history, that ideas become related or embodied in real life. So to understand human nature, and the political action that turns abstract ideas into reality, we have to see both human nature and politics as historical, produced under definite historical conditions, themselves changing and developing.

However, Gramsci's historicism goes much further than this. What does he mean by calling Marxism 'the greatest form of "historicism"'? Gramsci is suggesting that Marxism is the culmination and transcendence of previous philosophies, and that it itself will eventually be superseded and made redundant through the passage from societies marked by conflict and necessity to a society of freedom where social contradictions will have disappeared. These ideas are extremely important, but need to be explained not just in abstract terms of philosophy but with reference to the somewhat cryptic allusions Gramsci makes to the Marxism of the USSR. Gramsci is suggesting that Marxism itself is the product of certain definite social conditions, it is itself a historical product, reflecting and giving expression to social contradictions, evidently those understood by Gramsci as class antagonisms. The role of Marxism, for Gramsci, is to maintain a dynamic contact with the mass of the population, so that it 'tends continually to raise new strata of the population to a higher cultural life', unlike Catholicism which 'tends to maintain a purely mechanical contact' with the mass of the population (SPN 397; Q16, §9, 1862).

In his critique of Bukharin's philosophy or his version of historical materialism, Gramsci insists that Marxism itself is not exempt from its general statement that all ideas are historically based and in that sense are transient. What Gramsci argues is 'that the philosophy of praxis thinks of itself in a historicist manner, that is, as a transitory phase of philosophical thought' (SPN 404; Q11, §62, 1487). He argues that Marxism was a continuation and at the same time a reform of Hegelianism, in that it saw itself as a historical product, as an expression of social contradictions which would eventually be superseded as humanity progressed from what Marx called the realm of necessity to the realm of freedom. Yet Gramsci argued that this could only be affirmed in general terms: 'At the present time the philosopher – the philosopher of praxis – can only make this generic affirmation and can go no further; he cannot escape from the present field of contradictions, he cannot affirm, other than generically, a world without contradictions, without immediately creating a utopia' (SPN 405; Q11, §62, 1488). Since Marxism was the product of a society divided by social contradictions (class antagonisms) and sought to analyse those contradictions, it could only anticipate in a very general way a society free from such antagonisms. It could not analyse such a society since the philosophy of praxis had itself emerged from a class-divided society. Gramsci held to the idea of the transition, as Marx put it, from the realm of necessity to the realm of freedom, but his argument was that the philosophy of praxis itself would then become redundant or superfluous, since it was the product of circumstances that themselves would have ceased to exist. Paragraph 62 of Notebook 11 has the rubric 'Historicity of the Philosophy of Praxis', where Gramsci clearly expresses a historicist attitude emphasizing the transience of any system of thought, including Marxism itself. He writes that 'the philosophy of praxis affirms theoretically that every "truth" believed to be eternal and absolute has had practical origins and has represented a "provisional" value (historicity of every conception of the world and of life)' (SPN 406; Q11, §62, 1489). Yet this provisional character of any system of thought applies equally to Marxism, which itself would be irrelevant in a society which would have realized the ideals held out by that philosophy of praxis. The philosophy of praxis would cease to be appropriate in a society free from social contradictions, and clearly Gramsci thought that such a prospect was conceivable, though not as a result of a mechanistic and inevitable process of history. He conceded that such an interpretation of the provisional nature of Marxism was difficult for its proponents to accept, since it seemed to undermine beliefs in the scientific nature of Marxism. Gramsci wrote that it was 'very difficult' to make people accept that the provisional nature of all belief systems 'is valid also for the philosophy of praxis itself, without in so doing shaking the convictions that are necessary for action'. But his warning should be taken seriously, when he suggested that 'even the philosophy of praxis tends to become an ideology in the worst sense of the word, that is to say a dogmatic system of eternal and absolute truths' (SPN 407; Q11, §62, 1489). It is hard to avoid the thought that here Gramsci was referring in a cryptic way to the dogmatization of Soviet Marxism, all the more so since the sentence just quoted is followed by a critical sentence referring to Bukharin's 'popular essay'. Gramsci states that in that text 'Marxism is confused with vulgar materialism, with its metaphysics of "matter" which is necessarily eternal and absolute' (SPN 406–7; Q11, §62, 1489).

The implication of this historicism seems clear. All systems of thought and political ideas are transient, created by and bound by the conditions of the society in which they originate. In a literary form one could see this illustrated by the words which Goethe puts into the mouth of Mephistopheles in *Faust*: 'denn alles, was entsteht, ist wert, daß es zugrunde geht' ('everything that is created is fit to be destroyed'). Marxism itself, while offering the fullest theorization of this process through which ideas and philosophies are created, is not immune from this interpretation. Gramsci holds on to the notion of the achievement of a society free from deep social antagonisms (class conflict), a society which could be called the reign of freedom, though as he points out, again showing the lack of dogmatism and of determinism which characterizes his analysis, 'the proposition about the passage from the reign of necessity to that of freedom must be analysed and elaborated with subtlety and delicacy' (SPN 406; Q11, §62, 1489). He envisages that 'the whole system of the philosophy of praxis may fall away in a unified world', suggesting here too the temporal limitations of Marxism. 'Unified world' is a way of suggesting a classless society, seen as the goal to be achieved, and in such a society Gramsci suggests that 'many idealist concepts, or at least certain aspects of them which are utopian during the reign of necessity, could become "truth" after the passage' (SPN 407; Q11, §62, 1490). So Marxism itself as an analysis of society would lose its relevance, but Gramsci proposes that the ideals which it holds out ('many idealist conceptions'), which could not be achieved in a class-divided society, might become realized ('truth') once that society had been overthrown.

In his study of *Gramsci's Historicism*, Esteve Morera usefully distinguishes between four meanings of the term, after noting that Gramsci 'consciously attempts to define the term in opposition to speculative thought and to abstract rationalism' (Morera 1990, 35). The four meanings or uses of historicism in Gramsci which Morera distinguishes start with the idea of historicism as transience – institutions and ideas (including, as we have seen, Marxism) are not eternal verities, but have validity only for a distinct period of history, and are destined to be superseded. The implication is that any study of ideas or institutions has to investigate the historical conditions under which those ideas and institutions developed, and the circumstances or developments which led to the supersession of those same ideas and institutions. Historicism also, according to Morera, involves some concept of historical necessity: some ideas and social phenomena necessarily develop in particular historical circumstances. Gramsci's view of Marxism seems to be that it is a necessary philosophy, necessary in the sense that it could not but develop on a particular terrain of history, since Marxism makes sense of the world as it is, and is in accord with the development of history, at least for a particular period of time. Third, again following Morera's analysis, Gramsci's form of historicism was realist, in that 'his historicist realism, as a guiding principle for historical research, consists in the injunction to explain history on the basis of historical phenomena and historical necessity and that none of this has a transcendent, religious or speculative meaning' (Morera 1990, 53). The final aspect of historicism distinguished by Morera is one of historicism as humanism, the idea that it is human agency and human will which are the crucial factors in historical development. Certainly in the last two respects Gramsci's historicism is clearly distinguished from what he sees as the speculative version of historicism presented by Croce. Yet the problem arises of how this emphasis on human will and agency can be reconciled with the realism entailed by concepts of historical necessity and the determining economic structure of a particular society, so that one of the fundamental themes of the *Prison Notebooks* is Gramsci's interrogations and intellectual wrestling with problems of base and superstructure, and the ways in which the historical movement arises on the basis of a particular economic foundation.

BASE, SUPERSTRUCTURE, HISTORICAL BLOC

The extracts from the *Prison Notebooks* assembled in the first chapter of Part III of the SPN under the heading 'The Study of Philosophy' thus show Gramsci's concept of philosophy as an activity carried on by all human beings, exemplified in the common sense of a particular society. The task of philosophy in the more technical sense (as carried out by specialized intellectuals) is to raise the level of such common sense, to change people's consciousness so that they attain a critical conception of the world, thinking for themselves. Gramsci evidently thinks that what he calls the philosophy of praxis, or Marxism, is the only philosophy or body of thought which, in the conditions of modernity, can achieve this task of linking intellectuals with the simple, in ways which neither religion (notably Catholicism) nor liberalism (in the form of Crocean idealism – analysed further in the section below) could manage. In that sense Marxism was not only up to the task, so to speak, but could provide an analysis of the features of contemporary society and spread to the mass of the people (the working class) a truthful perspective on social reality. It was thus, or could become, the 'religion of modern man', to borrow the title of Frosini's recent study of Gramsci's thought (Frosini 2010). However, much of Gramsci's writing in the *Prison Notebooks* was concerned to transform or develop Marxism and to combat what he saw as the distortion of Marxism in the direction of a vulgar or simplistic materialism. Such a one-sided picture of Marxism (reducing it to a positivist sociology based on a crude materialism) was what Gramsci saw exemplified in Bukharin's text *Historical Materialism,* and much of the second chapter of Part III of SPN, given the heading 'Problems of Marxism', is composed of extracts from Notebook 11, 'Introduzione alla filosofia' ('Introduction to Philosophy'). This notebook starts with a number of paragraphs given the general title 'Appunti e riferimenti di carattere storico-critico' ('Notes and References of a Historical-Critical Nature'); this section takes up eleven paragraphs, and is then followed by a general heading, 'Appunti per una introduzione e un avviamento allo studio della filosofia e della storia della cultura' ('Notes for a Preface and Introduction to the Study of Philosophy and to the History of Culture'), itself a very general heading. This heading is then followed by material divided into two sections, the first one 'Alcuni punti preliminari di riferimento' ('Some Preliminary Reference Points'), is composed of the long paragraph in which Gramsci presents his views on philosophy and common sense. This paragraph has already been analysed above (it constitutes the first extract in chapter 1 of Part III of SPN). Notebook 11 then continues with a second part, headed 'Observations and Critical Notes on an Attempted "Popular Essay of Sociology"', and this takes up a large part of the notebook (paragraphs 13–35), which in turn constitutes the bulk of the chapter on 'Problems of Marxism' in SPN (pages 419–70 are mainly extracts from this part of Notebook 11, one of the special notebooks).

The fact that Gramsci devoted a large section of one of the special notebooks to criticizing Bukharin's ideas shows how important to him was the project, though never explicitly stated as such, of reformulating historical materialism. Gramsci was concerned to do this through the critique of what he saw as a distortion of Marxism, all the more significant because written by one of the leading Bolsheviks, Nicolai Bukharin. Bukharin was to fall victim to the Stalinist purges and was executed after a show trial in 1938 (the year after Gramsci's own death), after having opposed Stalin's policy of rapid industrialization and forced collectivization of the peasantry (S. Cohen 1974). Bukharin had proposed the continuation of the New Economic Policy and a policy of 'riding to socialism on the peasant's nag', and certainly in his prison cell Gramsci was aware of the conflicts in the USSR which opposed Stalin's breakneck industrialization policy to Bukharin's more pro-peasant line. However, the critique in the *Prison Notebooks* of Bukharin's text

Historical Materialism takes a different line. It is in the course of criticizing Bukharin's presentation of Marxism that Gramsci developed a much more complex theory of the relationship between base and superstructure, and thus contributed an original analysis of one of the fundamental problems within Marxism as a theory of society. Through the critique of Bukharin Gramsci develops a distinctive approach to Marxism which makes it a much more subtle and defensible theory of society than the very deterministic, mechanistic Marxism exemplified in Bukharin's book, always referred to by Gramsci as the 'popular essay', *saggio popolare*, presumably as another coded way of putting the censor off the scent. For the same reason, as noted by the editors of SPN (SPN 419), Bukharin is never mentioned by name, but always just called 'the author'.

The crucial point on which Gramsci focuses his critique of Bukharin is stated as follows: 'This fundamental point is not dealt with: how does the historical movement arise on the structural base?' (SPN 431; Q11, §22, 1422). In an earlier (A text) formulation in Notebook 4, paragraph 38, Gramsci has a rubric to this paragraph which reads 'Relationships of Structure and Superstructures' ('Rapporti tra struttura e superstrutture'), and states that 'this is the crucial problem of historical materialism, in my view' (QE2, 177; Q4, §38, 455). It is interesting to note the use of the plural for the term 'superstructures.' The later version of this topic comes in Notebook 13, where it is phrased rather differently, in terms of 'relations of force': paragraph 17 has the rubric 'Analysis of Situations: Relations of Force', after which Gramsci goes on to say 'It is the problem of the relations between structure and super-structure which must be accurately posed and resolved if the forces which are active in the history of a particular period are to be correctly analysed, and the relation between them determined' (SPN 177; Q13, §17, 1578). The relationship between 'base' and 'superstructure' is one of the fundamental problems of Marxism, stemming from Marx's famous preface to *A Contribution to the Critique of Political Economy*. This text of 1859, along with the *Theses on Feuerbach*, were texts which Gramsci himself translated, and his translations of those texts are included as an appendix to the third volume of the Gerratana edition of the *Quaderni* (Q3, pp. 2355–60) and are now in the *edizione nazionale* in the four volumes of the *Notebooks* given over to Gramsci's translations. Evidently these two texts of Marx were fundamental for Gramsci and for his interpretation of Marxism (as indeed they have been for any discussion of Marxism ever since – see G. Cohen 1978). In this preface, Marx announced what he called 'the guiding principle of my studies', his 'general conclusion', which was that 'in the social production of their existence men enter into definite relations, which are independent of their will, namely relations of production appropriate to a given stage in the development of their material forces of production'. And the crucial sentence is the following one, where Marx wrote that 'the totality of these relations of production constitutes the economic structure of society, the real foundation, on which arises a legal and political superstructure and to which correspond definite forms of social consciousness' (Marx 1973a, 424–28). The economic structure of society is thus the base, while forms of consciousness are part of the superstructure.

The recent study of Gramsci's thought by Giuseppe Cospito argues that in the course of writing the *Prison Notebooks*, the rhythm of thought (*ritmo del pensiero*) exhibited in those notes led Gramsci to move away from this 'architectural' model of base and superstructure to develop a quite different concept of the relationship between these two elements (Cospito 2011a, 19–76). Certainly some versions of the Marxism of the Second International (the association of Marxist social-democratic parties, dominated by the German SPD, formed in 1889 and which collapsed with the outbreak of war in 1914) took a very deterministic or economistic perspective on this relationship. Ideas and forms of consciousness were seen as mere epiphenomena, determined mechanistically by the economic base of society, thus devaluing the role of ideas and indeed of human will and consciousness, and hence of political initiative, in social and political change. This was the problem with which Gramsci was wrestling throughout the *Prison Notebooks*, as expressed by his fundamental question: 'how does the historical movement arise on the structural base?' Indeed, in the paragraph earlier referred to (§38 of Notebook 4), immediately following the rubric 'Relationships between Structure and Superstructures', Gramsci wrote, as we have seen, that 'this problem is the crucial problem of historical materialism, in my view'. He followed this sentence by referring to two sentences from Marx's 1859 Preface to *A Contribution to the Critique of Political Economy*. The first of these was the sentence in which Marx wrote that 'no social order is ever destroyed before all the productive forces for which it is sufficient have been developed' and the second was that 'mankind thus inevitably sets itself only such tasks as it is able to solve, since closer examination will always show that the problem itself arises only when the material conditions for its solution are already present or at least in the course of formation' (Marx 1973a, 426). Gramsci, writing from memory, inverted the order of those two sentences, citing the second one first in these words: 'the principle that "no society sets itself tasks for the accomplishment of which the necessary and sufficient conditions do not already exist"'. He followed this up with a citation from memory of the other Marx sentence, writing it as '"no society perishes until it has first developed all the forms of life implicit in its internal relations"', after which he added the words '(check the exact wording of these principles)' (QE2, 177; Q4, §38, 455).

These sentences are quoted again in Notebook 11, paragraph 22, in which Gramsci noted that only on the basis of those sentences could 'all mechanism and every trace of the superstitiously "miraculous" be eliminated'. That was the only way in which to pose 'the problem of active political groups' and also 'in the last analysis, even the problem of the historical function of great personalities', in Gramsci's words (SPN 432; Q11, §22, 1422). If then he thought that the relationship between base and superstructure was the crucial problem of historical materialism, how did he approach this problem? It is certainly one of the key themes which run through the *Prison Notebooks*. Gramsci could be called a Marxist of the superstructure, in the sense that he sees culture and ideas, and political activity, not in terms of being simplistically determined by the economic base or structure of society, but as factors which have their own crucial importance and cannot simplistically be explained merely as reflections of the economic base. He uses the concept of the historic bloc as a way of departing from the simplistic architectural metaphor of base and superstructure, which carries with it the implication that the economic structure of society is the fundamental factor in comparison with which other elements, such as culture, ideas, political action, are secondary and of less significance. A paragraph in Notebook 8, the third in the series of 'Appunti di filosofia', which appears at SPN 366, has the heading 'Structure and Superstructure', and this paragraph uses the concept of historical bloc (*blocco storico*). Gramsci writes that 'structures and superstructures form an "historical bloc"', followed by the statement that 'the complex, contradictory and discordant *ensemble* of the superstructures is the reflection of the *ensemble* of the social relations of production'. The paragraph in the *Quaderni* (and in SPN) ends by invoking 'the necessary reciprocity between structure and superstructure, a reciprocity which is nothing other than the real dialectical process' (SPN 366; Q8, §182, 1051). One could thus interpret this by suggesting that Gramsci was protesting against a variety of Marxism which underplayed the role of ideas and of culture. He saw Marxism as a moment of modern culture, and in his critique of Croce (see page 242 below) he denied that the philosophy of praxis paid no attention to ethical-political history, as Croce charged. So ideas and forms of consciousness have effectiveness in their own right and cannot be seen as less significant than the economic structure of society. Ideologies have thus an independent validity and strength, as is made clear by a paragraph from an earlier notebook, number 7, paragraph 21, this time from the second series of 'Appunti di filosofia'. Gramsci here again uses the concept of 'historical bloc' (*blocco storico*) 'in which precisely material forces are the content and ideologies are the form', though Gramsci immediately adds that the distinction between form and content is a purely formal or didactic one: 'the material forces would be inconceivable historically without form and the ideologies would be individual fancies without the material forces' (SPN 377; Q7, §21, 869).

A historical bloc thus seems to be for Gramsci a totality in which the economic structure and the ideas of a society organized on such an economic base mutually reinforce and influence each other. In the contemporary world (ours) of neo-liberalism, to give a present-day example, the economic structure of a globalized world of free markets and global flows of money and trade constitute the content or basic structure on which arise ideologies of globalization and a particular concept of freedom as freedom of trade and consumption, with the state generally seen as a potential enemy of these forces. Yet those ideologies themselves, as exemplified in and practised by powerful institutions such as the World Bank and the International Monetary Fund, often assisted by national governments, react on the economic base and themselves sustain it, by giving legitimacy to practices and economic structures which are seen as normal or natural (Steger 2005). Such ideologies present the world of global free markets as the inescapable structure to which all states have to conform. The ideologies have a causal influence in their own right. This interaction or mutual interdependence between base and superstructure is what is meant by a historic bloc, and the idea has been developed by contemporary international-relations (IR) theorists like Robert Cox who seek to apply Gramscian concepts to the international world of today (further discussed in the concluding chapter below).

Gramsci's own approach was to use this idea of the historic bloc as a way of developing a perspective on the problem of base and superstructure which undermined a mechanistic and fatalistic view of Marxism. He wrote that the idea that every movement of ideas or culture could be seen as a direct result of changes in the material base (economic structure of society) was a myth or infantile delusion. The concept of historical bloc occurs again in Gramsci's Notebook 10 on Croce, analysing the ideas of common sense and good sense, when Gramsci answers his own question of 'What is man?' by stating that 'man is to be conceived as an historical bloc of purely individual and subjective elements and of mass and objective or material elements with which the individual is in an active relationship' (SPN 360; §10 II, §48, 1338). Evidently Gramsci wants to develop historical materialism (Marxism) in ways which give heightened significance to superstructural factors – forms of consciousness and an activist view of humanity. This leaves open the idea that it is through political action in the broadest sense that human beings would or could become controllers of their destiny, not just beings determined by an economic structure which they cannot control. Gramsci uses the term catharsis to suggest the transition from a society where people are dominated by the economic structure and are thus passive to a situation where new forms of culture and society could be created.

This again involves the concept of a movement from necessity to freedom, to a situation where 'structure ceases to be an external force which crushes man, assimilates him to itself and makes him passive' (SPN 367; Q10 II, §6, 1244). This is reminiscent of the words of another Marxist, Trotsky, for whom generally Gramsci has harsh words, seeing him as the practitioner of a war of manoeuvre inappropriate to the complex superstructures of modern liberal democracy (this was discussed in Chapter 5 above). Trotsky wrote that 'as long as man is not yet master of his social organisation, that organisation towers above him like Fate itself' (Trotsky, *Literature and Revolution*, quoted in Deutscher 1959, 193). But how did Gramsci envisage this happening? Clearly it was through the creation of a new culture and through political activity in which the party (the modern Prince) played a crucial role.

Leaving aside the role of the party (discussed earlier), how was this new culture to be created? Gramsci is arguing against a view which sees the economic structure of society and its evolution as determining social changes, irrespective of the actions of human beings and independently of their ideas and forms of consciousness. He regarded the view that changes in the economic base would automatically lead to transformations in the superstructure, in the realm of ideas, as a form of vulgar or mechanist Marxism, a characteristic typical of a subaltern or subordinate class that hoped for its salvation through the fatalistic unfolding of forces over which it had no control. Marxism was the set of new ideas, a total philosophy, which in Gramsci's view would create a new culture through which hitherto subordinate groups (the working class – and other subordinate groups like the peasantry) would be able to construct a new society. The philosophy of praxis thus had two tasks, to be carried out by the new organic intellectuals that the movement would create. The first task was 'to combat modern ideologies in their most refined form, in order to be able to constitute its own group of independent intellectuals'. The second task was 'to educate the popular masses, whose culture was medieval' (SPN 392; Q16, §9, 1858). These ideas are contained in the section headed 'The Philosophy of Praxis and Modern Culture' (SPN 388–99), which is taken from paragraph 9 of Notebook 16 ('Argomenti di cultura 1'), and Gramsci gave as the rubric for this paragraph 'Some Problems for the Study of the Development of the Philosophy of Praxis'. Here Gramsci is not so much criticizing Bukharin as trying to explain how Marxism has influenced other currents of modern culture which have tried to absorb or integrate aspects of Marxism. Gramsci's concern was that in its focus on the second task, that of educating the masses, Marxist intellectuals had failed to develop the philosophy of praxis adequately, even though 'the new philosophy was born precisely to supersede the highest cultural manifestation of the age, classical German philosophy, and to create a group of intellectuals specific to the new social group whose conception of the world it was' (SPN 393; Q16, §9, 1858). In his critique of Croce, which we come to next, Gramsci tried to show how Marxist thought could take on the most prominent intellectual of the day (which was how he saw the figure of the Italian liberal thinker Benedetto Croce) and develop a totalistic view of the world which was not only intellectually superior to that of the idealist liberalism of Croce but also popular, able to inspire the broad masses of society and give them a worldview enabling them to grasp the complex world of modernity.

Some critical remarks may be in order here. How do Gramsci's views on Marxism look from the perspective of the early twenty-first century? Part of the problem is that what Gramsci called the philosophy of praxis or Marxism has lost its capacity to inspire popular action and to be a broad philosophy for the mass of people. This is for several reasons. The first is that it remains associated with the history of the Soviet Union, where it was realized (or the attempt was made to practise it) in conditions of material poverty and cultural backwardness. This meant that, in Gramscian terms, the philosophy of praxis, at least in that Russian or Soviet context, never rose above the economic-corporate level and was unable to offer the flowering of culture and analysis of modernity that Gramsci wanted that philosophy to offer. There are references, again rather cryptic, to this in Part III of the SPN. On page 397 Gramsci shows his awareness of some of the problems encountered by Marxism in the attempt to become a total philosophy of modern culture. Continuing his references to Renaissance and Reformation, and the unwillingness of Renaissance intellectuals like Erasmus to associate with popular culture and with the

Reformation, Gramsci observed that 'something similar has happened up to now with the philosophy of praxis. The great intellectuals formed on the terrain of this philosophy, besides being few in number, were not linked with the people, but were the expression of traditional intermediary classes, to which they returned at the great "turning points" of history' (SPN 397; Q16, §9, 1862). With reference to the USSR, Gramsci notes that 'only after the creation of the new State does the cultural problem impose itself in all its complexity and tend towards a coherent solution' (SPN 398; Q16, §9, 1862). The 'new State' here (although in the original Italian the text says only 'creation of the State', '*Solo dopo la creazione dello Stato* ... ') refers to the Soviet Union, but whatever solution was present in that context was limited by the development of the economic base through Stalin's revolution from above. Marxism was never able to develop freely in that new society's superstructures, which in any case were impoverished and stunted by the low level of economic development. The second reason is the control of the superstructure in Western societies by cultural forces and powerful institutions which paint Marxism and socialist ideas generally in the blackest of colours, and which permit little space for the kind of development of Marxism which Gramsci attempted to carry out from his prison cell. The third reason is the fundamental problem of agency, the fragmentation of society which renders much more problematic the formation of the *uomo collettivo* (collective man) and the totalistic philosophy which Gramsci saw as part of the development of the society of his own time (these issues are taken up again in the concluding chapter below).

THE CRITIQUE OF CROCE

In order to understand the *Prison Notebooks*, it is necessary to see them in part as a critique of, or even dialogue with, the ideas of the Italian philosopher Benedetto Croce. Notebook 10 is entitled 'La filosofia di Benedetto Croce', and consists of two parts, which deal mostly (though not exclusively) with analysis of and criticism of Croce's ideas. Several sections of this Notebook 10 appear in Part III of SPN, in its first chapter headed 'The Study of

Philosophy', but it should be noted that the most substantial translation of sections of Notebook 10 and Gramsci's critique of Croce is to be found in Derek Boothman's edition of *Further Selections from the Prison Notebooks* (FSPN), so that reference will be made to the paragraphs in that edition, as well as to the full Italian edition of Notebook 10. Indeed references to Croce abound throughout the *Quaderni*, not just in the special notebook (Notebook 10) in which Gramsci revised and extended many of the A texts which had appeared in earlier notebooks. Notebook 10 also contains many B texts, notes and paragraphs which appeared for the first time in that notebook, as original notes which were not revisions of earlier notes and which were not crossed out and revised to reappear as C texts elsewhere in the *Quaderni*. Croce's ideas were also discussed in other sections of the *Notebooks*, in particular with reference to Croce's historical writings, and some of the relevant material here appears in the chapter of SPN entitled 'Notes on Italian History'. The final pages of that section (partly discussed in Chapter 4 above) contain Gramsci's critical thoughts on Croce's historical work, his *History of Europe* and his *History of Italy*, but in this present chapter we return to those pages in the context of a fuller discussion of the critical dialogue between Gramsci and Croce.

In order to understand more clearly the intellectual dialogue which Gramsci carried on with the ideas of Croce throughout many of the pages of the *Prison Notebooks*, it is helpful to complement reference to the *Notebooks* with some important letters which Gramsci wrote to his sister-in-law Tania in 1932. These letters, as Vacca points out, are 'richer' (in intellectual content) than what Vacca calls the 'very schematic' notes of Notebook 10 (Vacca 2012, 203). The four letters (of 18 and 25 April and 2 and 9 May 1932) express in a rather clearer form the way in which Gramsci recognized the importance of Croce and at the same time wanted to show the differences between Croce's historicism (his idea of 'ethical-political history') and the view of history presented by Marxism. In his letter of 18 April 1932 Gramsci noted that 'Croce has a lofty concept of his position as a leader of world culture' (Gramsci uses the English word 'leader' in his letter, *'il Croce ha un alto concetto di questa sua posizione di* leader *della cultura mondiale'* (LP2, 164, emphasis added). Gramsci noted in a further letter, that of 25 April 1932, that the influence of Croce's writings stemmed partly from the clarity of his literary style, and from his 'serenity', the conviction that 'history is in essence rational' (*la storia è razionalità*). What is interesting is that Gramsci noted that through his numerous short articles written 'without pedantry' Croce's ideas were absorbed into 'good sense or common sense', since 'to many people Croce's thought does not present itself as a philosophical system, massive and as such difficult to assimilate'. In that way his thought infiltrated itself into the newspapers and into everyday life, so that there were many Croceans expressing his ideas who possibly did not even know that Croce existed (LP2, 166–67). It is hard to avoid the idea that this was what Gramsci wanted Marxism to be, at least at one level: a sort of common sense which addressed concrete problems of everyday life and did not present itself as a complex or refined philosophical system. Indeed, one recent study of *Gramsci and the History of Dialectical Thought* (Finocchiaro 1988) suggests that while Gramsci criticized Croce's presentation of Marxism, Gramsci himself practised a Crocean style of criticism. Croce interpreted religion in a broad sense, as an ethical system which presented norms of conduct and a way of life. For Croce modern civilization was one in which human beings could find norms of conduct in non-religious (in the narrower sense) ways, in a secular morality which could guide them on how to live. Finocchiaro in his study suggests that for Gramsci Marxism could be a religion exactly in that secular sense, and therefore that despite his criticism of Croce's ideas Gramsci was practising a distinctly Crocean line of thought. Finocchiaro suggests that 'his (Gramsci's) criticism of Croce is in part a defence of him', since Gramsci was implicitly using Croce's style of criticism to defend a view of Marxism as a new kind of (secular) religion.

One other crucial point which emerges very clearly from these letters of 1932 is that Gramsci recognized the importance of Croce as pointing to the idea of hegemony and the significance of ideas and culture as maintaining a particular form of society. Yet Croce's view of history, his concept of ethical-political history was in Gramsci's view too one-sided, it gave too much importance to the moment of hegemony. In a letter to Tania of 2 May 1932 Gramsci wrote that 'we can concretely say that Croce, in his historic-political activity, makes the stress fall exclusively on that moment in politics that is called the moment of "hegemony", of consensus, of cultural direction, to distinguish it from the moment of force, of coercion, of legislative, governmental, or police intervention' (LP2, 169). Croce as the leader of a form of revisionism of Marxism sought to liquidate the philosophy of praxis. But, using another English phrase, Gramsci wrote that it seemed to him that 'Croce is not "*up-to-date*" on the research and bibliography of his favourite studies or has lost his capacity to be critically oriented' (LP2, 169). One could say, in more colloquial terms, that Gramsci thought Croce had 'lost the plot' as far as Marxism was concerned, since 'precisely during the same period in which Croce was shaping this self-styled cudgel of his, the philosophy of praxis, in its greatest modern theorists, was being elaborated in the same direction and the moment of "hegemony" or cultural direction was precisely being re-evaluated in opposition to the mechanistic and fatalistic concepts of economism' (LP2, 169). This letter gives the gist of the ideas which appear in Notebook 10 of the *Quaderni*: Croce was right in pointing to 'that moment in politics that is called the moment of "hegemony"' but where Croce went wrong was in putting the emphasis solely on that 'moment', and also in not keeping 'up to date' with developments in Marxism that showed that the philosophy of praxis had the capacity to grasp that aspect or moment of political domination.

One further point emerges from these 'Croce letters' of 1932. Tania had sent Gramsci a copy of Croce's *History of Europe*, on the pretext that she was writing a review of the book and wanted Gramsci's help in giving her some points of orientation for her work. In reality she had sent him this book on the suggestion of Gramsci's friend the economist Piero Sraffa who wanted to give Gramsci a focus for his intellectual activity, and draw his mind away from his personal and familial preoccupations. From the letter of 9 May 1932 it emerges that although Tania had sent Gramsci Croce's book, it had been withheld from him in his prison cell. As he wrote to Tania in that letter, for each book which had been sent to him, in order to have access to it he had to write a letter of application to the fascist prison administration, which was, as he wrote, 'absurd besides being tedious'. But giving his views to Tania all the same, he suggested that Croce claimed 'that it was his intention to free modern thought from any and all traces of transcendence, of theology, and thus of metaphysics in the traditional sense' (LP2, 171). However, in Gramsci's view Croce had not succeeded in this, and his (Croce's) view of history remained purely speculative. It was not the case that a genuinely ethical-political history was incompatible with historical materialism: 'Ethico-political history is not excluded from historical materialism since it is the history of the "hegemonic" moment, whereas "speculative" history as well as all "speculative" philosophy are excluded' (LP2, 171). So it was only the philosophy of praxis that could claim to be genuinely free from any transcendence, since it was 'absolute historicism, really and not just in words freed from all transcendental and theological residues' (LP2, 171).

Why did Gramsci spend so much intellectual effort in this critical dialogue with Croce? His engagement with Croce's ideas should be understood not just as an intellectual exercise but as a profoundly political task, as part of the struggle for hegemony. This critique was necessary because Croce symbolized for Gramsci the most eminent representative of contemporary European liberal culture. Critique of his ideas was needed if Marxism or the philosophy of praxis could show its superiority as a worldview over liberalism. While Croce's views were historicist, in a sense to be explained, they represented for Gramsci an idealist or abstract historicism, seeing history as the process of development of Spirit and the realization of what Croce called 'the religion of liberty'. Gramsci saw Croce's philosophy as indeed a modern philosophy, combating religion, and opposed to a transcendental view of values as stemming from extra-human agency (i.e. from the power of God). But Croce's rejection of transcendentalism did not go far enough, and represented an attempt to denigrate the philosophy of praxis by characterizing it as a form of economic materialism or historical materialism which did not grasp the importance of culture and of ideas. Gramsci wanted to criticize Croce's ideas as such, but was also concerned to show that Croce offered a distorted view of Marxism. Croce then in certain respects was not the Olympian figure of the disinterested philosopher dealing with eternal ideas, but was in part an ideologist of the existing order. In a note which opens Notebook 10, a kind of jotting down of key points of his proposed 'essay on B. Croce', Gramsci wrote as the second point: 'Croce as intellectual leader of the revisionist tendencies of the 1890s: Bernstein in Germany, Sorel in France, the economic-juridical school in Italy' (FSPN 328; Q10 I, introd., 1207). So the criticism of Croce on the part of Gramsci was an intensely *political* critique: Croce represented the most sophisticated and intellectually impressive ideas which had to be combated if Marxism were to establish itself as the philosophy of the age, and create its own stratum of organic intellectuals. Yet this criticism, as Gramsci put it, was not a crude denigration which put the views of Croce (or any other philosophy to be opposed) on trial. In Gramsci's words, 'In the formulation of historico-critical problems it is wrong to conceive of scientific discussion as a process at law in which there is an accused and a public prosecutor whose professional duty it is to demonstrate that the accused is guilty and has to be put out of circulation.' Gramsci states in this same paragraph that in the context of scientific discussion, as compared with a court of law, 'since it is assumed that the purpose of discussion is the pursuit of truth and the progress of science, the person who shows himself most "advanced" is the one who takes up the point of view that his adversary may well be expressing a need which should be incorporated, if only as a subordinate aspect, in his own construction' (SPN 343–44; Q10 II, §24, 1263). The implication was that Croce's views (and other philosophies too) had to be critically superseded and incorporated in the philosophy of praxis which could present a different and intellectually superior form of historicism and critique of transcendence. Gramsci insisted that 'to understand and to evaluate realistically one's adversary's position and his reasons (and sometimes one's adversary is the whole of past thought) means precisely to be liberated from the prison of ideologies in the bad sense of the word – that of blind ideological fanaticism' (SPN 344; Q10 II, §24, 1263). These seem important words: Gramsci was perhaps differentiating himself, implicitly, from Bolshevik-style condemnation of liberalism and 'bourgeois thought' seen as 'bourgeois ideology' to be 'liquidated' by the superior truth of Marxism–Leninism. It was not a question of 'blind ideological fanaticism' which was something which had to be avoided, but of understanding the body of thought in question and seeing the truths it contained, which could be reframed in other ways by the philosophy of praxis.

So the critique of Croce was not just an intellectual exercise in ideas, but a task of political significance, in line with Gramsci's ideas that philosophy could not be separated from politics. Certainly Gramsci saw him as, in his (Gramsci's) words, 'intellectual *leader* of revisionist currents at the end of the 19th century' (FSPN 335; Q10 I, §2, 1213), with the word 'leader' again appearing in English in the original Italian. Croce was a figure not just of Italian significance but one of the leading intellectuals in European thought at the end of the nineteenth century and up to his death in 1952. His work covers an enormous range, dealing with aesthetics, historiography, literary criticism, political and moral philosophy as well as historical works, notably (at least from the point of view of those works discussed in the *Quaderni*) his *History of Europe in the Nineteenth Century* and his *History of Italy 1871–1915*. For Croce, history was the story of liberty, of the triumph of the religion of liberty, seen as an idea or manifestation of Spirit. Just to give some of the flavour of Croce's approach to history, at the risk of oversimplifying a complex philosophy, it is worth quoting from his *History of Europe*. This work ends up with an invocation of the religion of liberty, and has an epilogue where Croce condemned communism, which had not solved 'the fundamental problem of human relations, which is that of liberty, in which alone human society flourishes and bears fruit, the only reason for the life of man on the earth and without which life would not be worth living' (Croce 1934, 357). The first chapter of Croce's book is indeed called 'The Religion of Liberty', where Croce outlines his philosophy of history, which is a Hegelian view of history as the realization of freedom. In the modern period, wrote Croce, 'no longer did history appear destitute of spirituality and abandoned to blind forces, or sustained and constantly directed by alien forces. Now it was seen to be the work and the activity of the spirit, and so, since spirit is liberty, the work of liberty. It was all the work of liberty, its unique and eternal positive moment' (Croce 1934, 9). In a sentence which is Hegelian but could also be seen as one which Gramsci could endorse, Croce wrote that 'the philosophy of an age must not be sought only among its philosophers or even its great philosophers, but must instead be dug out of all the manifestations of that age' (Croce 1934, 9). Croce saw the liberal idea as a religion, as offering norms of conduct and guiding principles. History was the history of liberty, with liberty affirming itself against various enemies, among which Croce numbered democracy. For him democrats 'postulated a religion of quantity', in contrast to liberals who adhered to 'a religion of quality, of activity, of spirituality', opposing what Croce called 'the horror of democratic and Jacobin revolution with its spasmodic and bloody convulsions' (Croce 1934, 32), a judgement in marked contrast to Gramsci's much more positive view of Jacobinism as having linked up city and country in a revolutionary movement. For Croce another enemy of liberalism was Romanticism, which he saw as an alternative religion to that of liberalism, in the Crocean sense of religion as a way of life and norms of conduct. Romanticism sentimentalized the past, and according to Croce distorted the principle of nationality by pushing it into a racist form. Presumably Croce was thinking of philosophers like Fichte who saw nationalism as associated with language and common descent rather than the political nationalism of the Italian Risorgimento, which Croce described in his *History of Europe* as 'the masterpiece of the liberal-national movements of the nineteenth century' (Croce 1934, 225).

However, Croce's view of history, certainly as presented in his *History of Europe in the Nineteenth Century*, was one of the ultimate triumph of liberalism against its various opponents. In one sense Croce's view of liberalism seems to be similar to that of Gramsci's view of Marxism: just as Gramsci saw the philosophy of praxis as the summation and transcendence of other schools of thought, Croce saw liberalism as being able to absorb its challengers and rise superior to them. He wrote of 'the inevitable necessity and the virtue of the liberal idea, which is capable of attracting and bending to its own ends men and institutions that it should only have wished to cast down' (Croce 1934, 131). Croce cannot really be accused of blind optimism or complacency, but he firmly asserted the final victory of liberalism over its successive opponents in the course of history – absolutism, Catholicism, democracy, socialism, communism and indeed fascism. The epilogue to his *History of Europe* referred in a rather cryptic way to the 'activist' challenge to liberalism, seeing the genesis of activism as 'morbid romanticism', and making a hostile reference to futurism. His remarks on the mood of Europe before 1914 showed awareness of the irrational dark forces which threatened liberalism: 'Warfare, bloodshed, slaughter, harshness, cruelty, were no longer objects of deprecation and repugnance and opprobrium, but were regarded as necessities for the ends to be achieved, and as acceptable and desirable' (Croce 1934, 341). However, the core idea of what Croce called his 'history inspired by the liberal idea' was that the religion of liberty could survive these enemies and win out in the end.

It was partly through working out his criticism of Croce that Gramsci arrived at a clearer exposition of his own ideas, all the more so as according to his own admission he had been very much influenced by Croce's philosophy. In paragraph 11 of part 1 of Notebook 10 Gramsci alludes to one of his own pre-*Prison Notebook* writings in which he criticized Croce's essay on 'Religione e serenità' (this essay appears in Croce 1994, 29–32). Looking back on that essay Gramsci admitted that at that time he was unclear about the concept of the unity of theory and practice, or of the unity between philosophy and politics. He attributed this lack of clarity to the fact that 'I was tendentially somewhat Crocean' (FSPN 355; Q10 I, §11, 1233). But in that page of his *Notebooks* he reaffirmed the core idea of his earlier essay, which was that the philosophy of Croce was the basis for a renewal (*una ripresa*) of the philosophy of praxis for Gramsci's time, for his generation. Gramsci thus saw Crocean idealism as something which provided the stimulus for Marxism, which Marxism had to incorporate but also transcend. On the positive side, Gramsci attributed some important features to Croce's philosophy, which were to be taken up by the philosophy of praxis. Croce's thought had an instrumental value because 'it has forcefully drawn attention to the study of the factors of culture and ideas as elements of political domination, to the function of great intellectuals in state life, to the moment of hegemony and of consensus as the necessary form of the concrete historical bloc' (FSPN 332; Q10 I, introd., 1211). While in other places in the *Prison Notebooks* Gramsci attributed the importance of the concept of hegemony to Lenin, here he is crediting Croce with pointing to the importance of intellectuals and of ideas and culture as crucial aspects of political power and hegemony. This recognition goes along with the criticism that Croce's view of history was too idealistic and that Croce misunderstood Marxism or historical materialism. Gramsci insists that Croce's theory of ethical-political history (history as the victory of liberty and the progress of Spirit) was speculative history rather than genuine history, which was what Marxism could offer. Nevertheless, Gramsci attributes to Croce the recognition of the importance of ideas in historical change, and later on in the same Notebook Gramsci insisted that 'Croce's historiographical conception of history as ethico-political history must not be judged as futile, as something to be rejected out of hand' (FSPN 357; Q10 I, §12, 1234). Indeed Gramsci argued that just as Marxism had taken from Hegel the idea of history as a rational process but had seen this process not in purely speculative terms as the story of Spirit realizing itself, so Marxism in the contemporary form of the philosophy of praxis had to carry out the same operation on Croce's philosophy, keeping what was of value in it (the emphasis on ideas and on culture as elements of political domination) but rejecting the way in which Croce saw this as purely an intellectual process. Gramsci could be said to be giving credit to Croce for his opposition to economism and comparing him in an elliptical way to Lenin, because immediately after affirming that Croce's emphasis on cultural factors in the historical process was very significant, Gramsci wrote that

> in the same period as Croce, the greatest modern theoretician of the philosophy of praxis has – on the terrain of political organisation and struggle and with political terminology – in opposition to the various tendencies of 'economism', reappraised the front of cultural struggle and constructed the doctrine of hegemony as a complement to the theory of the state-as-force and as a contemporary form of the 1848 doctrine of 'permanent revolution'.
>
> (FSPN 357; Q10 I, §12, 1235)

The reference in the last sentence of the quote to 'the greatest modern theoretician of the philosophy of praxis' must be taken as a reference to Lenin, seen here together with Croce as the critic of economism and the kind of mechanistic Marxism which Gramsci saw exemplified in Bukharin's *Historical Materialism*. Thus Croce's view of history, albeit in a purely speculative form, was of instrumental value in properly assessing what in Marxist terms could be called superstructural factors, in seeing political power as not resting purely on force, but on consensus achieved through the power of ideas.

At the beginning of his Notebook 10 Gramsci listed some of the reasons for Croce's popularity, and singled out Croce's style of writing, and his lack of pedantry and scholasticism. Gramsci presents Croce's philosophy as one which is the expression of 'sound common sense' (*del commune buon senso*) (FSPN 338; Q10 I, §4, 1217) and which engages with the problems which are thrown up by the very process of historical development. So Croce's philosophy appealed more, according to Gramsci, to the Anglo-Saxon countries, since it appeared not in terms of a great and jumbled-up system of thought, but in the form of essays which seemed to be the expression of common sense, oriented to particular problems posed by the course of historical development. So the other positive side of Croce's philosophy, according to Gramsci's critical analysis, is its focus on particular practical ethical problems, destroying traditional prejudices. Thus Gramsci seems to value Croce's theory of history for offering a critique of transcendence, in other words rejecting a view of history which sees it as following God's will. In that sense Croce was offering an 'immanent' view of historical development, even though that immanence was presented in terms of the history of ideas, of what Croce called ethical-political history.

If Croce represented the highest point of liberal and idealist thought, it remained for Gramsci the object of criticism as well as of recognition for having drawn attention to the importance of culture and philosophy in the historical process. In the *Prison Notebooks* Gramsci insisted that Croce's understanding of Marxism was distorted; after expressing initial sympathy for Marxism Croce had reverted to a simplistic view of it as purely a form of economic materialism or even determinism. Gramsci insisted that the philosophy of praxis was in no way guilty of underplaying the significance of ideas or cultural factors. Gramsci expressed this in a very clear sentence: 'The philosophy of praxis does not exclude ethico-political history' (FSPN 329; Q10 I, introd., 1208). Marxism evidently was a form of historicism that was realistic, that gave due attention to factors of culture but saw them as related to particular forms of society and to the economic foundations of those forms of society. Croce did indeed offer a historicist perspective, but Gramsci makes the distinction between 'speculative historicism and realist historicism' (*storicismo speculativo e storicismo realistico*) (FSPN 330; Q10 I, introd., 1208). Croce's historicism was speculative, as Gramsci says: 'history becomes a formal history, a history of concepts, and in the last analysis a history of the intellectuals, rather an autobiographical history of Croce's thought, a history of those who have an exaggerated view of their own importance'. In that way Croce was guilty of the opposite mistake to that perpetrated by Bukharin's mechanistic Marxism: 'Croce is falling into a new and strange form of "idealistic" sociologism, no less quaint and no less inconclusive than positivist sociologism' (FSPN 370; Q10 II, §1, 1241).

Gramsci criticized what he saw as Croce's failure to properly understand Marxism. Gramsci argued that Croce was in a way obsessed by historical materialism, in the sense that Croce's own philosophy was not free of the influence of Marxism, yet Croce himself devalued Marxism by presenting it as nothing but a canon of historical research drawing attention to the significance of material factors in history. So at one and the same time Croce was reducing Marxism to a kind of economism, while simultaneously using Marxism to make his own philosophy less speculative and more rooted in reality. Croce was less an Olympian figure standing above the struggles of contemporary history, and more of an ideologist, who sought to deny Marxism the status of a complete philosophy while at the same time using Marxism in his own philosophy, seeking to absorb it and almost emasculate it by failing to understand its superior grasp of the historical process. One of the clearest expressions of Gramsci's critique is in paragraph 8 of part 1 of Notebook 10, whose first sentence reads

'Transcendence–theology–speculation', Gramsci recognized the efforts of Croce to link philosophy to real life, and to struggle against any idea of transcendence, at least in a religious form. But Gramsci insisted that Croce's philosophy remained a speculative one. Croce saw history as a rational process, which was the story of Spirit realizing the goals of the religion of liberty. The philosophy of praxis, on the other hand, was in Gramsci's words 'the historicist conception of reality, liberated from any residue of transcendence and theology even in their latest speculative incarnation; idealist Crocean historicism is still at the theological speculative stage' (FSPN 348; Q10 I, §8, 1225).

Gramsci's criticisms of Croce are complex and manifold. The importance which the thought of Croce had for him can be gauged from the fact that in the first part of Notebook 10 Gramsci suggested that, faced with Croce's furious critique of Marxism, there should be carried out an intellectual reckoning: there should be an *Anti-Croce*, which would have the same significance for the present generation (Gramsci's own) that Engels's massive statement of Marxist philosophy, *Anti-Dühring*, had had for the pre-First World War generation – and that it would be 'worth the trouble of a whole group of people dedicating ten years of their life to a work of this type' (FSPN 356; Q10 I, §11, 1234). Gramsci was of the view that the philosophy of praxis could supersede liberalism in its most sophisticated and up-to-date form, as represented by Croce. Marxism was not, as Croce maintained, merely a useful indicator pointing to the importance of material factors in history. Nor was the philosophy of praxis blind to the significance of spiritual or ideal factors in history, the ones which Croce's concept of ethical-political history highlighted. The philosophy of praxis indeed absorbed or took over from Croce's theory of history a number of elements, as Gramsci noted in paragraph 13 of the first part of Notebook 10 where he listed the 'elements of ethico-political history in the philosophy of praxis'. These elements were the 'concept of hegemony, reappraisal of the philosophical front, systematic study of the function of intellectuals in historical and state life, doctrine of the political party as the vanguard of every progressive historical movement'. Croce was playing an ideological role in seeking to portray Marxism as just a form of economism: 'In his reduction of the philosophy of praxis to an empirical canon of historical inter-pretation, by which the attention of historians is drawn to the importance of economic factors, Croce has done nothing other than reduce it to a form of "economism"' (FSPN 358; Q10 I, §13, 1235–36). Croce was also in error in presenting the Marxist idea of economic structure as a 'hidden God' which explained in an abstract fashion the course of history as depending on that one factor alone. Gramsci argues that Croce's view of history was too one-sided and idealistic, and therefore fundamentally not a truly historical theory, only a speculative one. The Gramscian concept of historical bloc offered a much richer way of understanding history. This sentence expresses the idea clearly: 'Ethico-political history, in so far as it is divorced from the concept of historical bloc, in which there is a concrete correspondence of socio-economic content to ethico-political form in the reconstruction of the various historical periods, is nothing more than a polemical presentation of more or less interesting philosophical propositions, but it is not history' (FSPN 360; Q10 I, §13, 1237). In other words, Gramsci argued that Marxist historiography could apply the insights of Croce's historicism, but purge that philosophy of its speculative and transcendent aspects, and develop a true study of history on the terrain of absolute humanism and based on real factors in history, not just a succession of concepts.

IMMANENCE AND TRANSCENDENCE

Another concept which is crucial to understanding Gramsci's ideas on philosophy and on Marxism, as developed in these paragraphs from the *Quaderni* extracted in Part III of SPN, is the idea of immanence. As Frosini says in his study of the *Prison Notebooks*, the significance given to the concept of immanence is unusual in Marxist thought, and he notes 'the exceptional nature of Gramsci's interest in this concept' (Frosini 2010, 116). Gramsci's use of the idea of immanence has to be explained, according to Frosini, in terms of the 'eccentric orbit which Gramsci underwent in his formation', and his engagement with the ideas of Croce and Croce's criticism of Hegel, and also Gramsci's critique of Gentile. But what did Gramsci understand by immanence, and how can the idea be clarified?

One important paragraph in the Notebooks appears in the 'Croce' notebook as paragraph 9 of the second part of that notebook, and in SPN on page 399. The rubric which Gramsci gives to this paragraph is 'Introduction to the Study of Philosophy: Speculative Immanence and Historicist or Realistic Immanence' (SPN 399; Q10 II, §9, 1246). It can be said that in general immanence suggests an approach to history which sees historical developments as in some sense emerging out of factors present in society as currently constructed. When Marx wrote of the coming of socialist society as emerging from the womb of the existing society, this involved the idea of a future society as immanent in the present one, rather than (as the utopian socialists envisaged) a future associative society being an abstract intellectual construction spun out of thought and held out as desirable just as an ideal. In the Marxist perspective, there were elements in the existing (capitalist) society which were laying the basis for a future (socialist) society, which was in that sense immanent in its predecessor. The growing cohesion of the working class, as envisaged in classical Marxism, was one such feature, in which the development of capitalist society was laying the basis for the agency, and hence for the emergence, of an entirely different social formation which could transcend or supersede the previous one. The emergence of a new social order was thus immanent in the old one. For his part Gramsci in his pre-prison writings used the concept of immanence as a way of explaining the historic process. In June 1918 he wrote that 'I thus conceive of history as immanent necessity, which is justified in culture, in economic forms, in the modes of human sociability [convivenza] determined by the development of the past' (quoted in Frosini 2010, 120). Human beings would come to develop consciousness of this historical process, so that in that way human activity would help bring about the ends immanent in the existing society. Frosini, to follow him again, suggests this idea brings about a 'short-circuit between presupposition or precondition and result' (Frosini 2010, 121), meaning that the concept of immanence does not refer to scientific laws which operate irrespective of human will and action, but refers to a concept of social reality of which human beings become aware, and in such awareness they come to actualize and bring to fulfilment the potentialities contained in the existing social order. They thus realize, in the sense of making real, the possibilities of the presently existing society.

In the *Prison Notebooks*, in the paragraph under discussion in which Gramsci opposed 'speculative immanence' to 'historicist or realist immanence', these ideas are given clearer exposition. Gramsci's analysis starts from the affirmation made by Lenin that Marxism brought together the three great strands of modern thought and action, French politics (post-French Revolution), English political economy, and German idealistic philosophy. Gramsci also frequently refers to Engels's statement, at the end of Engels's essay on 'Ludwig Feuerbach and the End of Classical German Philosophy', that 'the German working-class movement is the inheritor of German classical philosophy' (Engels 1970, 376). Engels meant by that sentence that what was presented in abstract philosophical form by philosophers like Hegel would be realized in practice by the working-class movement. The idea of the progress of history and the replacement of one form of society by another, as expressed in philosophical form by Hegel in his philosophy of history, was made practical and real through a particular social force, that of the German working-class movement. This agency was thus realizing in a very practical way the tendencies immanent in contemporary reality. For his part Gramsci took the idea of the three elements of Marxism as presented by Lenin (French socialism, English political economy, German idealism) as giving rise, in Marxism, to a distinctly new philosophy which was a synthesis of the three elements, and he wrote that 'the unitary "moment" of synthesis is to be identified in the new concept of immanence, which has been translated from the speculative form, as put forward by classical German philosophy, into a historicist form with the aid of French politics and English classical economics' (SPN 400; Q10 II, §9, 1247). The idea here seems to be that Marxism has in a way brought Hegelian ideas of historical progress down to earth, combining them with the study of the reality of the capitalist economy as analysed by classical economists like Ricardo, so that Gramsci asserts that 'one could say in a sense, I think, that the philosophy of praxis equals Hegel plus David Ricardo' (SPN 400; Q10 II, §9, 1247). He added to this statement a series of questions to be studied, one of which was 'to establish the connection of Ricardo with Hegel and with Robespierre', which seems a strange juxtaposition. What it seems to mean is that for Gramsci Marxism could offer what he called in the next sentence a 'new conception of immanence, freed from all traces of transcendence and of theology' (SPN 402; Q10 II, §9, 1248). Gramsci was suggesting that Marxism could take over the historicist philosophy of Hegel, but was making this real or realistic by combining with it in a new synthesis the study of the workings of the capitalist economy as analysed by economists like Ricardo. In this way immanence became realistic, concerned with observing or analysing the real features of contemporary society and the potentialities to which those features gave rise. Linked to this was the idea of the 'determined market' – *mercato determinato*. Classical political economy claimed to study economic laws, and operated with a concept of *homo economicus*, seeing those laws as the necessary eternal features of any society. Gramsci referred to these laws as 'laws of tendency'. His note here argues that the philosophy of praxis universalized the discoveries of Ricardo, 'extending them in an adequate fashion to the whole of history and thus drawing from them, in an original form, a new conception of the world.' What Marxism had done was to use classical political economy as a constituent part of its own new world view. The way in which it extended Ricardo's discoveries was to historicize those ideas, to see them (and indeed to see the whole formation of economic science) as expressions of 'the development of the bourgeoisie as a "concrete world class" and (of) the subsequent formation of a world market' (SPN 401; Q10 II, §9, 1247).

These rather condensed ideas can be clarified in this way: Gramsci is making the contrast between a kind of immanence that is purely speculative and one that is realistic, concrete, historical and historicist. The former he saw exemplified in the ideas of Croce. Crocean idealism and Marxist historicism were both philosophies of immanentism, in that they were opposed to transcendentalism. Transcendental philosophy was one which viewed history as (for example) the process of God's will, the product of forces outside human action and independent of their will and consciousness. In that sense, as Gramsci himself stated, he had been influenced in his early years and writings by Croce, and the critique of religion which Croce's ideas had unfolded. In a letter (17 August

1931) to his sister-in-law Tania, Gramsci referred to one of his teachers at the University of Turin, Professor Umberto Cosmo, an expert on Dante, and explained how despite some differences in their ideas, the two of them found themselves 'on a common ground': 'we were participating wholly or in part in the movement of moral and intellectual reform initiated in Italy by Benedetto Croce, whose first point was this, that modern man can and must live without religion, revealed, positive, mythological, or whatever else you want to call it'. Gramsci goes on to say in this letter that 'this point seems to me even today the major contribution to world culture made by modern Italian intellectuals. I regard it as a civil achievement that must not be lost' (LP2, 56). So in that respect Crocean philosophy and Marxism were so to speak on the same side, of immanentism as opposed to transcendentalism, of a this-worldly perspective as opposed to some idea of values coming from some external source, external to the human world. It is true that for Croce history was the sphere of Spirit realizing itself. Nevertheless Croce's view of ethico-political history firmly rejected a religious interpretation and saw history as the struggle of human beings to achieve certain ideals, notably those encapsulated in the religion of liberty. As one commentator summarizes what he calls 'Croce's "ethico-political" interpretation of history', 'society advanced via the struggle of intellectuals to realise certain "moral ideals" of mankind' (Bellamy 1987, 90). History was the story through which the idea of liberty was fought for and eventually grasped, in opposition to those forces which sought to repress liberty, which as we have seen ranged from absolutism to democracy and communism.

While these ideas of Croce, like those of Marxism, could come under the heading of immanentism, in the sense that they saw history as a this-worldly or terrestrial process, Gramsci argued that it was only Marxism that could develop immanence in a realistic and totally humanistic way. The laws of the determined market which economists like Ricardo had discovered were (seen from a Marxist perspective) not scientific laws of a deterministic kind, but were laws in a historicist sense. They were valid for a particular kind of society, that of the determined market, 'an environment which is organically alive and interconnected in its movements of development' (SPN 401; Q10 II, §9, 1248). So

Gramsci's views of immanence can perhaps be summed up in a simplified form like this: Croce saw history as an immanent process, but this was presented as the process or progress of an idea, the liberal one. So this view of history, while an immanentist one, remained purely theoretical or speculative, in the sense that it did not engage with the study of the economic features of society, the laws of tendency which Ricardo (among others) had discovered. Marxism, by contrast, was a totalistic philosophy of immanence, but not in a speculative sense – it saw the laws of economics as historicist, as bound up with a particular kind of society which was developing the forces or agency which would lead to its supersession. It was in that way realistic, and that was how Gramsci understood the often-quoted, by him, sentence from Engels about the German proletariat being the heir to German idealist philosophy. The argument here is that there is present in society an active agent which would put into practice the ideals of historic change developed by Hegel and others, and would make philosophy a living force. Gramsci came back to this sentence of Engels on several occasions, one such reference coming in part 2 of Notebook 10 on Croce, in paragraph 31. He quotes Croce's comments on the Engels sentence, in which Croce argued that the relationship of the German proletariat to classical German philosophy was that of an heir 'undertaking work of a different and opposed nature'. Gramsci's view was that this was not the case, since, as he wrote, 'the "heir" continues its predecessor's activity, but does so "in practice" since it has deduced from mere contemplation an active will capable of transforming the world' (FSPN 384–85; Q10 II, §31, 1271). Thus we are led back by Gramsci to the critique of a purely speculative concept of immanence. In opposition to such an abstract concept the passage previously quoted goes on to focus on the practical and transformative nature of the philosophy of praxis, and the way in which the working class is indeed, in a real this-worldly or terrestrial way, the heir to German philosophy: 'the nature of the philosophy of praxis is in particular that of being a mass conception, a mass culture, that of a mass which operates in a unitary fashion, i.e. one that has norms of conduct that are not only universal in idea but "generalised" in social reality' (FSPN 385; Q10 II, §31, 1271). Gramsci accuses Croce of having reversed the step forward made by Marxism: Marxism moved from German idealism to practice, so in that way the movement was from a speculative philosophy to philosophy that was 'concrete and historical' (*concreta e storica*), from theory to practice (or a combination of the two). Croce backtracked – he 'has translated the progressive acquisitions of the philosophy of praxis back into speculative language', though Gramsci was of the view that 'in this retranslation lies the best of his thought' (FSPN 385; Q10 II, §31, 1271).

CRITICAL EVALUATION

What can be said by way of evaluation of these ideas? What can we derive from a reading of these sections of the *Prison Notebooks* from the perspective of twenty-first-century developments both in the realm of philosophy and in terms of changes in the real world? It is clear that Gramsci thought of Marxism as a totalistic philosophy, as a distinctive all-embracing view of the world but one rooted in reality in two ways. First, it was a distinctively modern philosophy which could offer an explanation of social reality and of the contradictions in existing society. In his analysis of Bukharin's ideas, Gramsci agrees with Bukharin that the meaning of immanence is metaphorical, and argues that Marxism uses an old concept (immanence) but applies it in a new way: 'The philosophy of praxis continues the philosophy of immanence but purifies it of all its metaphysical apparatus and brings it onto the concrete terrain of history' (SPN 450; Q11, §28, 1438). Second, it was rooted in reality in that it envisaged a particular agent or agency, that of the working-class movement, which would absorb Marxism and which would be the force, in very realistic and practical terms, for the realization of its ideas. This seems to be the reason why Gramsci refers so frequently to Engels's statement that the German working class is the heir of German philosophy. If philosophy was something that was living, in the sense that it became part of popular culture, there had to be some agency to bring about this union of philosophy and politics. As we have seen, Gramsci took the view that Marxism could become a widespread philosophy, and that it articulated a distinctively new culture. If humanity could live without religion, without any transcendent religious worldview, as Gramsci suggested in his letter of 17 August 1931, quoted above, then Marxism could be the worldview which could grow up on the soil of modernity and become both a mass philosophy and a set of ideas developed by the intellectuals. Gramsci acknowledged that this would be a long and difficult process. The long paragraph which opens up Notebook 11 states that 'critical self-consciousness means, historically and politically, the creation of an elite of intellectuals' and that this process is 'long, difficult, full of contradiction, advances and retreats, dispersals and regroupings, in which the loyalty of the masses is often sorely tried' (SPN 334; Q11, §12, 1386).

It is clear then, if we are to evaluate some of the key ideas in this section of SPN, that Gramsci saw Marxism as providing a broad culture for the masses, and as being a genuinely new moment of modern culture, covering philosophy in the narrow sense but offering a kind of secular religion, or norms of conduct, a set of standards by which people could orient their life. This was not to be understood in any totalitarian sense as imposing a philosophy of life on to people, in the way in which Marxism became a state philosophy or set of dogmas in the Soviet Union. It seems that Gramsci's view was that the philosophy of praxis was a humanistic philosophy which saw progress as coming about through human activity; in that sense it was a philosophy of absolute historicism and earthliness. Marxism or the philosophy of praxis was thus a total philosophy, though not totalitarian in the fascist or Soviet communist sense. This view of the possibility and desirability of a total philosophy has come under attack in recent times. Can a single broad worldview offer such a total perspective, or have knowledge and social interests become fragmented and specialized so that no such total view is possible? Certainly in academic work it seems that knowledge has become much more partial and specialized, so that the acceptance of an all-embracing worldview is seen as impossible and viewed with scepticism. The idea of Marxism coming to be the realistic worldview which penetrates and takes over popular culture seems a remote possibility in the conditions of twenty-first-century politics. Postmodern scepticism towards grand narratives does not have to be accepted without question, indeed it does not have to be accepted at all, but Gramsci's view of the philosophy of praxis as a unified synthesis of previous currents of thought seems problematic in a much more fragmented society. The possibility of a unified body of knowledge which could become a shared common sense which raises the cultural level of society as a whole rests on a view of society at odds with a much more 'liquid' form of modernity (Bauman 2000). It is worth pondering the words of Gramsci in paragraph 31 of Notebook 10, the second part of his notebook on the philosophy of Croce (p. 385 of FSPN), quoted earlier, in which Gramsci wrote that 'the nature of the philosophy of praxis is in particular that of being a mass conception, a mass culture, that of a mass which operates in a unitary fashion, i.e. one that has norms of conduct that are not only universal in idea but "generalised" in social reality' (FSPN 385; Q10 II, 1271). This seems to assume that there is in society a mass operating in such a coherent and cohesive way. In contemporary society, divided by several lines of division – cultural, ethnic, national, gendered – it might be difficult to establish or identify such a mass operating in a unitary fashion.

One may also question whether Gramsci's view that Marxism could be the unified philosophy that creates a new mass culture is feasible or realistic in the contemporary world, for several reasons. Can ideas of Marxism and communism be separated from the experience of the Soviet Union, at least in the popular perception of Soviet communism as an oppressive system in which one worldview was imposed on people through a repressive state? And when Gramsci talks of a mass culture, which is what he thought Marxism could become, is this not optimistic or unrealistic when mass culture as it really exists in contemporary capitalist societies is very much dominated and controlled by media magnates and the possibility of the manipulation of mass culture is facilitated by modern means of communication? This is to echo the point made in Chapter 3 above with respect to Gramsci's view of the creation of organic intellectuals of the working class. As Jerome Karabel argues, it might be more difficult to find the institutional and organizational space for such new organic intellectuals in a world with greater possibilities for the manipulation of mass consciousness and culture (Karabel 1976). Jürgen Habermas's study of *bürgerliche Öffentlichkeit* (*The Structural Transformation of the Public Sphere*, in the English translation) suggests that the emergence of an independent and critical public opinion flourished in the early stages of modernity, with its institutional basis in coffee houses and in bourgeois society (Habermas 1989). Yet his argument seems to be to the effect that that gave way to a much more manipulated public opinion, in which the institutional bases for a critical public opinion became eroded and weakened. This obviously has implications for Gramsci's view of civil society as the terrain on which the creation of a new culture could take place. It also relates to his view of the political party as the vehicle for the formation of new intellectuals and the development of a new overarching culture (that of Marxism) which would become the shared popular philosophy of modern society. If, as suggested above, political parties in contemporary politics are far from performing the functions which Gramsci thought they should perform ('parties are the elaborators of new integral and totalitarian intelligentsias' is what Gramsci writes) (SPN 335; Q11, §12, 1387) then it becomes difficult to see how this new culture represented by Marxism could emerge in a world in which the agency, institutions and economic base for such a new culture are all eroded by the hegemony of market forces, organized on a global scale.

Some of these thoughts are of course possible to accept within the framework of the ideas developed by Gramsci in these sections of the *Prison Notebooks*. We have seen that his criticism of Croce was that the form of immanence which he offered was purely speculative and not free of teleology or transcendence, despite Croce's claims. Marxism offered a form of immanence that was genuinely earthbound and historicist, in other words related to the real conditions of society. If therefore those conditions changed then the philosophy of praxis had to reflect those conditions, and not remain in the realm of speculation. It is clear that Gramsci was rejecting two worldviews which were in a sense rivals to Marxism. The first was a form of Marxism, as exemplified by Bukharin in his text *Historical Materialism*, but this represented a mechanically deterministic Marxism which should, in Gramsci's view, be buried with full honours. It might function as a kind of drug, to give people a belief in the inevitable victory of their socialist cause, but this was a poor substitute for the activist view of the philosophy of praxis and the much more open view of history which Gramsci offered. There is no certainty of victory or possibility of predicting the future. The only form of prediction was a commitment to action, to try and realize a particular outcome, but the only thing that could be predicted, according to Gramsci, was the struggle, not the way in which that struggle between contending classes would develop. This put paid to the idea of Marxism as a science on the model of the natural sciences with the ability to predict the future. The other rival philosophy or view of the world was Crocean liberalism, seen by Croce as a successful attempt to overcome Marxism. But Croce had, according to Gramsci, fundamentally misinterpreted the nature of Marxism and wrongly dismissed it as unable to take account of ideas and culture. Croce had not kept up to date with the recent developments of the philosophy of praxis.

SUGGESTIONS FOR FURTHER READING

The best book on Gramsci's philosophy and the idea of 'the philosophy of praxis' is by Fabio Frosini, *La religione dell'uomo moderno: Politica e verità nei Quaderni del carcere di Antonio Gramsci* (Rome: Carocci, 2010). In English, the same author has a useful article dealing with the analysis of Renaissance and Reformation in the *Notebooks*, which is also relevant to issues discussed in other chapters: 'Reformation, Renaissance and the State: The Hegemonic Fabric of Modern Sovereignty', *Journal of Romance Studies* 12, no. 3 (2012): 63–77. Peter Thomas's book mentioned in the further reading to the previous chapter, *The Gramscian Moment*, is also important for the issues discussed in this chapter. On historicism, Esteve Morera's book, *Gramsci's Historicism: A Realist Interpretation* (London: Routledge, 1990), is useful, and so too is Maurice Finocchiaro's study, *Gramsci and the History of Dialectical Thought* (Cambridge: Cambridge University Press, 1988), though this is heavy going in places. For material on the figure of Croce, who appears so often in the *Notebooks*, there are the book by David Roberts on *Benedetto Croce and the Uses of Historicism* (Berkeley: University of California Press, 1987) and the essays by Richard Bellamy in *Croce, Gramsci, Bobbio and the Italian Political Tradition* (Colchester: ECPR Press, 2014).

7

THE AFTERLIFE AND INFLUENCE OF GRAMSCI'S *PRISON NOTEBOOKS*

This chapter seeks to indicate some of the pathways through which Gramsci's *Prison Notebooks* became established as a classic of twentieth-century political thought, and some of the ways in which discussion of this text has influenced a range of disciplines in the humanities and made it a classic text on a worldwide scale. The discussion has to be somewhat selective, and focuses firstly on debates in Italy and the way in which Gramsci's *Prison Notebooks* became a key point of reference in political debates in post-war Italy. However, the phenomenon worthy of note is the increasingly international interest in Gramsci and in particular in the *Prison Notebooks*, both as a political text and in the context of academic studies. Here our focus is on the phenomenon of what has come to be called neo-Gramscianism, a term which denotes the use of categories and concepts derived from the *Prison Notebooks* in particular fields of academic enquiry, notably (for our present purposes) the fields of IR (international relations) and international political economy (IPE), on the one hand, and cultural studies on the other, understanding cultural studies to include the study of so-called mass culture and the political uses of culture. At least in the United Kingdom, one of the ways in which the *Prison Notebooks* became known to a wider audience was through the publication of the SPN in 1971, which made Gramsci's writings in the prison period more easily available to English-speaking readers. In particular, debates around the phenomenon of Thatcherism, especially through the analysis by the cultural and political theorist Stuart Hall, gave much wider currency to basic Gramscian concepts such as hegemony and common sense. Hall's influential analysis of the impact of Margaret Thatcher as British prime minister, and more particularly of the way in which she articulated and drew political support from a wide strand of popular opinion, drew on Gramscian ideas, and as we shall see developed a line of cultural analysis very influential in the 1980s in the British context.

What follows is therefore necessarily a highly selective account of the impact of the *Prison Notebooks*. The story it tries to tell in short outline is one of the way in which those notebooks written in a fascist cell became a text of global significance, and the very different readings to which that text has been subjected. The final question to be posed is that of the significance of the *Prison Notebooks* now: have they become a classic text in the sense of a document of historical significance, as part of the canon of political and social theory, perhaps at the expense of their political relevance? Can the *Prison Notebooks* help us to make sense of the contemporary world, or is the world of present-day liquid modernity (Bauman 2000) one so far removed from Gramsci's aspiration of creating a collective will that the *Prison Notebooks* remain classic but predominantly the preserve of academic study rather than furnishing material for political debate and analysis of contemporary reality? To adapt the question which Croce asked of Hegel, 'what is living and what is dead' in the thought of Antonio Gramsci as it appears in the *Quaderni*? And has neo-Gramscianism given Gramsci's thought a new lease of life, whether in academic circles or in a broader context?

GRAMSCI AND POST-WAR ITALY

It has to be recalled that at the end of the Second World War, eight years after Gramsci's death in 1937, his name was familiar only within a restricted circle of members of the Italian Communist Party, and of course the *Notebooks* and their existence hardly known at all. It was Palmiro Togliatti, the leader of the Italian Communist Party (known since the dissolution of the Comintern in 1943 as the Partito Comunista Italiano, PCI, and no longer as the PCd'I, Partito Comunista d'Italia), who presided over the first series of publications of the *Notebooks*, in thematic volumes rather than in one complete chronologically arranged edition, which only saw the light of day in 1975 with the publication of the Gerratana edition. The following account relies heavily on the very informative survey of the Gramsci scholar Guido Liguori, in his book *Gramsci conteso*, which surveys in detail the contested legacy of Gramsci in Italy and the use made of Gramsci's writings in political debate (Liguori 2012). It was through Togliatti's agency that the *Prison Notebooks* first appeared in printed form, in successive volumes organized thematically. Liguori notes that in 1945 the memory of Gramsci remained marginal, known in restricted circles. However, it was Togliatti who not only was responsible for the publication of the *Prison Notebooks* (and other writings by Gramsci), but who gave a particular reading of the *Notebooks*, and lined up Gramsci's political perspective with that of the post-war PCI. The *svolta di Salerno* (the Salerno 'turn') proclaimed the democratic and pluralist nature of the Italian Communist Party, making it into a mass party rather than a cadre party, and emphasizing its full acceptance of pluralism and political democracy. The idea was that the party was now a new party, committed to the 'Italian road to socialism', a democratic path to socialism which accepted the distinct national framework within which the struggle for socialism had to be carried out. In other words, 'the emphasis was on the *democratic* and *national* character of the action of the PCI' (Liguori 2012, 55). Gramsci's ideas were invoked to legitimize this political strategy, with Togliatti arguing that Gramsci saw the working class as 'the first, the only, the true national class, which has the task of solving all the problems left unresolved by the bourgeoisie and by the bourgeois revolution' (Togliatti 2001, 78), and certainly these were themes highlighted in the *Prison Notebooks* through Gramsci's concept of passive revolution and his analysis of the Risorgimento. Gramsci's ideas on intellectuals and the concept of the national-popular were clearly in accordance with this new line of the Italian Communist Party, and Gramsci's intellectual legacy was used to appeal both to intellectuals and indeed to a wider mass public and so give the Italian Communist Party a much broader political appeal. In an article in the party newspaper *Unità* of 30 April 1944 Togliatti wrote that 'he [Gramsci] created our party. He fixed the national function of the proletariat in the struggle for its emancipation' (quoted in Liguori 2012, 70). In a speech given in Cagliari on 27 April 1947 Togliatti proclaimed that 'Gramsci's patrimony belongs to all, all Sardinians, all Italians' (Togliatti 2001, 128). Of course these statements were made before the first appearance of extracts from the *Prison Notebooks*, the first volume of which (the notes on Croce and historical materialism) was published in 1948, a year after the publication of the *Letters from Prison*, which were given the Viareggio Prize the same year.

It seems then that the first reading of the *Prison Notebooks* was that strongly influenced by Togliatti, who emphasized Gramsci's work as exploring Italian culture and Marxism, and who focused on the specifically national implications of Gramsci's theories. These ideas were seen as offering a distinctively Italian path to socialism, picking up on Gramsci's idea of the differences between East and West, and on his idea that in the West 'the state was only an outer ditch, behind which there stood a powerful system of fortresses and earthworks; more or less numerous from one State to the next, it goes without saying – but this precisely necessitated an accurate reconnaissance of each individual country' (SPN 238; Q7, §16, 866). Despite Togliatti's attempt to reconcile Gramsci's ideas with those of orthodox Marxism–Leninism, it was obvious that in many fundamental respects the ideas of the *Prison Notebooks* were in opposition to the dogmas of Soviet-type Marxism–Leninism, in particular his critique of determinism and the whole idea of the philosophy of praxis as something in many respects different from both dialectical materialism and from historical materialism in their orthodox manifestations. By 1951 the publication of the *Prison Notebooks* in thematically organized volumes had been concluded, and certainly by then Gramsci's ideas had percolated to a wider audience in Italy. The *Prison Notebooks* seem then to have had their initial impact through the lens of Togliatti's reading of Gramsci as a political leader who opened up the idea of a national and democratic road to socialism. These ideas were to gain wider currency in the 1970s with the phenomenon of what came to be called Eurocommunism, whose leading protagonists were the mass communist parties of Italy, France and Spain, all of whom proclaimed their adherence to pluralism and the electoral road to socialism, rejecting the concept of the dictatorship of the proletariat. This political strategy also emphasized the distinctly national character of each of these communist parties and the importance of the national context of class struggle. Hence Eurocommunism involved a rejection, whether implicit or more explicitly stated, of Bolshevism and Soviet Marxism as the only valid strategy for gaining power and as the point of reference for Marxist politics. Gramsci's idea of the war of position and his statement of the distinction between East and West were invoked as justifications and anticipations of this Eurocommunist strategy.

The impact of the *Prison Notebooks* in Italy was linked to the fortunes and issues debated in the Italian Communist Party, since it was through the PCI and above all through its leader Togliatti that the *Notebooks* had become known to a wider public. Liguori tells us that 'the action of the [Italian] Communist Party had been the most important vehicle thanks to which the thought of the author of the *Quaderni* had been spread', and in his view the ideas of Gramsci had been 'the principal medium through which the PCI had succeeded in talking to different generations and to various types of intellectuals and of militants' (Liguori 2012, 251). It was through debates in and beyond the PCI that the impact of the *Prison Notebooks* was felt. In a somewhat schematic way, one could highlight three issues of contemporary politics in Italy, and more broadly beyond Italy, which raised themes basic to the *Prison Notebooks* of crucial importance for understanding contemporary reality. These are the issues of *the role of the political party*, the question of *civil society*, and the *war of position* and its applicability in practice.

Togliatti's reading of Gramsci insisted on the compatibility of his ideas with Leninism, and on the importance Gramsci gave to the role of the political party, even in the pre-*Prison Notebooks* period of the Turin factory councils. Togliatti in his various speeches and articles on Gramsci highlighted the idea of 'the revolutionary party of the working class', and argued that 'this is the other essential element of the Leninist doctrine that Gramsci makes his own, elaborating it and deepening it, linking it to the reality of our country, translating it into action, into practical work [*in una pratica di lavoro*]' (Togliatti 2001, 255). Togliatti's interpretation of Gramsci stressed the latter's concern with discipline and organization, the need for the mass of the workers (indeed any mass of human beings) to be organized. In support of this Togliatti quoted those lines from the *Prison Notebooks* where Gramsci writes that 'a human mass does not "distinguish" itself, does not become independent in its own right without, in the widest sense, organising itself; and there is no organisation without intellectuals, that is without organisers and leaders, in other words, without the theoretical aspect of the theory–practice nexus being distinguished concretely by the existence of a group of people "specialised" in conceptual and philosophical elaboration of ideas' (SPN 334; Q11, §12, 1386). This interpretation of Gramsci was challenged in the 1960s by critics from the Left (the *Manifesto* group) who laid more emphasis on the Gramsci of the workers' councils, seeing that aspect of his thought as more fruitful, and criticizing the idea of the hegemony of the party as the 'modern Prince' (Liguori 2012, 245). The idea of the modern Prince and the leading role of the party in Gramsci's thought was also criticized from a liberal perspective by the leading Italian political philosopher Norberto Bobbio, and more generally by those who thought that Gramsci's invocation of the modern Prince, which 'takes the place of the divinity or the categorical imperative' (SPN 133; Q13, §1, 1561), was incompatible with ideas of pluralism and democracy. Such a criticism had been raised even earlier by the liberal philosopher who figures so prominently in the *Notebooks* themselves, Benedetto Croce. Croce wrote in 1950 that Gramsci was unable to 'develop a new outlook and to carry out the important revolution that is attributed to him'. The reason for this failure, in Croce's view, was that Gramsci's purpose 'was solely to create in Italy a political party, a task which has nothing to do with the dispassionate search for truth' (quoted in Liguori 2012, 101). In his turn, Bobbio, focusing on the theme of civil society, suggested that Gramsci's ideas were incompatible with the reality of a pluralist society, which could be threatened by the hegemony of a single party. In an interview published in the newspaper *La Repubblica* on 24 September 1976, Bobbio argued that in a situation of modern democracy where pluralism was necessary 'we must abandon the concept of the hegemonic party' (Liguori 2012, 253), a criticism echoed by another author, Biagio de Giovanni, who argued that in contemporary conditions 'the hegemony of the workers movement nowadays passes through the exaltation of political pluralism' (Liguori 2012, 262).

Thus the impact of the *Prison Notebooks* made itself felt through debates on the role of the party as it was presented in some central passages of the *Notebooks*. Was Gramsci a (more or less) orthodox Leninist, as Togliatti claimed, and if so, was his praise of organization and the role of the party one with totalitarian implications, and hence incompatible with the values of pluralism and democracy which the PCI proclaimed, and which in any case constituted the core values of contemporary liberal democracy? The English scholar Richard Bellamy more recently echoed some of these concerns in arguing that Gramsci 'showed no awareness of the role the state plays in protecting the diversity of society by upholding the rule of law and the rights of individuals', and stating that Gramsci's writings 'contain no adequate theorisation of bourgeois democracy' (Bellamy 2014, 159–60). Debates over the themes of the *Prison Notebooks* also focused on the question of whether there was a decisive break between the Gramsci of the factory councils period and the Gramsci of the *Prison Notebooks*, with the latter giving much more emphasis on the directing and organizing role of the political party. In turn this raised the question, as liberal critics suggested, that the *Notebooks* presented a potentially dangerous, monist view of politics, with the idea of the (single) party as a hegemonic force. The charge was that this allowed no room for the pluralism and diversity fundamental to a modern liberal democracy, hence the claim that the ideas of the *Notebooks* were inadequate as a 'theorisation of bourgeois democracy', as Bellamy puts it. With regard to the question of whether there is a fundamental difference between the Gramsci of the pre-prison period and the Gramsci of the *Notebooks*, the Italian historian of the PCI, Paolo Spriano, emphasized the clear break evident between the reflections in prison and the whole of the earlier period, giving a positive evaluation to that break, since in his view as summarized by Liguori 'the victory of fascism allowed to mature in Gramsci a new way of considering the relationship between democracy and socialism, with alliances considered without any concerns of instrumentality, and also taking into consideration the *national* element' (Liguori 2012, 177). It seems that in the 1960s some of the New Left theorists, critical of the PCI, accepted this idea of a break between early and later Gramsci, but, unlike Spriano, saw more of value in the Gramsci of the factory councils than in the theorist of the modern Prince, and used ideas of the former as an example of workers' democracy and popular power in opposition to what they saw as the Italian Communist Party's acceptance of the structures of parliamentary democracy, an issue to which we will return below in discussion of the war of position.

If the question of the political party and its role both in the ideas of the *Prison Notebooks* and in contemporary political debate was one way in which those notebooks had an impact, the next question was precisely the role of *civil society*, again seen in this double perspective of a theoretical question and in terms of its contemporary political relevance. Here it was the political theorist Norberto Bobbio who posed the issue, seeing Gramsci as the theorist of the superstructure, whose most important idea was that of civil society, seen as the master concept of Gramsci's thought. The implications of Bobbio's famous article on Gramsci and civil society, which was first delivered as a contribution to a congress held in Cagliari, Sardinia, in 1967, were clear (Bobbio 1988). If civil society (rather than hegemony) was the core concept of the *Prison Notebooks*, the emphasis then switched from the idea of a subaltern class (and its allies) achieving hegemony, to the idea of civil society in opposition to the state, as a means of (so to speak) cutting the state down to size. Civil society could be seen in

Gramscian terms as the whole range of groups, associations and institutions (the media, the schools, the educational system) which constituted 'the "trenches" and the permanent fortifications of the front in the war of position', as Gramsci wrote (SPN 243; Q13, §7, 1567). Gramsci was thus presented as a theorist different from Marx, since Gramsci unlike Marx did not see civil society as the sphere of the economy – and also different from Lenin, since it was on the terrain of civil society and its diverse institutions that political struggle and social conflicts could be fought out, rather than through a single party aspiring to hegemonic power. This 'civil society Gramsci' *was* compatible with pluralism and with advanced forms of liberal democracy, and Bobbio had as far back as 1955 criticized Italian Marxists for having made of Gramsci 'an inventory of five or six formulae with which one could explain everything, and making of Gramsci's books a pile of maxims or quotes to be cited as arguments to be accepted on authority' (Liguori 2012, 132).

The interpretation of Gramsci as the theorist of the super-structure (in a new way – different from Marx) whose key concept was civil society certainly opened up a new perspective on Gramsci, and fitted in with, or perhaps helped initiate, the rediscovery of civil society, seen both as the arena for struggle against one-party rule in communist systems and as the sphere of diversity and difference characteristic of liberal-democratic society (Ehrenberg 1999 gives a good overview of the concept of civil society). These were themes of great topicality in the 1970s and 1980s and indeed have remained so today, so one could say that Bobbio's reading of Gramsci's *Prison Notebooks* showed both the impact of those writings and helped give them more actuality and relevance to the present day, given the centrality of themes of diversity and associative life. Both Liguori and Vacca are critical of Bobbio's reading, suggesting that this is a liberal perspective which cuts out Gramsci's own political concerns with the gaining of hegemonic power by subaltern groups. Liguori argues that Bobbio (and others) turned Gramsci into the figure of a classic (of political and social philosophy), 'beyond and outside time and space and above all distant from present-day problems' and in that way, Liguori claims, 'dissolving the real forms of Gramsci as a historic figure'

(Liguori 2012, 199–201). But certainly the intervention of Bobbio and his interpretation of Gramsci showed the significance of the *Prison Notebooks*, not just within the Italian context but more broadly in terms of the debate on civil society and a new emphasis on the different identities and groups that constituted it. Vacca's criticism is that Bobbio, in treating structure and superstructure as a dichotomy, distorts Gramsci's thought, since Gramsci himself presented the distinction of those two levels as purely methodological, not organic, and the same was true of Gramsci's distinction between civil society and political society. According to Vacca, Bobbio's perspective remains the liberal one which sees civil society in opposition to the state, acting as a curb or check on state power, whereas Gramsci sought to develop (as we saw in Chapter 5 above) the idea that state and civil society were not necessarily antagonistic, indeed that the idea of an enlarged state or state in its fullest sense included and incorporated civil society (Vacca 1999, 159–64).

Equally significant for the impact and reading of the *Prison Notebooks*, both in Italy and in the wider context of contemporary liberal democracy, was the debate on the war of position and what exactly this meant in practical terms. Here again the debate related to the policies pursued by the PCI after the *svolta di Salerno* and more generally the themes raised by Eurocommunism in the 1970s and debates about the abandonment of Soviet-style interpretations of the dictatorship of the proletariat. Did the war of position in its Gramscian interpretation mean a gradual takeover of the trenches and earthworks of civil society, and in what ways, if any, did this differ from a reformist acceptance of the institutions and processes of liberal democracy? The war of position was interpreted by some as equivalent to what the German social democrat Karl Kautsky had in the pre-First World War period referred to as the *Ermattungsstrategie*, or war of attrition, waged through a protracted struggle to capture institutions of civil society in a gradual process of permeation of those institutions. Indeed, according to Liguori, one expert on both Kautsky and Gramsci, the Italian scholar Massimo Salvadori, suggested that the Italian Communist Party in its Eurocommunist phase was nearer to Kautsky than to Gramsci (Liguori 2012, 254). But in any case critics of the concept of the war of position, at least as interpreted by the PCI, saw it as a classic case of integration into the existing order, so that the PCI was becoming 'caged inside the administration of the existing order', as Liguori puts it (Liguori 2012, 269). If the war of position meant the revolutionary party taking over the running of municipalities, for example, like the PCI's control for many years of the city of Bologna, did this mean a position not so different from that of the classic revisionist Edouard Bernstein for whom 'the movement is everything and the final goal is nothing'? It seems that for some critics of the *Prison Notebooks* like Bobbio, Gramsci's ideas were irrelevant to a modern pluralist society, because (according to Bobbio) Gramsci ignored thinkers of the liberal tradition like de Tocqueville since he, Gramsci, operated with an unrealizable idea of a harmonious or conflict-free society. Gramsci had not, in this perspective, paid enough attention to the question of how to limit the power of the state, and his totalizing or organicist philosophy was highly problematic. On the other hand, critics of the idea of the war of position, or of what some people in the 1960s in Italy and beyond called 'the long march through the institutions', suggested that the war of position could never lead to any radical transformation of the existing order, because it meant becoming bogged down in precisely the administration of the existing order, and so the ideas of the *Prison Notebooks* lost much of their relevance to political problems of the present day. Comparing discussions at the 1987 conference on the theme of 'Morality and Politics in Gramsci' with the conference held ten years earlier, which had been devoted to questions of politics and history, Liguori suggests that while the earlier meeting had presented Gramsci as not just a theorist of the political but on occasion 'as a reference point for political processes actually taking place', the later congress in its overall approach 'proposed a metapolitical and academic reading of the author of the *Quaderni*, who was treated as a classic of philosophy, distant from any possibility of actualization and, in places, remote from any historic contextualization' (Liguori 2012, 311).

For some later interpreters and scholars of Gramsci the equation of Gramsci's ideas and his war of position with Eurocommunism and more generally with the idea of a peaceful transition to socialism is totally erroneous. The British Gramsci scholar Joseph Femia argued in 1979 that Gramsci cannot be considered a defender of an idea of a gradual evolution towards socialism through parliament, and that the so-called war of position does not exclude the direct assault on the parliamentary system, since (according to Femia) 'Gramsci never deviated from a belief in total revolution brought about in part through the intervention of armed force' (Femia 1979, 501). This seems to underestimate the way in which throughout the *Notebooks* Gramsci wrestles with the idea of new forms of political action and criticizes other revolutionaries like Trotsky and Rosa Luxemburg for promoting the idea of a war of manoeuvre and its direct assault on the centres of political power.

In the Italian context, before the period of Eurocommunism, the impact of the *Prison Notebooks* was mediated through the work of Togliatti in getting the *Notebooks* known to a wider public and in the use of these writings in connection with the Italian road to socialism and the wider debates in the Communist Party. These debates, as we have shown, focused on the issues of the party and its role, the topic of civil society highlighted by Bobbio, and the topic of whether the war of position was a defensible strategy for coming to power in an advanced liberal democracy. Togliatti's own interpretation started by emphasizing Gramsci as the party man, the person who in theoretical terms freed Marxism from being, as Togliatti put it, 'banal economic determinism' and restored Marxism 'as an integral conception of the world and as an absolute historicism' (Togliatti 2001, 204). But it is noteworthy that in his later, and final, reflections on the significance of Gramsci's life and writings Togliatti stated that 'the persona of Gramsci transcends the historic events of our party' and that Gramsci represents the 'critical conscience of a century of our country's history', thus broadening out the significance of Gramsci's writings and political activity well beyond the history of the Communist Party and its strategy (Togliatti 2001, 309). However, in the period since Togliatti's death in 1964 the *Prison Notebooks* have had an impact well beyond the world of Italian politics and the debates within and about the PCI's Italian road to socialism. At least some of this broader impact must be indicated, even though this account is highly selective and focuses on two areas, those of IR and IPE (international political economy), on the one hand, and the area of culture on the other, represented in the British context by the cultural theorist and analyst Stuart Hall. Both can be seen as representing aspects of neo-Gramscianism, if this term is understood to refer to later attempts to interpret some of the ideas of the *Prison Notebooks* and use them to analyse the reality of the present-day world.

NATIONAL AND GLOBAL: DEBATES OUTSIDE ITALY

The debates in Italy referred to above took place in a specific political environment, concerned with questions of political strategy and party policy, and the issue of applying some of Gramsci's core ideas to justify (or also to criticize) political choices. The broader impact of the *Prison Notebooks* outside Italy was less concerned with a particular party and its policy and more related to academic debates. These debates sought to extend Gramsci's ideas, using some of his key concepts in ways left implicit or undeveloped in his own writings, but claiming to be faithful to his mode of analysis. This does raise the question, to which we will return in our final section, of whether in their later impact the *Quaderni* should be seen more as an academic text or source of academic analysis than as a direct guide to political action. In recent years it has been in the field of IR and IPE that the so-called neo-Gramscians have made the most impact. What has been called 'the Italian school' in IR and IPE represents an attempt to extend Gramscian concepts, notably the idea of hegemony, from the predominantly national context in which Gramsci employed them and to extend them to the sphere of IR and world politics generally. The protagonists of this Italian school were above all academics in British and American universities, who wished to understand the new world order of the late twentieth and twenty-first century, and found Gramscian ideas helpful for this purpose.

One of the key figures in this so-called Italian school of neo-Gramscians has been the American IR scholar Robert Cox. In general it can be said that the neo-Gramscians seek to apply Gramsci's ideas to a world much more globalized than the society in which Gramsci wrote his *Prison Notebooks*. However, there are some extremely interesting passages in the *Prison Notebooks* which could be said to be highly prescient in anticipating issues of nationalism and cosmopolitanism, those very issues taken up and developed by the neo-Gramscians. Some of these passages identify the contradiction between the cosmopolitanism of the economy (what now would be called a globalized economy) and the increasingly out-of-date framework of the nation-state. Notebook number 15 (one of the miscellaneous notebooks), contains some significant reflections on the 'crash' of 1929 and the subsequent Great Depression. Paragraph 5 of this notebook is headed 'Past and Present: The Crisis', referring to the crisis of 1929, with Gramsci insisting that it was a complex process 'that shows itself in many ways, and in which causes and effects become intertwined and mutually entangled. To simplify means to misrepresent and falsify' (FSPN 219; Q15, §5, 1755). Gramsci saw the crash of 1929 as part of the ongoing crisis opened up by the First World War, but the crucial point in the present context is that he noted that one of its 'fundamental contradictions' was the opposition between the internationalism or rather cosmopolitanism of economic life contrasted with the fact that the operations of the state remained within the framework of the nation-state. In his words, 'One of the fundamental contradictions is this: that whereas economic life has internationalism, or better still cosmopolitanism, as a necessary premiss, state life has developed ever more in the direction of "nationalism", of "self-sufficiency" and so on' (FSPN 220; Q15, §5, 1756). Gramsci followed this observation with the statement that one of the most obvious characteristics of the present (1929) crisis was an exasperated nationalism, referring in this paragraph to economic nationalism, the nationalist perspectives of economic life evident in restrictive foreign-exchange policies and restrictions of trade to bilateral trade treaties. This contradiction between the national framework of political life and the cosmopolitan context of economic life is ever more evident in our contemporary globalized world. Philosophers and social observers like Jürgen Habermas analyse this same tension in Habermas's concept of 'the post-national constellation' and the evident failure of the nation-state to achieve control over global economic forces. For Habermas the need is for a new global *Schliessung* or closure, through which political and democratic forces could regain some control over what have been hitherto unregulated or dominant flows of economic forces (Habermas 2001).

There are other passages in the *Prison Notebooks* which dwell on this contrast of the gap between the increasingly outmoded framework of the nation-state and the need for a new cosmopolitanism. In another of the miscellaneous notebooks, this time Notebook 6, Gramsci anticipates and analyses the formation of a common European cultural consciousness, which would in due course, if not exactly render nationalism redundant, then at least put it on a par with feelings of municipal localism: 'There is today a European cultural consciousness and there exists a whole series of declarations by intellectuals and politicians who maintain that a European union is necessary' (FSPN 119; Q6, §78, 748). Given that this was written in the early 1930s (Notebook 6 seems to have been composed from 1930 to 1932), it was highly prescient of Gramsci to be writing that 'it may also be said that the historical process tends towards this union and that there are many material forces that will only be able to develop within this union. If this union is brought to fruition in *x* years, the word "nationalism" will have the same archaeological value as "municipalism" has at present' (FSPN 119; Q6, §78, 748). This is all the more significant given Gramsci's emphasis on the force of the national-popular, because it suggests Gramsci's awareness that the nation-state was increasingly under threat as an adequate framework for economic forces.

If for Gramsci economic tendencies were pushing towards a common European awareness, his analysis here of the dynamic of modernity is comparable with what he wrote on Americanism and Fordism (discussed in Chapter 4 above). The analysis there was that Fordism as mass production represented the mode of production of modernity, but that it had to be controlled and harnessed by the working class, which had to make itself the master of these new methods of production. If they did not do so, then Americanism became just a means of using modern productive methods to exploit the workers and extract a higher rate of surplus value. Similarly, in Notebook 19, under the heading of 'Italian Risorgimento' Gramsci reflects on the need for a new form of cosmopolitanism, which would be based on work, on what he calls the *uomo-lavoro*, man as worker and the intellectuals associated with such 'humanity-as-labour'. This would be the modern form of cosmopolitanism of which the working class and its allies would be the bearers. Such cosmopolitanism was in the interest of the mass of the Italian people. Gramsci writes that 'Italian expansion can only be that of humanity-as-labour and the intellectual who represents this humanity-as-labour is no longer of the traditional type, a rhetorical windbag recounting yesteryear's yellowing pages' (FSPN 253; Q19, §5, 1988). Gramsci seems to be rejecting previous forms of cosmopolitanism, arguing that traditional Italian cosmopolitanism should give way to 'a modern type of cosmopolitanism such, that is, as to ensure the best conditions for the development of Italian humanity-as-labour [*uomo-lavoro*] in whatever part of the world it is to be found. Not the citizen of the world in as much as *civis romanus* [a citizen of Rome] or a Catholic but as a producer of civilisation [*civiltà*]' (FSPN 253; Q19, §5, 1988). He suggested that the Italian people were '"nationally" more interested in a modern form of cosmopolitanism', and that this was true not just of the workers but also of the peasants and specially the peasantry of the south. Their national development was compatible with the reconstruction of the 'world economically in a unitary way'.

It is noteworthy that Gramsci rejected what he labelled 'nationalism of the French type', calling this 'an anachronistic excrescence in Italian history.' By 'nationalism of the French type' he presumably meant the nationalism of such right-wing and populist nationalists as those who had emerged in the anti-Dreyfus campaign, thinkers like Charles Maurras and Maurice Barrès, the latter being one of the leaders of *le parti nationaliste*, which combined themes of nationalism with a socialistic appeal to the (national) workers, which anticipated later fascism and National Socialism (Girardet 1966). But it could also be taken as a covert reference to Italian fascist notions of the nation and of national expansion, since Gramsci stated that 'collaborating in reconstructing the world economically in a unitary fashion is in the tradition of the Italian people and of Italian history, not in order to dominate it hegemonically and appropriate the fruit of others' labour, but to exist and develop properly as the Italian people'. This marks the contrast between fascist forms of nationalism and national expansion, on the one hand, and on the other the modern form of cosmopolitanism which would not be an 'anachronistic excrescence'. In Gramsci's words, 'The "mission" of the Italian people lies in taking up once again Roman and medieval cosmopolitanism, but in its more modern and advanced form': this was the only way in which the concept of a proletarian nation (a concept used by nationalists of the Right, like Corradini) could be acceptable (FNSP 253–54; Q19, §5, 1988–89). Only in that way could Italy play a part in the economic reconstruction of the modern world.

Gramsci's remarks on nationalism and cosmopolitanism are highly suggestive and interesting, not merely because of their prescient nature, anticipating later developments of a global economy and the supersession, at least in economic terms, of the nation-state, but as exemplifications of one of the core ideas of the *Prison Notebooks*. This idea is of the working class and its allies as the representatives of modernity and of the bearers of a cosmopolitanism of a new type, one appropriate to the realities of a globalized world. The so-called neo-Gramscians in IR developed those arguments further, in their attempt to explain what Robert Cox calls 'a globally-conceived civil society, i.e. a mode of production of global extent which brings about links among social classes of the countries encompassed by it' (Cox 1993, 61). If Gramsci's *Prison Notebooks* indicate the development of a new form of cosmopolitanism and a world going beyond the nation-state, the neo-Gramscians sought to develop those insights further and give a positive answer to the question which Cox posed: 'Is the Gramscian concept of hegemony applicable at the international or world level?' (Cox 1993, 59).

The ideas of the *Prison Notebooks* are thus taken up by these IR/IPE scholars focusing on two crucial themes, which were anticipated or sketched out in the *Quaderni*. The first is the idea of a world order, which calls out for analysis via the concept of hegemony. However, 'hegemony' in this global context is something more than, indeed different from, the hegemony of one state. The hegemony exercised in a world order is the dominance of a set of values and practices to which even dominant states are subject.

Such practices are, at least in the contemporary world, policed and controlled by international organizations, in the present context exemplified by institutions like the International Monetary Fund and the World Bank, which maintain and enforce the rules of the game. Following the seminal analysis of Robert Cox, one would thus see the contemporary world as a system in which market rules of a neo-liberal sort are the hegemonic rules of the system, into which all states are incorporated, though of course states differ widely in the degree of manoeuvre they have within such rules. Cox makes a distinction between hegemonic periods and non-hegemonic ones. In hegemonic periods there is one dominant state which represents and expresses the hegemonic values of the system as a whole, which are presented in such a way as to gain the consent of all other states in the system. As Cox expounds this idea, 'a state would have to found and protect a world order which was universal in conception, i.e., not an order in which one state directly exploits others but an order which most other states (or at least those within reach of the hegemony) could find compatible with their interests'. As an example of hegemonic periods he offers that of 1845–75, a world order of free trade and the gold standard, in which Britain was the dominant power whose sea power and Empire gave it the ability to police the system and 'enforce obedience by peripheral countries to the rules of the market' (Cox 1993, 60). The other example of a hegemonic period is the post-Second World War era, up to the mid-1960s, in which it was the United States which was the dominant power in the hegemonic world order, policing and controlling a market-dominated society. One could take this further (though in his 1983 article Cox was not able to do this) by referring to the contemporary world as one of a world order of hegemonic neo-liberalism, in which a set of values (of market relations) is enforced on all states worldwide (with penalties for those states infringing the rules of the game), as is an ideology of globalization (Steger 2005) that expresses and almost codifies the market relations which have to be followed and imposed on all aspects of social life, and which individual states have to respect (Harvey 2005). The main enforcers of this 'market discipline' on a global scale would be the already mentioned institutions such as the World Trade Organization (WTO) and the World Bank (on WTO see Paterson 2009).

One other concept prominent in the *Prison Notebooks* is employed in the writing of the Italian school, namely that of war of position, interpreted in this context as a countermovement of a global civil society, showing yet another Gramscian idea developed and taken up in conditions of contemporary politics. Cox talks about a movement of counter-hegemony, which would seek to create a new historic bloc of forces capable of opposing the dominance of the current world order by the ideals of neo-liberalism, enforced by international organizations. He is insistent that such organizations could not be challenged by a direct attack or even by a war of position inside such institutions, since (to use yet another Gramscian idea) they practice their own variety of *trasformismo*, co-opting elites from peripheral countries into their mechanisms of power. In a striking image he notes that 'hegemony is like a pillow: it absorbs blows and sooner or later the would-be assailant will find it comfortable to rest upon'. Thus he comes to the conclusion that if there were to be a counter-hegemonic movement which would challenge or change the world order, this would have to begin 'with the long, laborious effort to build new historic blocs within national boundaries' (Cox 1993, 65). In what is possibly a more optimistic analysis, another of the neo-Gramscian analysts, Stephen Gill, talks of a 'postmodern Prince' which could challenge neo-liberal hegemony, and would involve institutions and organizations of a global civil society, in contemporary terms exemplified by the alternative globalization movement. Gill suggests the possible components of such a new oppositional movement: 'Organisations and movements which might form part of a counter-hegemonic bloc include Amnesty International, Green parties and ecological groups, socialist think-tanks like the Transnational Institute, peace groups such as European Nuclear Disarmament, development agencies such as Oxfam, and religious organisations such as the World Council of Churches' (Gill 1993, 122). This rather heterogeneous assemblage of groups could articulate values and policies in opposition to the orthodox policies and decisions taken by the international organizations and states of the existing world order.

It is not possible here to explore in depth the strengths, weaknesses and limitations of such neo-Gramscian analyses of the present world order. The purpose is merely to illustrate how the conceptual framework and some of the key concepts developed in the *Prison Notebooks* have been given a new lease of life by being explored in contemporary academic debate analysing the shape of world politics, the new world order and the possible emergence of counter-hegemonic movements opposing the dominant historic bloc and seeking to wage a war of position, whether through Gill's idea of a newly constituted global civil society (the postmodern Prince) or Cox's concept of building 'new historic blocs within national boundaries' (Cox 1993, 65). Some scholars (e.g. Femia 2009) remain deeply sceptical of these attempts to apply Gramsci's concepts to IR, at least in the way in which this has been done by those within the so-called Italian school. There is a whole range of writing which uses the framework of ideas derived from the *Prison Notebooks* to extend Gramsci's concept of modern forms of cosmopolitanism, itself an idea discussed in a wide literature which debates whether cosmopolitanism can furnish a convincing alternative to what some authors call methodological nationalism (e.g. Beck 2006). It is not the case, of course, that all of these authors directly invoke Gramsci or refer to his concepts. However, Gramsci's analysis of the tension between economic internationalism and political nationalism, as expressed in the *Prison Notebooks*, is certainly a significant contribution to the debate concerning forms of solidarity and community in contemporary politics. In that sense the *Prison Notebooks* are the work of a classic author, as laid out by Gerratana, of someone whose interpretation of his own time remains relevant at all times (quoted in Liguori 2012, 310).

GRAMSCI AND THE ANALYSIS OF THATCHERISM

In investigating the 'afterlife' of the *Prison Notebooks* and the influence which Gramsci's concepts have had on political and social theory, one important example is the use of ideas derived from the *Quaderni* to analyse British politics and the phenomenon of Thatcherism. The main reference here is to the work of the cultural theorist Stuart Hall, who applied a Gramscian framework in an influential analysis of British politics in the 1980s. Hall used core concepts of the Gramscian lexicon to discuss the crisis of the British state and society and the way in which Margaret Thatcher was able to articulate a new form of common sense and develop what Hall called a form of authoritarian populism to achieve hegemony. The interesting thing here is Hall's deployment of concepts of organic crisis, hegemony and an idea of regressive modernization as a form of passive revolution. In a series of articles, many of which appeared in the journal *Marxism Today*, Hall offered a view of the transformation of British conservatism seen through a Gramscian lens. In an article entitled 'Gramsci and Us', Hall made it clear that he was not proposing that 'Gramsci "has the answers" or "holds the key" to our present troubles', but that he thought 'we must "think" our problems in a Gramscian way' (Hall 1988, 161). At the risk of simplifying Hall's nuanced analysis, one can say that he saw the new form of British conservatism represented by Margaret Thatcher as an attempt to achieve hegemony for a distinct set of ideas, and as a response to an organic crisis of the social-democratic consensus of post-war Britain. While not equating the new forms of British conservatism with the fascism of post-First World War Italy, Hall's discussion follows a Gramscian path. In Hall's view, 'Gramsci gives us, not the tools with which to solve the puzzle, but the means with which to ask the right kinds of questions about the politics of the 1980s and 1990s' (Hall 1988, 163). Hall's perspective seems to be that the *Prison Notebooks* were a wide-ranging attempt to analyse the defeat of the Left in the 1920s and what Hall called 'the capacity of the right – specifically of European fascism – to hegemonise that defeat' (Hall 1988, 162). The analytical tools and concepts which Gramsci developed in that intellectual effort could be applied to come to a better understanding of another defeat of the Left and victory of the Right, perhaps on a less epochal scale, namely the electoral victory in Britain of Thatcher and her brand of conservatism in 1979, and the failure of the British Left to understand the implications of her victory and the new terrain of political struggle which it implied.

According to Hall's analysis, Thatcher's politics was a form of regressive modernization and more fundamentally represented what he called 'authoritarian populism'. The former concept can be seen as comparable with Gramsci's idea of passive revolution, while the latter idea is similar to that of Caesarism. By regressive modernization Hall implies that Thatcherism succeeded in overcoming some of the obstacles of tradition and hierarchy which impeded the full onset of modernity in Britain. According to Hall 'the British social formation ... had never, ever, properly entered the era of modern bourgeois civilisation', and Britain 'never institutionalised, in a proper sense, the civilisation and structures of advanced capitalism – what Gramsci called "Fordism"' (Hall 1988, 164). This analysis echoes some of the thoughts Gramsci developed about Italian 'backwardness', both in his pre-prison journalism (see Chapter 1 above) and in his discussion of Italian history in the *Prison Notebooks* (see Chapter 4). Thatcherism pushed Britain forward by attacking some of its traditional hierarchical institutions and substituting a brash market-oriented modernity. Yet this partial attempt to modernize British society went along with a nostalgic backward-looking invocation of Victorian values and by a ruthless suppression (as with the miners' strike of 1984–85) of any opposition to the market society which the state was imposing – in the words of Andrew Gamble's classic analysis, 'the free market and the strong state' (Gamble 1994). In those ways Thatcherite modernization was regressive, and there are parallels here with Gramsci's analysis of fascist corporatism and the way in which fascism in some respects was a modernizing force (see discussion in Chapter 4 above), while being deeply reactionary and regressive in other respects. A similar approach underlies the idea of Thatcherism as a form of authoritarian populism. In Hall's view, Thatcher articulated a set of beliefs which had considerable popular resonance, appealing to (and indeed partially constructing) a mentality of independence, holding on to one's assets and feeling hostile to paternalistic state power and opposing it by a sense of self-reliance, 'standing on one's own two feet'. In that way Hall thought that the ideology of Thatcherism was one which 'in the course of "representing" corporate capital ... wins the consent of very substantial sections of the subordinate and dominated classes' (Hall 1988, 165). While that explained the populist part of the concept, the authoritarian element came in the exaltation of values of tradition and patriotism, used to invoke support for the Falklands War, and in the determined use of state power to limit the power of working-class institutions and ride roughshod over local government and any countervailing power to the Thatcherite project.

More generally, Hall saw Thatcherism as an attempt to establish hegemony and create a new form of politics, and to offer a coherent political response in conditions of crisis. The crisis was one of the post-Second World War social-democratic consensus and compromise in an age when the traditional institutions of Empire and the solidarity expressed in welfare-state policies were wearing thin, unable to be sustained by the weaker state of the British economy and the challenges it faced from an increasingly globalized world market. Again, we can see here the influence of Gramsci's idea of organic crisis, and Hall's insistence that while Thatcher saw the need to build up a new set of ideas, the Left in Britain was blind to the need to establish a counter-hegemonic ideology. In words that read like a paraphrase of Gramsci's statement that 'there can and must be a "political hegemony" even before assuming government power', Hall wrote that 'no social or political force can hope to create a new type of society or raise the masses to a new level of civilisation without first becoming the leading cultural force and in that way providing the organising nucleus of a wider-ranging set of new conceptions' (Hall 1988, 9). His critical judgement on the British Labour Party reads like a version of Gramsci's severe strictures on the Action Party in the Italian Risorgimento, analysed in Chapter 4. Hall suggested that 'Labour commands no intellectual presence ... it has not organised a core of "organic intellectuals"'. In his view the Labour Party 'still looks like a party which has never heard of the strategy of a "war of position"', so that it was not in a position from which it could make 'itself the focal point of popular aspirations, the leading popular political force' (Hall 1988, 207). The conclusion of Hall's analysis is that in terms of waging the war of position and establishing a hegemonic outlook, it was the right, in the form of Thatcherism, that had been more successful than the left, and indeed it was the right that understood better the kind of politics needed to capture popular consent and become *dirigente* or leading, as Gramsci would have put it. What Hall called 'the

Great Moving Right Show' was one in which the Thatcherites understood better than the Labour Party the idea of a war of position and the need to establish hegemonic positions.

This highly influential analysis provides one example of how the Gramscian political vocabulary and the concepts developed in the *Prison Notebooks* were put to use in a very different political context from their original setting and used to illuminate a phenomenon which showed parallels with the situation that those notebooks were analysing. Ideas of an organic crisis, the failure of the left to develop hegemonic policies, and the analysis of regressive modernization were all concepts taken from Gramsci's *Prison Notebooks* and used as tools to understand developments in British politics. In that way this can be seen as proof of the attraction and analytical validity of the new language of politics which Gramsci developed. Along with the neo-Gramscian development of ideas of hegemony in an international setting, Hall's dissection of Thatcherism is an example of the influence of Gramsci's *Prison Notebooks* in the contemporary age.

CONCLUSION: THE *PRISON NOTEBOOKS* TODAY

What then is the status of the *Prison Notebooks* now? We have seen how they informed the policies of the Italian Communist Party in the post-Second World War period, in particular because of the personal link between Gramsci and the leader of the PCI, Palmiro Togliatti. In the English-speaking world, the availability of the *Prison Notebooks* in translation, above all through the publication of the SPN in 1971, fitted in with New Left ideas which rejected Cold War politics. Gramsci's ideas were seen, rightly, as opening up a form of Marxism very different from the rigid framework of Marxism–Leninism and from Soviet orthodoxy, and giving greater attention to matters of culture and ideology as a crucial field of struggle. Beyond the anglophone world, ideas of war of position and the importance of building up consent for radical change were part of the relatively short-lived Eurocommunist phase, in which mass communist parties, above all those of Italy, France and Spain, rejected the concept of the dictatorship of the proletariat and made a firm commitment to democracy and pluralism. This implied a jettisoning of ideas of one-party rule and more generally of the Soviet model as universally valid. This phenomenon of Eurocommunism could draw on Gramsci's ideas of the national-popular and the need for intellectuals to join the mass political movement and give it leadership. One could say then that in the period up to the fall of the Berlin wall and the emergence of 'post-communism' the ideas of the *Prison Notebooks* were linked with and used to support actual political strategies and movements. But is that still the case now? How should we read the *Prison Notebooks* today? They can certainly be said to take their place as a classic of twentieth-century political theory, offering novel analyses of its key concepts. Ideas of the state, the role of the political party, the nature and significance of civil society, the nature of revolution in complex societies, all these and more are developed in the *Prison Notebooks* in ways which no other set of reflections within Marxism, and indeed within political theory generally, can offer. But does that mean that the *Prison Notebooks* have achieved a classic status as a text fit for academic analysis and reflection, at the expense of a direct connection with political life and movements?

In some respects this seems to be the case. In the contemporary world of globalized capitalism and of what the influential socio-logist Zygmunt Bauman calls liquid modernity, the concept of a collective will seems difficult to realize (Bauman 2000). Gramsci's idea that 'it is necessary to study precisely how permanent collective wills are formed, and how such wills set themselves concrete short-term and long-term ends – i.e. a line of collective action' (SPN 194; Q8, §195, 1057) is problematic in an age when many of the agencies and institutions that could be the basis for such a 'collective will' are themselves fragmented. This could be said to be true of the working class itself, in an age when some theorists talk not of the proletariat but of the 'precariat' (Standing 2014), a group of workers whose position is not one of a salariat or traditional working class but who are defined by prospects of short-term and uncertain employment, not very propitious for the formation of a collective will. Similarly, as we have noted in our discussion of the modern Prince, political parties in the contemporary world are much more electoral machines, controlled from on high to make sure their members are on message, rather than the vehicles and agents of the moral and intellectual reform which Gramsci saw as a precondition for radical change. His idea of Marxism as a totalitarian all-embracing philosophy which sums up and transcends previous epochs and their philosophies meets the present-day scepticism towards grand narratives, and beyond that a hostility from those who think we are living 'in Enlightenment's wake' (Gray 1995) and who are opposed to any scheme of totalistic social renewal and revolution. Furthermore, as noted in our discussion of civil society, some sympathetic commentators use Gramsci's own ideas to show the difficulties of radical change in contemporary society. If one thing we can learn from Gramsci is the importance of what he calls the trenches and earthworks of civil society as constituting the defences of the existing order, and the need to overcome those defences before seeking to gain political power, then how could they be captured in a society where the media are privately controlled and inimical to ideas of socialist transformation, and where the schools and institutions of higher education are often seen as preparing their students to be part of the existing order rather than the organic intellectuals of an increasingly marginalized and precarious working class?

Gramsci's *Prison Notebooks* are not merely reflections on, and developments of, key concepts in political and social theory, carried on in highly adverse conditions, and in that sense a monument to one person's struggle for intellectual survival and resistance which manifest the determination to write something '*für ewig*', for ever, as announced in Gramsci's famous letter to his sister-in-law. Concepts of hegemony and the whole idea of subordinate groups developing their own independent philosophy and ideas as the means of emerging from their subaltern position remain as indispensable keys for understanding the politics of our time, in an age of neo-liberal hegemony being challenged by movements of various kinds, even if those movements are different from the collective will of an industrial working class. The idea of developing modernity and the latest methods of production, as analysed in the notebook, 'Americanism and Fordism', and of doing so in ways that avoid passive revolution and provide opportunities for subordinate groups to control the conditions of their lives, remains an inspiring and important one in an age of neo-liberal hegemony. The *Prison Notebooks* contain a theory of modernity and of the role of intellectuals, illustrated with a wealth of historical examples and reflections on the whole epoch opened up by the French Revolution, and indeed on earlier periods as well. The master concept of hegemony is explained not as an abstract idea but as a tool for understanding modes of domination and control, and the clue to challenging such forms of power. Gramsci rejects any kind of determinism or forms of economism, and shows how political action and philosophical reflection go together as the free creation of human beings. His radical historicism rejects any idea of transcendence and shows the impossibility of any philosophy as eternal or removed from the social conditions which give birth to that philosophy. The fact that the new language of politics developed in the *Notebooks* has been employed, as briefly indicated in this chapter, to analyse a whole range of political and social phenomena shows how fruitful are the ideas of the *Notebooks* in understanding political life in the broadest context. These are some of the reasons why the *Prison Notebooks* remain a great book, a classic text of twentieth-century political thought, with ideas and concepts indispensable for understanding the still evolving and no doubt quite different world of the twenty-first century. These notes were written, as we know, in a prison cell, and only saw the light of day in published form many years after the death of their author in 1937. Published at first in separate thematic volumes, only in 1975 as a complete text, in Italy they now form part of an *edizione nazionale* (national edition) of all of Gramsci's works, still in the process of production. The ongoing English translation of the complete *Prison Notebooks* will bring the whole text to the anglophone world. The discovery of further letters and documents, and the ending of the distorted perspectives of the Cold War, allow for a much more dispassionate study of this text, and the life and times of their author. This new season of Gramsci studies opens up for the first time a more adequate understanding of these complex reflections on history, philosophy, politics, language and culture, with their single theme underlying the many paragraphs and notes: how could subordinate groups end their subaltern position? How can a process of moral and intellectual reform be initiated and carried to a successful conclusion? These reflections certainly give us indispensable material for thinking through a politics of emancipation for the twenty-first century.

SUGGESTIONS FOR FURTHER READING

The collection of articles edited by Stephen Gill, *Gramsci, Historical Materialism and International Relations* (Cambridge: Cambridge University Press, 1993), remains a very good way in to debates about the neo-Gramscians and questions of IR and IPE (international relations and international political economy). A more recent survey is the collection edited by Allison J. Ayers, *Gramsci, Political Economy, and International Relations: Modern Princes and Naked Emperors* (Basingstoke: Palgrave Macmillan, 2013). Stuart Hall's Gramscian analysis of Thatcherism is contained in the essays collected in his book *The Hard Road to Renewal* (London: Verso, 1988). On Gramsci's views on international relations there is an important essay in Italian by Roberto Gualtieri, 'L'Analisi internazionale e lo sviluppo della filosofia della praxis', in F. Giasi (ed.), *Gramsci nel suo tempo*, 2 vols (Rome: Carocci, 2008), vol. 2, pp. 631–56.

For the wider impact of Gramsci and the *Prison Notebooks*, there is consideration of a range of perspectives on Gramsci in the three volumes of articles edited by, respectively, Joseph Francese, *Perspectives on Gramsci: Politics, Culture and Social Theory* (London: Routledge, 2009); Marcus E. Green, *Rethinking Gramsci* (London: Routledge, 2011); Mark McNally and J. Schwarzmantel, *Gramsci and Global Politics: Hegemony and Resistance* (London: Routledge, 2009). The final part of this last collection has a section on 'Gramsci and Contemporary British politics', which in part takes up some of the themes of Hall's analyses.

BIBLIOGRAPHY

Gramsci's own works, and the key to the way in which they are referenced, are listed on pages xiii–xiv. The following bibliography is organized into three parts: first, books and articles directly on Gramsci in English; second, books and articles directly on Gramsci in Italian; third, other books and articles referred to in the text.

BOOKS AND ARTICLES DIRECTLY ON GRAMSCI IN ENGLISH

Adamson, Walter L. (1980) *Hegemony and Revolution: A Study of Antonio Gramsci's Political and Cultural Theory*, Berkeley: University of California Press.

Anderson, Perry (1976–77) 'The Antinomies of Antonio Gramsci', *New Left Review* 100: 5–78.

Ayers, Alison J. (ed.) (2013) *Gramsci, Political Economy, and International Relations Theory: Modern Princes and Naked Emperors*, rev. edn, Basingstoke: Palgrave Macmillan.

Bellamy, Richard (2014) *Croce, Gramsci, Bobbio and the Italian Political Tradition*, Colchester: ECPR Press.

Bobbio, Norberto (1988) 'Gramsci and the Concept of Civil Society', in J. Keane (ed.), *Civil Society and the State: New European Perspectives*, London: Verso, pp. 73–99.

Borg, Carmel, Buttigieg, Joseph and Mayo, Peter (eds) (2002) *Gramsci and Education*, Lanham, MD: Rowman & Littlefield.

Callinicos, Alex (2010) 'The Limits of Passive Revolution', *Capital and Class* 34, no. 3: 491–507.

Cammett, John M. (1967) *Antonio Gramsci and the Origins of Italian Communism*, Stanford CA: Stanford University Press.

Carlucci, Alessandro (2012) 'Introduction: New Approaches to Gramsci: Language, Philosophy and Politics', *Journal of Romance Studies* 12, no. 3: 1–9.

——(2013) *Gramsci and Languages: Unification, Diversity, Hegemony*, Leiden: Brill.

Cox, Robert W. (1993 [1983]) 'Gramsci, Hegemony and International Relations: An Essay in Method', *Millennium* 12: 162–75; repr. in Stephen Gill (ed.), *Gramsci, Historical Materialism and International Relations* (Cambridge: Cambridge University Press, 1993), pp. 49–66.

Davidson, Alastair (1977) *Antonio Gramsci: Towards an Intellectual Biography*, London: Merlin Press.

Davis, John A. (ed.) (1979) *Gramsci and Italy's Passive Revolution*, London: Croom Helm.

Entwistle, Harold (1979) *Antonio Gramsci: Conservative Schooling for Radical Politics*, London: Routledge & Kegan Paul.

Femia, Joseph (1979) 'Gramsci, the *Via Italiana* and the Classical Marxist-Leninist Approach to Revolution', *Government and Opposition* 14: 66–95; repr. in James Martin (ed.), *Antonio Gramsci: Critical Assessments of Leading Political Philosophers*, 4 vols (London: Routledge, 2002), vol. 3, pp. 482–504.

——(1981) *Gramsci's Political Thought: Hegemony, Consciousness, and the Revolutionary Process*, Oxford: Oxford University Press.

——(2009) 'Gramsci, Epistemology and International Relations', in M. McNally and J. Schwarzmantel (eds), *Gramsci and Global Politics: Hegemony and Resistance*, Routledge: London, pp. 32–42.

Finocchiaro, Maurice A. (1988) *Gramsci and the History of Dialectical Thought*, Cambridge: Cambridge University Press.

Fiori, Giuseppe (1970) *Antonio Gramsci: Life of a Revolutionary*, translated by Tom Nairn, London: New Left Books.

Francese, Joseph (ed.) (2009) *Perspectives on Gramsci: Politics, Culture and Social Theory*, London: Routledge.

Frosini, Fabio (2012) 'Reformation, Renaissance and the State: The Hegemonic Fabric of Modern Sovereignty', *Journal of Romance Studies* 12, no. 3: 63–77.

Germino, Dante (1990) *Antonio Gramsci: Architect of a New Politics*, Baton Rouge: Louisiana State University Press.

Gill, Stephen (ed.) (1993) *Gramsci, Historical Materialism and International Relations*, Cambridge: Cambridge University Press.

Ginsborg, Paul (1979) 'Gramsci and the Era of Bourgeois Revolution in Italy', chapter 6 of John A. Davis (ed.), *Gramsci and Italy's Passive Revolution*, London: Croom Helm.

Green, Marcus E. (ed.) (2011) *Rethinking Gramsci*, London: Routledge.

Hart, Janet (1999) 'Reading the Radical Subject: Gramsci, Glinos and Paralanguages of the Modern Nation; Strange Rhapsody', in R. Suny and M. D. Kennedy (eds), *Intellectuals and the Articulation of the Nation*, Ann Arbor MI: University of Michigan Press.

Ives, Peter (2004) *Language and Hegemony in Gramsci*, London: Pluto Press.

Karabel, Jerome (1976) 'Revolutionary Contradictions: Antonio Gramsci and the Problem of Intellectuals', *Politics and Society* 6, no. 1: 123–72; repr. in James Martin (ed.), *Antonio Gramsci: Critical Assessments of Leading Political Philosophers* (London: Routledge, 2002), vol. 3, pp. 7–52.

King, Margaret L. (1978) 'The Social Role of Intellectuals: Antonio Gramsci and the Italian Renaissance', *Soundings* 61, no. 1: 23–46; repr. in James Martin (ed.), *Antonio Gramsci: Critical Assessments of Leading Political Philosophers* (London: Routledge, 2002), vol. 3, pp. 145–64.

McNally, Mark and Schwarzmantel, J. (eds) (2009) *Gramsci and Global Politics: Hegemony and Resistance*, Routledge: London.

Martin, James (1998) *Gramsci's Political Analysis: A Critical Introduction*, Basingstoke: Macmillan.

——(ed.) (2002) *Antonio Gramsci: Critical Assessments of Leading Political Philosophers*, 4 vols, London: Routledge.

Mayo, Peter (ed.) (2009) *Gramsci and Educational Thought*, Oxford: Blackwell.

Morera, Esteve (1990) *Gramsci's Historicism: A Realist Interpretation*, London: Routledge.

Morton, Adam David (2007) *Unravelling Gramsci: Hegemony and Passive Revolution in the Global Political Economy*, London: Pluto Press.

——(2010) 'The Continuum of Passive Revolution', *Capital and Class* 34, no. 3: 315–42.

Paterson, Bill (2009) '*Trasformismo* at the World Trade Organisation', in M. McNally and J. Schwarzmantel (eds), *Gramsci and Global Politics: Hegemony and Resistance*, Routledge: London.

Sassoon, Anne Showstack (1987) *Gramsci's Politics*, 2nd edn, London: Hutchinson.

Spriano, Paolo (1979) *Gramsci: The Prison Years*, translated by John Fraser, London: Lawrence & Wishart.

Thomas, Peter D. (2009) *The Gramscian Moment: Philosophy, Hegemony and Marxism*, Historical Materialism 24, Leiden: Brill.

Togliatti, Palmiro (1979) *On Gramsci, and Other Writings*, edited and introduced by Donald Sassoon, London: Lawrence & Wishart.

Williams, Gwyn A. (1975) *Proletarian Order: Antonio Gramsci, Factory Councils and the Origins of Communism in Italy 1911–1921*, London: Pluto Press.

BOOKS AND ARTICLES DIRECTLY ON GRAMSCI IN ITALIAN

Canfora, Luciano (2012) *Spie, URSS, antifascismo: Gramsci 1926–1937*, Rome: Salerno Editrice.

Cospito, Giuseppe (2011a) *Il ritmo del pensiero: Per una lettura diacronica dei 'Quaderni del carcere' di Gramsci*, Naples: Bibliopolis.

——(2011b) 'Verso l'edizione critica e integrale dei "Quaderni del carcere"', *Studi Storici* 52, no 4: 881–905.

Daniele, Chiara (ed.) (1999) *Gramsci a Roma, Togliatti a Mosca: Il carteggio del 1926, con un saggio di Giuseppe Vacca*, Turin: Einaudi.

——(2011) 'L'Epistolario del carcere di Antonio Gramsci', *Studi Storici* 52, no 4: 791–836.

Francioni, Gianni (1984) *L'Officina Gramsciana: Ipotesi sulla struttura dei 'Quaderni del carcere'*, Naples: Bibliopolis.

——(1992) 'Il bauletto inglese: Appunti per una storia dei "Quaderni" di Gramsci', *Studi Storici* 33, no. 4: 713–41.

——(2009) 'Come lavorava Gramsci', in G. Francioni (ed.), *Antonio Gramsci: Quaderni del carcere, Edizione anastatica dei manoscritti*, Milan: Biblioteca Treccani.

Frosini, Fabio (2010) *La religione dell'uomo moderno: Politica e verità nei 'Quaderni del carcere' di Antonio Gramsci*, Rome: Carocci.

Gagliardi, Alassio (2008) 'Il problema del corporativismo nel dibattito europeo e nei Quaderni', in F. Giasi (ed.), *Gramsci nel suo tempo*, 2 vols, Rome: Carocci, vol. 2, pp. 631–56.

Galasso, Giuseppe (1978) 'Gramsci e i problemi della storia italiana', in his *Croce, Gramsci e altri storici*, 2nd edn, Milan: Il Saggiatore.

Giasi, Francesco (2008a) 'I comunisti torinese e l'"egemonia del proletariato" nella rivoluzione italiana: Appunti sulle fonti di *Alcuni temi della quistione meridionale* di Gramsci', in A. D'Orsi (ed.), *Egemonie*, Naples: Edizioni Dante & Descartes, pp. 147–86.

——(ed.) (2008b) *Gramsci nel suo tempo*, 2 vols, Rome: Carocci.

Gualtieri, Roberto (2008) 'L'Analisi internazionale e lo sviluppo della filosofia della praxis', in. F. Giasi (ed.), *Gramsci nel suo tempo*, 2 vols, Rome: Carocci, vol. 2, pp. 581–608.

Izzo, Francesca (2008) 'I Marx di Gramsci', in Francesco Giasi (ed.), *Gramsci nel suo tempo*, Rome: Carocci, vol. 2, pp. 553–80.

Liguori, Guido (2012) *Gramsci conteso: Interpretazioni, dibattiti e polemiche 1922–2012*, rev. edn, Rome: Editori Riuniti.

Liguori, Guido and Voza, Pasquale (eds) (2009) *Dizionario gramsciano: 1926–1937*, Rome: Carocci.

Lo Piparo, Franco (2012) *I Due Carceri di Gramsci: La prigione fascista e il labirinto comunista*, Rome: Donzelli.

——(2013) *L'Enigma del Quaderno: La caccia ai manoscritti dopo la morte di Gramsci*, Rome: Donzelli.

Rapone, Leonardo (2011) *Cinque anni che paiono secoli: Antonio Gramsci dal socialismo al comunismo (1914–1919)*, Rome: Carocci.

Righi, Maria Luisa (2011) 'Gramsci a Mosca tra amori e politica (1922–23)', *Studi Storici* 52, no. 4: 1001–38.

Santucci, Antonio A. (2005) *Antonio Gramsci 1891–1937*, Palermo: Sellerio; trans. Antonio Santucci, *Antonio Gramsci* (New York: Monthly Review Press, 2010).

Togliatti, Palmiro (2001) *Scritti su Gramsci*, edited by Guido Liguori, Rome: Editori Riuniti.

Vacca, Giuseppe (1991) *Gramsci e Togliatti*, Rome: Editori Riuniti.

——(1999) *Appuntamenti con Gramsci: Introduzione allo studio dei Quaderni del carcere*, Rome: Carocci.

——(2012) *Vita e pensieri di Antonio Gramsci 1926–1937*, Turin: Einaudi.

OTHER WORKS REFERRED TO

Aristotle (1958) *The Politics*, edited and translated by Ernest Baker, Oxford: Oxford University Press.

Avineri, Shlomo (1969) *The Social and Political Thought of Karl Marx*, Cambridge: Cambridge University Press.

Banti, Alberto Mario (2004) *Il Risorgimento italiano*, Rome: Laterza.

Bauman, Zygmunt (1987) *Legislators and Interpreters: On Modernity, Post-modernity and Intellectuals*, Cambridge: Polity.

——(2000) *Liquid Modernity*, Cambridge: Polity.

Beck, Ulrich (2006) *The Cosmopolitan Vision*, Cambridge: Polity.

Beetham, David (1977) 'From Socialism to Fascism: The Relation between Theory and Practice in the Work of Robert Michels', *Political Studies* 25: 3–24, 161–81.

Beiser, Frederick C. (2011) *The German Historicist Tradition*, Oxford: Oxford University Press.

Bellamy, Richard (1987) *Modern Italian Social Theory: Ideology and Politics from Pareto to the Present*, Cambridge: Polity.

Bukharin, Nicolai (1925) *Historical Materialism: A System of Sociology*, New York: International Publishers.

Carr, Edward Hallett (1966 [1953]) *The Bolshevik Revolution 1917–1923*, vol. 3, Harmondsworth: Penguin.

Cohen, G. A. (1978) *Karl Marx's Theory of History: A Defence*, Oxford: Clarendon Press.

Cohen, Stephen F. (1974) *Bukharin and the Bolshevik Revolution: A Political Biography 1888–1938*, London: Wildwood House.

Collini, Stefan (2006) *Absent Minds: Intellectuals in Britain*, Oxford: Oxford University Press.

Cranston, Maurice (1986) *Philosophers and Pamphleteers: Political Theorists of the Enlightenment*, Oxford: Oxford University Press.

Croce, Benedetto (1934) *History of Europe in the Nineteenth Century*, London: George Allen & Unwin.

——(1994) *Etica e politica*, edited by Giuseppe Galasso, Milan: Adelphi Edizioni.

Cuoco, Vincenzo (1998 [1800]) *Saggio storico sulla rivoluzione di Napoli del 1799*, Naples: Generoso Procaccini.

Dante Alighieri (1949) *The Divine Comedy*, vol. 1: *Hell*, translated by Dorothy L. Sayers, Harmondsworth: Penguin.

Davidson, Neil (2012) *How Revolutionary Were the Bourgeois Revolutions?*, Chicago: Haymarket.

Davis, John A. (ed.) (2000) *Italy in the Nineteenth Century*, Oxford: Oxford University Press.

——(2006) *Naples and Napoleon: Southern Italy and the European Revolutions 1780–1860*, Oxford: Oxford University Press.

Deutscher, Isaac (1959) *The Prophet Unarmed: Trotsky: 1921–1929*, Oxford: Oxford University Press.

Di Palma, Giuseppe (2014) *The Modern State Subverted: Risk and the Deconstruction of Solidarity*, Colchester: ECPR Press.

Ehrenberg, John (1999) *Civil Society: The critical History of an Idea*, New York: New York University Press.

Engels, Frederick (1970 [1888]) 'Ludwig Feuerbach and the End of Classical German Philosophy', in *Karl Marx and F. Engels: Selected Works in Three Volumes*, Moscow: Progress Publishers, vol. 3, pp. 335–76.

Etzioni, Amitai and Bowditch, Alyssa (eds) (2006) *Public Intellectuals: An Endangered Species?*, Lanham MD: Rowman & Littlefield.

Ferguson, Adam (1995 [1767]) *An Essay on the History of Civil Society*, edited by F. Oz-Salzberger, Cambridge: Cambridge University Press.

Fleck, Christian, Hess, Andreas and Stina Lyon, E. (eds) (2009) *Intellectuals and Their Publics: Perspectives from the Social Sciences*, Farnham: Ashgate.

Gamble, Andrew (1994) *The Free Economy and the Strong State: The Politics of Thatcherism*, Basingstoke: Macmillan.

Girardet, Raoul (ed.) (1966) *Le nationalisme français 1871–1914*, Paris: Armand Colin.

Gray, John (1995) *Enlightenment's Wake: Politics and Culture at the Close of the Modern Age*, London: Routledge.

Griffin, Roger (ed.) (1995) *Fascism*, Oxford: Oxford University Press.

Habermas, Jürgen (1989) *The Structural Transformation of the Public Sphere: An Inquiry into a Category of Bourgeois Society*, Cambridge: Polity.

——(2001) *The Post-national Constellation: Political Essays*, Cambridge: Polity.

Hall, Stuart (1988) *The Hard Road to Renewal: Thatcherism and the Crisis of the Left*, London: Verso.

Harvey, David (2005) *A Brief History of Neo-liberalism*, Oxford: Oxford University Press.

Hayek, F. A. (1978) *New Studies in Philosophy, Politics, Economics and the History of Ideas*, London: Routledge & Kegan Paul.

Hegel, G. W. F. (1952 [1821]) *The Philosophy of Right*, translated by T. M. Knox, Oxford: Clarendon Press.

Kriegel, Annie (1972) *The French Communists: Portrait of a People*, Chicago: University of Chicago Press.

Lenin, Vladimir Ilyich (1973 [1902]) *What Is to Be Done? Burning Questions of Our Movement*, Beijing: Foreign Languages Press.

Lih, Lars T. (2008) *Lenin Rediscovered: What Is to Be Done? in Context*, Chicago: Haymarket.

Luxemburg, Rosa (1906) *The Mass Strike, the Political Party and the Trade Unions*, London: Merlin Press.

——(1961 [1904]) 'Organisational Questions of the Russian Social Democracy', in *The Russian Revolution*, Ann Arbor: University of Michigan Press.

Lyttelton, Adrian (ed.) (1973) *Italian Fascisms from Pareto to Gentile*, London: Jonathan Cape.

——(2002) *Liberal and Fascist Italy 1900–1945*, in *The Short Oxford History of Italy*, edited by John A. Davis, Oxford: Oxford University Press.

——(2004) *The Seizure of Power: Fascism in Italy 1919–1929*, rev. edn, New York: Routledge.

McClelland, J. S. (ed.) (1970) *The French Right: From de Maistre to Maurras*, London: Jonathan Cape.

Machiavelli, Niccolò (1988 [1532]) *The Prince*, edited by Quentin Skinner and Russell Price, Cambridge: Cambridge University Press.

Mair, Peter (2013) *Ruling the Void: The Hollowing of Western Democracy*, London: Verso.

Mannheim, Karl (1936) *Ideology and Utopia: An Introduction to the Sociology of Knowledge*, London: Routledge & Kegan Paul.

Marx, Karl (1973a) Preface to *A Contribution to the Critique of Political Economy*, in *Early Writings*, introduced by Lucio Colletti, translated by Rodney Livingstone and Gregor Benton, Harmondsworth: Penguin, pp. 424–28.

——(1973b [1848]) *Manifesto of the Communist Party*, by K. Marx and F. Engels, in *The Revolutions of 1848*, edited by David Fernbach, Harmondsworth: Penguin.

——(1973c [1869]) *The Eighteenth Brumaire of Louis Bonaparte*, in *Surveys from Exile*, edited by David Fernbach, Harmondsworth: Penguin.

——(1976) *Capital: A Critique of Political Economy, Volume 1*, Harmondsworth: Penguin.

Marx, Karl and Engels, F. (1975) *Selected Correspondence*, Moscow: Progress Publishers.

Michels, Robert (1959) *Political Parties: A Sociological Study of the Oligarchical Consequences of Modern Democracy*, New York: Dover.

Miliband, Ralph (1975) 'Teaching Politics in an Age of Crisis', Inaugural Lecture delivered on 7 October 1974, in *University of Leeds Review* 18, 129–45.

——(2009 [1969]) *The State in Capitalist Society*, Pontypool: Merlin Press.

Posner, Richard A. (2001) *Public Intellectuals: A Study of Decline*, Cambridge MA: Harvard University Press.

Putnam, Robert (2000) *Bowling Alone: The Collapse and Revival of American Community*, New York: Simon & Schuster.

Riall, Lucy (2009) *Risorgimento: The History of Italy from Napoleon to Nation State*, Basingstoke: Palgrave Macmillan.

——(2013) *Under the Volcano: Revolution in a Sicilian Town*, Oxford: Oxford University Press.

Roberts, David D. (1987) *Benedetto Croce and the Uses of Historicism*, Berkeley: University of California Press.

Schwarzmantel, John (1994) *The State in Contemporary Society: An Introduction*, Hemel Hempstead: Harvester Wheatsheaf.

Sorel, Georges (1950 [1907]) *Reflections on Violence*, translated by T. E. Hulme, introduced by Edward A. Shils, New York: Collier.

Spriano, Paolo (1967) *Storia del Partito comunista italiano*, vol. 1: *Da Bordiga a Gramsci*, Turin: Einaudi.

——(1975) *The Occupation of the Factories: Italy 1920*, translated and introduced by Gwyn A. Williams, London: Pluto Press.

Standing, Guy (2014) *A Precariat Charter: From Denizens to Citizens*, London: Bloomsbury.

Steele, Tom (2007) *Knowledge Is Power! The Rise and Fall of European Popular Educational Movements 1848–1913*, Oxford: Peter Lang.

Steger, Manfred (2005) 'Ideologies of Globalisation', *Journal of Political Ideologies* 10, no. 1: 11–30.

——(2008) *The Rise of the Global Imaginary: Political Ideologies from the French Revolution to the Global War on Terror*, Oxford: Oxford University Press.

Wolin, Sheldon (2004) *Politics and Vision: Continuity and Innovation in Western Political Thought*, rev. edn, Princeton: Princeton University Press.

INDEX